THE ... OF ...

# AMERIC. N
# OLITICS

For Nicola

# THE CONTOURS OF
# AMERICAN
# POLITICS

## AN INTRODUCTION

# JON ROPER

polity

320.973

First published in 2002 by Polity Press in association with Blackwell Publishers Ltd

*Editorial office*:
Polity Press
65 Bridge Street
Cambridge CB2 1UR, UK

*Marketing and production*:
Blackwell Publishers Ltd
108 Cowley Road
Oxford OX4 1JF, UK

*Published in the USA by*
Blackwell Publishers Inc.
350 Main Street
Malden, MA 02148, USA

**Library of Congress Cataloging-in-Publication Data**
Roper, Jon.
  The contours of American politics : an introduction / Jon Roper.
    p. cm.
  Includes bibliographical references (p. ) and index.
    ISBN 0-7456-2060-4 (alk. paper) — ISBN 0-7456-2061-2 (pbk. : alk. paper)
    1. United States—Politics and government.   2. Political culture—
  United States—History.   3. National characteristics, American.   I. Title.
  E183 .R666 2002
  306.2′0973—dc21                                                      2001007344

Typeset in 10.5 on 12pt Times New Roman
by Graphicraft Limited, Hong Kong
Printed in Great Britain by TJ International, Padstow, Cornwall

This book is printed on acid-free paper.

# Contents

# Preface

> Thus, in the beginning, all the world was America.
> *John Locke,* Second Treatise on Government (*1690*)

In the early years of the seventeenth century, a family of French Huguenots fled from religious persecution and found asylum in Britain. One of them, Samuel Louis – the name became anglicized as Lewis – settled in Wales. His son Robert emigrated to the United States in 1635, and five years later, his grandson, John, was born in America. The family became one of the most prosperous in colonial Virginia. In 1804, John's great-great grandson, Meriwether Lewis, was asked by his childhood friend, Thomas Jefferson – then president – to explore the land that the United States had acquired by the Louisiana Purchase. Lewis and William Clark led the expedition: a transcontinental journey from St Louis, across the Rocky Mountains, to the Pacific Ocean and back again. It took them two years.

The adventures of the Louis/Lewis family as religious refugees, as emigrants to the New World and as pioneers in it are not unique. But they are illustrative of the main themes of this book. Religious beliefs, together with patterns of immigration and migration westwards across the continent, are elements in the creation of the landscape of contemporary American political culture. Ideas, institutions and attitudes may best be understood in the context of such experiences. The contours of American politics have been moulded by the nation's history: its development from a cluster of British colonies on the eastern seaboard, to a federal democratic republic stretching from the Atlantic to the Pacific coasts; from a scattering of small, agrarian, mainly white, Anglo-Saxon, Protestant and male-dominated communities, to a complex, industrial, multi-ethnic, religiously pluralistic, multi-cultural society. In its complexity and diversity, America fascinates. Its politics – sometimes corrupt, sometimes unfathomable – are brash and exciting; its political impact upon the wider world is profound. It is thus important to understand not simply the mechanics of its political system but also the animating ideas and principles that shape its values and its attitudes.

In 1814, the publication of the story of Lewis and Clark's journey, chronicling their meetings with Native Americans, their observations of the landscapes they had encountered and their accounts of the wildlife of the wilderness, gave their readers valuable information about the territory of the frontier. In the same way, later travellers across America can provide useful insights into its society and culture. Bill Bryson, for example, in *The Lost Continent* (1990) records an account of his road trip through the small towns of the midwest. It is a reminder that although the United States has impressive cities – take New York, Chicago, Atlanta or Los Angeles as just a few of many examples – the perspectives of its citizens are also moulded by their experiences of life outside the metropolis, in what remains the rural heartland of the country. Again, Gavin Young in *From Sea to Shining Sea* (1996) explores the country through visiting places commemorated in its history of conflict – battlefields of the Civil War, the remains of the Alamo and the site of Custer's Last Stand – or which inspired such novelists as Herman Melville, Raymond Chandler, John Steinbeck and Jack London. America's frontier and its hinterland, its history and its literature, are thus connected to, and illustrative of, its contemporary society and ways of life. The present volume also draws on diverse material in its interdisciplinary approach to a wide-ranging subject: mapping the landscape of contemporary American political culture and identity with an appreciation of its past as a formative influence upon its present.

Meriwether Lewis and William Clark began their expedition in Missouri. It would become one of the United States of America in 1821, only after Congress had agreed a compromise by which slavery would be tolerated there but would be forbidden elsewhere in the territories of the Louisiana Purchase that extended north of a negotiated line of latitude. In 1835 Samuel Langhorne Clemens was born in Missouri, growing up in a small town called Hannibal. Later, like Samuel Louis, he took a different name: Mark Twain. And it is with an idea from *The Adventures of Huckleberry Finn*, the timeless story of the journey of a boy and a runaway slave on a raft down the Mississippi river, first published in 1884, that this book begins.

# Acknowledgements

David Held both invited and encouraged me to write this. I am grateful to him, and to everyone at Polity who has helped along the way, notably Sandra Byatt, Rachel Kerr, Louise Knight, Gill Motley, Pam Thomas, Ali Wyke and Justin Dyer. They have helped to make the end result a lot better than otherwise it might have been.

At the University of Wales, Swansea the Department of American Studies remains a congenial academic environment in which to work. I would like to thank David Bewley-Taylor and Craig Phelan for looking at early drafts of some of the chapters, and also Phil Melling, Steve McVeigh and Duncan Campbell for sharing their expertise.

Nigel Bowles was kind enough to read the first draft of the manuscript and I appreciated his comments on it. Criss-crossing the United States on innumerable visits over a number of years has enabled me to talk with colleagues – friends – there, and they have given me many useful insights into American politics, society and culture. Their names are too numerous to be listed here, but I hope they know who they are and how much I appreciate their help.

To all the gratitude is sincere, but for some it is, as ever, inadequate. This is undoubtedly true for Marjorie and for John. Caitlin, Aisling and Jack also deserve more than mere thanks. So too does Nicola, to whom this book is dedicated.

Jon Roper

# 1

# Lighting Out for the Territory

But I reckon I got to light out for the Territory ahead of the rest, because Aunt Sally she's going to adopt me and sivilize me and I can't stand it. I been there before.

*Mark Twain*, The Adventures of Huckleberry Finn (*1884*)

The concluding words of *The Adventures of Huckleberry Finn* encapsulate an enduring promise of American life. West of the Mississippi, in 'Ingean territory', Huck Finn will be free. Aunt Sally's civilized society demands conformity to its structures and rules. Huck rejects it. His preferred course of action is to find a place beyond the reach of her authority – beyond civilization itself. Until the end of the nineteenth century, when the US Census Bureau declared the American frontier closed, the New World had always offered that opportunity for escape. So, in common with both immigrants and migrants, Huck could take advantage of the safety-valve of America's 'virgin land'. The opportunity was there to 'light out for the Territory'. Once that idea became established as part of the nation's mythology, moreover, it could take on a life that transcended geographical or territorial limitations. For the historian Frederick Jackson Turner, the existence of the frontier as the dividing line between the wilderness and civilization, and the opportunities that it provided for the shaping of a unique national character, became a central motif that meant that his 'frontier thesis' could explain America's unique and exceptional history. Even after the frontier closed, it was possible still to escape into the 'American Dream': a myth that continues to shape America's political and cultural identity.

Imagine if Huck had nowhere to go. Then he would have faced a different choice: to stay and submit to his aunt's plans or to remain and rebel against them. It is because he lives in America that he does not have that decision to make. He can move on. The fact of that opportunity, moreover, is what makes America different from those nations – indeed most of the rest of the world – that do not provide the prospect for such an escape. This, then, is a defining characteristic of the belief in American exceptionalism. In the imagination of those who live there, and indeed of those who aspire to go there to live, it is what creates America as a world apart: the history of America is contained in that vision of being able to 'light out for the Territory' whenever authority threatens.

## The Psychology of Escape

In the day we sweat it out on the street/of a runaway American dream.

*Bruce Springsteen, 'Born to Run' (1975)*

Among the initial emigrants from Europe to America were those who, as Louis Hartz put it, 'fled from the feudal and clerical oppressions of the Old World'. In *The Liberal Tradition in America* (1955), Hartz argued that it follows from this that 'the outstanding thing about the American community in Western history ought to be the non-existence of those oppressions, or since the reaction against them was in the broadest sense, liberal, that the American community is a liberal community.' It is true that another significant feature of American political life has been the comparative absence of ideological debate and conflict along European lines and a history unpunctuated by the experience of periodic radical reconstructions of the social order. The reason for this, Hartz suggested, is that 'in a real sense physical flight is the American substitute for the European experience of social revolution. And this, of course, has persisted throughout our national history, although nothing in the subsequent pattern of flight, the 'safety-valve' notwithstanding, has approximated in significance the original escape from Europe.'[1]

How, then, has America's political culture been shaped by these circumstances of its settlement by Europeans – and particularly by the British who came to this New World from the sixteenth century onwards? The timing was critical. The impact of the Renaissance and the Reformation transformed Europe's cultural, political and religious landscape just as the mapping of this New World – America – opened up opportunities of exploration, exploitation and escape. The colonization of America happened as the rigidities of contemporary Europe – its political certainties and religious dogmas – were being eroded from within. When Christopher Columbus made his historic voyage of contemporary discovery in 1492, Martin Luther was nine years old. Twenty-five years later, in 1517, he is said to have nailed his Ninety-five Theses to a church door in Wittenberg. These discussion points for a proposed debate on the medieval papacy's practice of selling indulgences – promissory notes whereby sins committed on earth would receive a reduced punishment in purgatory – sparked the Protestant reformation. Renaissance ideas and the new theologies of Protestantism in turn would convulse European societies; and as the civil and spiritual order of the medieval world decayed, the result was political, social and religious turmoil. America beckoned.

If it appeared to be a place of refuge, it was also seen as having a deeper historical and symbolic significance. So the discovery of America was described by Francisco López de Gómara in 1552 as 'the greatest event since the creation of the world, apart from the incarnation and death of Christ'. Moreover, for many Protestants, the existence of America, only now revealed to them, seemed proof that God had kept the New World as a place where their new faith might flourish. But even though some early colonists were inspired by a sense of mission that would in turn have a profound influence upon American political culture, still more came to the New World for other reasons.

As Adam Smith observed in *The Wealth of Nations* (1776) – published in the year Jefferson wrote America's Declaration of Independence from British rule – it was thus 'not the wisdom and policy, but the disorder and injustice of European governments, which peopled and cultivated America'.[2] Those satisfied with the status quo in their own societies – conservatives – had no reasons to leave and vested interests to defend. But those who rejected the established order could either seek to change things, or look for asylum elsewhere. For Hartz, then, these contemporary 'liberals' were defined by the choice they made; they had differing political agendas, and it is important to recognize that fact.

> It is interesting how romance has been thrown alike around the European liberals who stayed home to fight and the American liberals who fled their battle. There are two types of excitement here, that of changing familiar things and that of leaving them, which both involve a trip into the unknown. But though one may find a common element of adventure in flight and revolution, it is a profound mistake to confuse the perspectives they engender. They are miles apart – figuratively as well as literally.[3]

The map of America's unique political culture thus can be drawn
from the circumstances and the history of its settlement and in subsequent patterns of immigration and migration. What Hartz referred
to in testimony he gave to the Senate Committee on Foreign Relations
as 'the psychology of escape'[4] became a substitute for the 'psychology
of revolution' that inspired those who remained elsewhere to battle
with the social, political, religious or economic structures that they felt
were oppressing them. Those who went to America wanted to avoid
that fight, to have a better life. Otherwise, why go?

So the contours of American politics are shaped by the aspirations of those who arrived there with the hope of transcending the
perceived religious, political or economic injustices they had experienced elsewhere. Of course, that is not true of all those who have
inhabited the 'last best hope for mankind'. If America became the
refuge for religious and political dissidents, and the magnet for economic migrants and opportunists, it was also home to slaves and
Native Americans. Yet, while not forgetting the ways in which both
blacks and Native Americans have helped to shape American society,
it is the first two groups who set the mould of America's democratic
polity. As their power supplanted Spanish influence in the New World,
moreover, it was the British who, through their colonial experiences
in Virginia and in New England, mapped the political landscape of
the United States.

## The Promise of American Life

Give me your tired, your poor,
Your huddled masses yearning to breathe free
The wretched refuse of your teeming shore.
Send these, the homeless, tempest tost to me,
I lift my lamp beside the golden door!
    *Inscription on the Statue of Liberty – from Emma Lazarus,*
                           *'The New Colossus' (1883)*

Despite their different motivations for making the long Atlantic
crossing, emigrants to America were united in one respect: they were
prepared to reject their own culture and society, and to accept the
challenges of re-creating their lives in a new, unfamiliar and initially
hostile environment. It was a gamble. Little more survived of the first
attempts to settle Virginia in the fifteenth century than the colony's
name. In 1607, however, Jamestown was established there, and the

settlement survived. Others followed. This initial scattering of settlements along the eastern sea-board – isolated one from another, and with different purposes and agendas – would in time impact upon the framework of the nation's political institutions. Yet these first successful migrants were not seen necessarily as the potential architects of a new world order. For Alexis de Tocqueville,

> [t]he men sent to Virginia were seekers of gold, adventurers without resources and without character, whose turbulent and restless spirit endangered the infant colony and rendered its progress uncertain. Artisans and agriculturalists arrived afterwards; and, although they were a more moral and orderly race of men, they were hardly in any respect above the level of the inferior classes in England. No lofty views, no spiritual conception, presided over the foundation of these new settlements.[5]

One hundred and fifty years later, however, Virginia would be home to, among others, George Washington, Thomas Jefferson and James Madison: inspirational and indispensable influences in the creation of an independent America.

In 1620, at about the same time as the first slaves came to Jamestown, the *Mayflower*, sailing from Plymouth, brought its small congregation of puritans – Pilgrims – and others who had joined them on their journey to New England. The *Mayflower* Compact, agreed as they established the settlement, was signed out of necessity. It recognized the reality that a colony established so far from home would necessarily be largely politically autonomous, and that for the new community to survive, the colonists would have to be involved in the decisions that affected their futures and indeed their lives. In other words, government of the people would only work if it was government *by* the people. The *Mayflower* Compact represented an early example of a form of written constitution on American soil, and the Pilgrims made a significant contribution to the development of a new political culture there. Their efforts were to be supplemented, if not surpassed, by the example of spiritual and moral leadership given by later puritan immigrants to the Massachusetts Bay colony under the influence of John Winthrop. For the puritans, America indeed became the promised land.

Winthrop's contemporary was another puritan leader, Oliver Cromwell. Indeed, Cromwell and Winthrop encapsulate Louis Hartz's argument. While one stayed and fought and won a civil war, overcoming – temporarily – the entrenched power of the British monarchy, the other left for America. Cromwell's audacious victory came sixteen years after Winthrop founded his colony in the New World.

The contrast between their different but related experiments in creating fresh forms of civil and political society is illuminating. Britain's short-lived flirtation with republican government failed. It was almost as if the change brought about – and the execution of the king that accompanied it – was too dramatic for contemporary mainstream political discourse to rationalize and accept. Despite the attempts to establish a puritan democracy, with the monarchy and the House of Lords swept away, the political gulf between the radical and democratic demands of levellers, on the one hand, and the royalist desire to restore the political system from which they had formerly benefited, on the other, was too wide to bridge. Political power came to rest where it had traditionally been concentrated. Cromwell was king. The sovereign authority took the form of a limited monarchy during Cromwell's 'Protectorate' but after that it was re-established in the symbolic shape that has since remained. In 1651, during the interregnum, Thomas Hobbes published *Leviathan*, a philosophical justification of the necessity of such absolute power; by the end of that decade Cromwell had died and the monarchy was about to be restored. The belief that kings – and the occasional queen – had a divine right to rule was finally destroyed only with the success of the constitutional revolution of 1688. Two years later John Locke published his *Two Treatises of Government* to lend philosophical weight to that new political reality.

Meanwhile, puritanism in Massachusetts had survived and prospered. The early New England colonists viewed America as both an opportunity and a refuge. In the nineteenth century, Lord Macaulay saw them leaving in 'despair of the destiny of their country'. They 'looked to the American wilderness as the only asylum in which they could enjoy civil and spirtual freedom'. It was there though that

> a few resolute Puritans, who, in the cause of their religion, feared neither the rage of the ocean nor the hardships of uncivilised life, neither the fangs of savage beasts nor the tomahawks of more savage men, had built, amidst the primeval forest, villages which are now great and opulent cities, but which have, through every change, retained some trace of the character derived from their founders.[6]

So Winthrop lit a slow-burning fuse. A little over a century after the collapse of Cromwell's commonwealth, an American military commander, George Washington, once more defeated the forces of a British king. This time, however, it was the principles and practices established in colonies like New England that contributed to a climate of opinion ensuring that America's revolution brought to an end what was then regarded by many as the pernicious influence of monarchy in contemporary political life. Moreover, in seeking a philosophical justification for their actions, Americans now had John Locke's ideas at hand. So the spirit of puritanism, which had sparked a civil war in Britain in the seventeenth century, but which had failed to achieve permanent and radical change there, survived as a source of political inspiration in America when, a century later, a new national identity was in the process of being formed.

## Destiny and Mission

Religion stands on tip-toe in our land
Readie to passe to the American strand.
                    *George Herbert, 'The Church Militant' (1633)*

The puritan migration was not only an escape. Winthrop's mission was to forge a new society, based upon the principles of Protestant beliefs. The disciples had become apostles. As Christianity had spread westwards from the Holy Land, contemporaries saw America as inevitably its next destination. The puritan 'errand into the wilderness' thus established a religious element at the core of American political culture. Indeed, puritan ideas have moulded American attitudes, and the rhetoric in which they are expressed can be traced in contemporary political statements of America's purpose.

Central to this idea was the concept of the covenant. This went beyond the purely political accommodations of the Pilgrim's *Mayflower* Compact. It mapped out an 'idea of America': the spiritual purpose of the enterprise of settlement, which later became the basis for its secular sense of destiny and mission. 'Thus stands the case between God and us: We are entered into a covenant with Him [and if He] shall please to hear us then hath He sealed our commission.' Winthrop's words in a sermon to his small congregation aboard the *Arbella* in 1630 took on a significance that transcended the circumstances in which they were spoken. The 'Model of Christian Charity' that Winthrop outlined to his fellow-travellers aboard a small ship in mid-Atlantic is widely regarded as providing the rationalization and legitimization of the puritans' mission, and as establishing a dominant narrative voice in American history. It emphasizes the puritan adventure as central to America's image of itself as fulfilling a providential mission. If the puritan community obey the terms of their covenant with God, then their community will prosper. If they neglect the covenant, however, 'the Lord will surely break out in wrath against us.' So if things go well in America, then it is a sign that the covenant remains intact. If they do not, the puritans have fallen from grace, departing from their destiny, and God may extract His revenge.

The more famous passage of Winthrop's sermon imbues the covenanted community with a vision of its mission. 'For we must consider that we shall be as a city upon a hill. The eyes of all people are upon us.' If America is to be the New Jerusalem, then it becomes a symbol of hope for the rest of the world. At the time, Winthrop's suggestion that the community was the object of global attention was manifestly an exaggeration; indeed, the domestic events leading to civil war would continue to preoccupy even those puritans in Britain who might be expected to retain most interest in the experiment in America. Yet again, in future years, as the United States did indeed become the most familiar – and arguably the most fascinating – country in the world, even to those who had never visited it, his words would seem prophetic. This is despite the tendency to ignore the remainder of his sentence, which contains another important admonition. Given the assumption of universal interest in their mission, the community should beware that 'if we shall deal falsely with our God . . . we shall be made a story and a by-word throughout the world.' For Winthrop the stakes were high: if successful, the puritan experiment would become a beacon and an inspirational model for all other nations; if not, it would constitute a failure of global proportions.

So to fulfil its providential mission, to act as that beacon of hope, America has to prove an unparalleled success as a new religious and political community. From the perspective of the immigrants, moreover, it was. Subsequent history – the War of Independence, the establishment of the United States itself, westward expansion under the auspices of 'manifest destiny', even the preservation of the union through the trauma of a civil war, and underlining it all the motor of unprecedented economic development and growth – meant that a little over three hundred years after Winthrop's sermon, Henry Booth Luce would style the twentieth century 'the American Century'.

There is, of course, another history that can be written here: one that retrieves and respects the experiences of minorities, whether characterized by race, class, gender or sexual orientation, who have struggled to find political and cultural accommodations within the American Dream. But the story of the nation is more often retold in the celebratory images of its past. As Tocqueville put it: 'I think I see the destiny of America embodied in the first Puritan who landed on those shores, just as the whole human race was represented by the first man.'[7] In these terms, John Winthrop becomes an 'American

Adam', the influence of his ideas imprinting themselves upon the nation's political consciousness. So in his inaugural address as president in 1965, Lyndon Johnson could remind his audience of the nation's origins and its future prospect:

> They came here – the exile and the stranger, brave but frightened – to find a place where a man could be his own man. They made a covenant with this land. Conceived in justice, written in liberty, bound in union, it was meant one day to inspire the hopes of all mankind. And it binds us still. If we keep its terms we shall flourish. . . . Under this covenant of justice, liberty, and union we have become a nation – prosperous, great, and mighty. And we have kept our freedom. But we have no promise from God that our greatness will endure . . . the judgment of God is harshest on those who are most favored. If we succeed it will not be because of what we have, but it will be because of what we are; not because of what we own, but rather because of what we believe.

The new president reinvents the nation in a vision shared with the puritan of old. Johnson's rhetorical commitment to building the 'Great Society' borrows the language of Winthrop, outlining his 'idea of America' to his few compatriots on the Atlantic crossing to the New World. Similarly in his 1992 election campaign, Bill Clinton talked of the need for a 'new covenant, a solemn agreement which we must not break', if America was to move forward.

## The Melting-Pot and Frontier Dreams

> And as long as our dreams outweigh our memories, America will be forever young. That is our destiny. And this is our moment.
> *Bill Clinton, State of the Union address (2000)*

America as an escape; America as a reaction against the feudal and religious hierarchies of Europe; America as a promised land: the place where visions of destiny and mission can be projected upon a land of opportunity and abundance – these intertwining ideas are part of a continuing debate about 'the meaning of America'. Yet they also impart a dynamic sense of significance to the development of 'the first new nation'. The sense of exceptionalism, difference, importance, creates a climate of expectations and an unshakeable sense that the 'idea of America' is indeed special. Whether it is articulated in the language of religious conviction or secular rhetoric, it has contributed to the nation's sense of itself and has defined its political culture.

As Neil Campbell and Alasdair Kean point out,

> American national myths, like the promised land or Turner's frontier thesis, 'attempt to put us at peace with ourselves and our existence' . . . by confirming certain qualities and attributes. These could become the focus for attempting to define the 'national character' and aspirations by suggesting that all people held these beliefs as common and shared. American Studies has often followed and explored, even helped to define, some of these mythic frameworks.

Furthermore, '[o]ne means by which America has unified itself is through an imaginary communal mythology that all could share and that provided a cluster of beliefs through which the nation could be articulated, both to itself and to the world.'[8] Central to that mythology are two beliefs: that 'becoming American' involves a process of personal reinvention that results in a reconfiguration of cultural identity; and that it was the American frontier that was the natural theatre for such a dramatic transformation.

The idea of America as 'the melting-pot' can be traced to colonial times. Hector St John de Crèvecoeur's famous 'letter from an American Farmer', written in 1782, saw those who had migrated to the New World as transformed by that experience. 'Urged by a variety of motives, here they came. Every thing has tended to regenerate them: new laws, a new mode of living, a new social system.' Furthermore, '[h]ere individuals of all nations are melted into a new race of men.' So once again, from that initial definition of American character, produced by the alchemy of the melting pot, flows the argument for American exceptionalism. The recipe is simple. Take immigrants – typically European, and preferably Caucasian – throw them into the melting pot of American life, and what will be distilled is a new, different, improved race: Americans.

In 1893, Frederick Jackson Turner identified the frontier as the catalyst for this powerful forging of a fresh cultural identity. The immigrant, projected into that wilderness, was forced to change: to adapt was to survive. To light out for the territory was to become an American. Thus, the pioneer encounters the wilderness as 'a European in dress, industries, tools, modes of travel and thought. It takes him from the railroad car and puts him in the birch canoe. It strips off the garments of civilization and arrays him in the hunting shirt and the moccasin.' And as the wilderness is tamed, 'the outcome is not the old Europe . . . here is a new product that is American.'[9] Such encounters with the unique environment of the frontier shaped not only America's national character but also its political values. The 'frontier thesis' separates America from Europe, driving a wedge between the dynamism of American democracy and the traditionalism of European social structures. At the same time, however, such frontier dreams, like the myth of the melting-pot, are only one way of mapping the contours of American politics.

## Other Voices

Perhaps thirty thousand years ago, the first settlers arrived in the land that would come to be known as North America. These pioneers did not travel by ship, nor did they claim territory for any monarch, but they did discover America. . . . They sought not empires to swell national treasuries but new hunting grounds to feed growing populations.
*Peter Iverson, 'Native Peoples and Native Histories' (1994)*

This is a different account of the settlement of the New World, one that precedes European voyages of discovery and colonization, and one that has to be retrieved from a history preoccupied with covenants, missions, destiny, myths and dreams. Those who became Native Americans – named Indians by the disoriented later arrivals to the continent – had walked to their new homeland during the Ice Age, across a land bridge over the Bering Strait. Theirs is a story of north–south settlement that would spread eventually as far as Patagonia. They too encountered a wilderness – a frontier – but evidently it did not mark their characters in the same way as it was to shape the European immigrants of subsequent eras in their movement from east to west. Instead their societies were destroyed; their culture and their history marginalized. They could not light out on their own for the territory – instead that was where they were placed upon reservations – nor indeed could they escape into the American Dream.

As Chief Seattle put it in an address to the governor of Washington Territory in 1854,

[w]e are two distinct races with separate origins and separate destinies. There is little in common between us. . . . Day and night cannot dwell together. The Red Man has ever fled the approach of the White Man, as the morning mist flees before the morning sun. . . . I think that my people . . . will retire to the reservation you offer them. Then we will dwell apart in peace. . . . It matters little where we pass the remnant of our days.

Such a combination of realism and resignation is resonant of the fact that of all those whose influence upon the political culture of the United States has been in the main unspoken, the Native American voice is the one that echoes least in most accounts of the nation's development. Instead, as Indians, they would became foils by which to judge the achievements of the all-American heroes who would battle them on the ever-expanding – ever-receding – frontier. And when the migration from east to west eventually reached the Pacific Ocean, Seattle's name would be taken by an American city. His territory would become a state in a Union in which he had neither historical interest nor political capital. Native Americans were not granted full US citizenship until 1924.

Other voices have not been so forgotten. Six years prior to Seattle's speech, in July 1848, the Women's Rights Convention was held in Seneca Falls, New York. The 'Declaration of Sentiments and Resolutions' took in part the form of an ironic parody of Jefferson's Declaration of Independence. It demanded for women 'the equal station to which they are entitled'. Furthermore, 'in view of this entire disfranchisement of one-half the people of this country, their social and religious degradation . . . and because women do feel themselves aggrieved, oppressed, and fraudulently deprived of their most sacred rights, we insist that they have immediate admission to all the rights and privileges which belong to them as citizens of the United States.' It would take another seventy-two years before the ratification of the nineteenth amendment to the Constitution assured that '[t]he right of citizens of the United States to vote shall not be denied or abridged by the United States or by any states on account of sex.' That was progress. But women's rights extend beyond the franchise, and there remained and remains more to be achieved.

'I have borne thirteen children, and seen most all sold off to slavery, and when I cried out with my mother's grief, none but Jesus heard me! And ain't I a woman?' Sojourner Truth's speech at a New York City Convention in 1851 contains in its famous refrain a plea for recognition, not simply in terms of gender but also in respect of race. Hers is a voice that addresses the fundamental political, social and cultural faultline in America's democratic polity, but from a position of subordination. Yet the 'peculiar institution' into which slaves were sold, traded and subsequently born did impact upon the nation's historical and political development like no other. The existence of slavery in its southern states meant that until the Civil War national politics was haunted by the question: how could a democratic community call itself such? Slaves were by status unequal and by definition unfree. The war was fought in part to resolve that dilemma.

Reconstruction demonstrated once more, however, that changing habits of the mind was to prove far more difficult than amending the Constitution itself. So the legacy of the controversies that led to the Civil War rumbled on after it. The southern surrender did not end the matter: racism remained.

Sojourner Truth's plea was to be recognized on the basis of her common humanity. But early in the twentieth century William Du Bois understood still that the fact of racial difference in a racist society gave rise to a fundamental psychological trauma.

> It is a peculiar sensation, this double-consciousness, this sense of always looking at one's self through the eyes of others, of measuring one's soul by the tape of a world that looks on in amused contempt and pity. One ever feels his twoness, – an American, a Negro; two souls, two thoughts, two unreconciled strivings; two warring ideals in one dark body, whose dogged strength alone keeps it from being torn asunder.[10]

If one response might be to withdraw into the privatized world of Ralph Ellison's *Invisible Man* (1952), another was to take part in the civil rights movement, among the most courageous and ultimately most effective mass protest that any group within America has organized in the hope of political change. Yet as Samuel DuBois Cook argued at the time of the Bicentennial celebrations of America's independence in 1976, '[i]n a tortuous and anguished way, racism has been, on the ultimate level, both the affirmation and the negation of the American Dream.' So '[i]n black politics today, there is a profound and somewhat painful and melancholic groping for power and meaningful participation in the heart of the American political system. There is a strange mixture of alienation, hope, despair, confidence, frustration, apathy, feeling of futility of effort, and feverish activism about political things.'[11] A quarter of a century later, such sentiments may appear still valid.

On the other hand, there is no doubt that the pace of social and cultural change in the United States quickened dramatically in the last half of the twentieth century. In the 1950s, it was possible – even essential – for many Americans to identify with a common national culture. During the 1960s, however, such a cultural and political consensus fell apart, not least because of the divisions caused by America's war in Vietnam, but also as a result of the success of the civil rights movement and the recognition of the contemporary political reality that America was a multi-cultural society. In discussing this move 'beyond consensus', therefore, Hans Lofgren and Alan Schima observe that

[i]f ever there was a stable and congruous understanding of what con-
stituted the United States as a nation, as a people, as an ideal site of
life, liberty, and the pursuit of happiness, the civil unrest and political
movements of the 1960s undeniably challenged the sense of national
unity. Consciously ambiguous, 'after consensus' is a term that connotes
the social and political tensions that emphatically marked the United
States after the assassinations of President John Kennedy and civil
rights leader Martin Luther King, after the national traumas of the
Vietnam War and Watergate scandal, and, since the collapse of the
Soviet Union, after the long-standing politics of containment.[12]

In this new cultural dynamic, therefore, Native Americans, women
and African-Americans form sections of the chorus of voices whose
heterogeneous histories run counter to the narrative that projects the
'idea of America' as an unparalleled success. For many groups –
minorities – within America's increasingly multi-cultural society, the
'American Dream' is indeed a myth that is given the lie by their experience. And yet, with the possible exception of the Native Americans,
most groups at some level seek to define themselves not simply in
opposition to the prevailing myths of American national identity. At
core, what they seek is inclusion. Discrimination, whether on the basis
of race, gender, sexual preference or some other criteria of exclusion,
is a denial of access to the political and economic benefits of living
in American society. These other voices seek political change as part
of a process of recognition: that they too can become stake-holders
in the 'American Dream' rather than the forgotten victims of it. In
so doing they are part of an important dynamic. They are the new
pioneers who are mapping, in contemporary terms, the changing
contours of American politics.

## The Politics of Spectacle

The Declaration of Independence I always considered as a
theatrical show. Jefferson ran away with all the stage effect of
that . . . and all the glory of it.
                    *John Adams, letter to Benjamin Rush (1811)*

In an essay that attempts to answer the question 'is there an American Culture?', Allan Lloyd Smith observes that '[w]hat most strikes
foreign observers of the American political scene is the element of
*spectacle* involved: American politics seems to outsiders – and to many
insiders – to have a show business ethos.' In such an atmosphere, he

suggests, the political agenda can be manipulated 'through the politics of "spectacle" '.[13] In the absence of fierce ideological conflict, where the widespread agreement on the cultural norms that find expression in the idea of exceptionalism, the myth of the frontier or the pervasive temptations of the 'American Dream' is giving way to the kaleidoscopic images of multi-culturalism, style may matter more than substance in American politics. To a great extent, it has always been true; but the politics of spectacle – whether reflected in the organized hysteria of presidential nominating conventions, the advertising campaigns that market candidates as more or less interchangeable commodities, or the focus on political personalities rather than policies – may also be the consequence of attempts to reverse a progressive alienation from the political process. In such circumstances, politics has to be loud, brash, colourful, to attract any attention to itself in a society and culture both preoccupied with other concerns and wise to the ways of its elected representatives. For those who feel excluded from the American Dream, the concerns of mainstream politics are irrelevant: although they may have won the democratic franchise, they may not even vote. Indeed, for Michael Barone, 'Americans today are engaged in a search for autonomy and empowerment, trying to live and work and engage in Tocquevillian community life outside and beyond the big units that have become corrupt and unresponsive and in some cases have withered away and died.'[14] Local issues may matter more than even the various acts of state politicians or the ongoing dramas of national political life.

As John Kingdon points out, therefore,

> [g]overnment in the United States is much more limited and much smaller than government in virtually every other advanced industrialized country on earth. . . . Public policies to provide for health care, transportation, housing, and welfare for all citizens are less ambitious. . . . Our constitutional system of separation of powers and federalism is more fragmented and less prone to action, by design, than the constitutional systems of other countries. Our politics are more locally based, and centralizing features like cohesive national political parties are weaker than in other countries. This description of public policies, together with governmental institutions, adds up without undue distortion to one phrase: limited government.[15]

Why is this so? Simply because, like Huck Finn, historically most Americans have had a healthy suspicion of authority and power.

The American republic was formed in the crucible of a reaction against what was seen by contemporaries to be the arbitrary use of tyrannical power by the British monarchy in its overseas colonies.

'No taxation without representation' may not be the most inspiring revolutionary slogan ever devised, but it reflects an outraged sense of justice and a pragmatic sense of purpose. After the War of Independence had turned off the tap of imperial power in the New World, and after a number of experiments in the newly independent states, when they constructed their federal republic, Americans were very careful as to how it was turned on again. So they devised an intricate system of government: a network of interlocking institutions at various levels of political authority through which power could flow, both diffused and defused. Power often became merely the power to persuade, or indeed to influence. The animating principles of American constitutionalism – federalism, the separation of powers, the division of the legislature into two separate houses and the intricate system of checks and balances – combine to define the parameters of power within the structure of government. The aim was to prevent the abuse of power through frustrating its use. From this perspective, if there is 'gridlock' in the American political system, things are working well.

The transparent desire to limit power is simple enough to understand, yet it has produced a complex political system, the very intricacies of which may seem to provide opportunities for clandestine manipulation and political corruption. Suspicion of power in America has been accompanied by scepticism about politics and its practitioners that has, at times, been translated into a fascination with the idea that the 'government of the people, by the people, for the people' is in reality a massive conspiracy against them. It is a view that has been reflected in popular culture, particularly when Hollywood has turned its attention to such subjects.

So the political culture of the United States has been shaped by an awareness and a wariness that government can misuse and abuse power if not kept under strict control. And if government is under suspicion, so too are those who run government: politicians. As his mother puts it in describing her son's initial disability in the film *Forrest Gump* (1994), he was born 'with a back as crooked as a politician'. That brief aside encapsulates an image that resonates through America's political history. Political scandal has tainted the administrations of numerous presidents, among them Ulysses S. Grant, Warren Harding and, more recently, with an apparently quickening pace, those of Richard Nixon, Ronald Reagan and Bill Clinton. Indeed, Nixon's 'breach of faith', when he was forced to resign under threat of impeachment following the revelations of Watergate, unleashed what has now become a world-weary cynicism about the political process.

In its broadest context, then, government has tended to be seen as a threat to individual freedom in the United States, and corrupt politicians – indeed the corruption of the political process itself – is seen as compounding that threat. That is a strand in the nation's political culture, and one that was questioned only a couple of times during the twentieth century: during Franklin Roosevelt's New Deal in the 1930s, and briefly during Lyndon Johnson's Great Society in the 1960s. On both occasions, government activity to help individuals was seen in a more positive light. But the dominant public philosophy in America, reflected too in Hollywood movies – from westerns such as *High Noon* (1952) or *Shane* (1953), to the *Dirty Harry* series (1972–88), for example – is to rely on the integrity of the individual in preference to the government or the corrupt agents of authority.

This, then is a prevalent and powerful image: the ordinary American individual has a core integrity that professional politicians lack. The nineteenth-century poet Walt Whitman, in an essay he wrote just prior to the Civil War, complained about the professionalization of American politics, in which political offices, including the presidency, were 'bought, sold, electioneered for, prostituted, and filled with prostitutes'. He argued that, instead, ordinary people should take on the responsibilities of government. 'I expect to see the day when . . . qualified mechanics and young men will reach Congress and other official stations, sent in their working clothes, fresh from their benches and tools, and returning to them again with dignity.'[16] Successful politicians in the United States often run 'against government'. They go to Washington to 'clear up the mess': witness 'honest Abe' Lincoln, in Whitman's time, moving from his symbolic log cabin to the White House, and more contemporary examples such as Jimmy Carter in the immediate post-Watergate era, and indeed Ronald Reagan in the 1980s. A message on candidate George W. Bush's campaign website on the internet during the 1999–2000 primary season claimed: 'of the major candidates, I'm the only one who does not have a DC zip code. I come from outside the system with a record of reform and a record of results.' Hollywood's version of this is most obvious in the movie *Mr Smith Goes to Washington* (1939), starring James Stewart.

Yet, if Stewart went to the nation's capital to represent Wisconsin in the Senate at a critical time in contemporary politics – as war in Europe broke out and Franklin Roosevelt was about to embark on an unprecedented campaign for a third term as president – it is in the post-war period that the politics of spectacle began to compete with, and even overtake, such celluloid scenarios. During the 1950s, another senator from Wisconsin, the all too real Joseph McCarthy, would inflame the politics of fear and hysteria that accompanied the anti-communist witch-hunts of the decade. Hollywood would find itself in the front line of his indiscriminate accusations. The 1960s would be marked by Kennedy's assassination, filmed by a bystander named Abraham Zapruder but ironically missed by the television cameras – although they were there to capture the shooting of Lee Harvey Oswald. Vietnam would become the 'living-room war', fought each evening on the network news broadcasts. Images from the 1970s also resonate. Richard Nixon's trip to China in 1972 allowed media coverage of his historic meeting with Mao Tse Tung. Two years later, back in the United States, the president would announce to the nation on television his intention to resign. The following day the cameras would record the scene as he was helicoptered away from the White House for the last time. President Ford, Nixon's unelected successor, along with the rest of the nation, would witness via television Americans being forced to abandon the nation's embassy in Saigon as the North Vietnamese invaded the city. And Jimmy Carter's apparently spontaneous decision to stop his motorcade and walk down Pennsylvania Avenue after his inauguration was as much an action choreographed for the cameras as it was a symbolic populist gesture. In the 1980s, the unsuccessful attempt to assassinate Ronald Reagan was a televised event, and in the last decade of the century, George Bush's war in the Gulf appeared as a made-for-TV special, a drama that proved more of a ratings success than the soap opera of Bill Clinton's impeachment.

As these few random illustrations suggest, the politics of spectacle are given life through the presence of the media, and in particular by television. In an American world of 'infotainment', political life too may be about both informing and entertaining: a fact not lost on those like Jesse 'the Body' Ventura, the former wrestler elected governor of Minnesota in 1998.

## Conclusion: The Map of American Politics

'Tis the star-spangled banner: O long may it wave
O'er the land of the free, and the home of the brave!
*Francis Scott Key, 'The Star-Spangled Banner' (1814)*

In 1787, Minnesota could not have been imagined as a state of the Union by the fifty-five delegates from thirteen states who met in Philadelphia to frame a Constitution for the United States. They wrestled with different, though no less formidable, problems than those that confront politicians who now operate within the contours of the political system that they designed. At the same time, the continuing hold of their achievement upon the American political imagination cannot be underestimated. The next chapter of this book thus considers the 'politics of nostalgia', illuminating how America's political system still looks to the past for the ideas and the framework within which contemporary political activity is structured. It looks in particular at the influence of religion on American nationalism, and the way in which political values have been, and continue to be, shaped by religious beliefs.

Chapter 3 discusses aspects of America's Constitution. The intention is to convey a sense of the challenges that the former colonists faced after winning their independence from Britain: how to 'invent' America as 'the first new nation'. What was created was a democratic republic that could draw strength through expanding its sphere of political influence. By creating a system that allowed new states to join the Union, the founders imparted a dynamic to their constitutional settlement that would allow Thomas Jefferson's 'empire for liberty' eventually to span the continental United States, and to extend its influence beyond its natural borders to Hawaii and Alaska.

In chapter 4 the framework of American government is described. Concentrating on the political dimensions of the system of government – one in which separated institutions (executive, legislature and judiciary) share powers – the chapter analyses the changing dynamics of the relationships between president, Congress and Supreme Court. Political institutions are organic, and the operation of the political system is affected thus by changing circumstances, technologies and alterations in the dominant political mood of the nation.

Chapter 5 – 'Playing the Political Game' – begins with a discussion of power. The workings of the American political system are considered through an analysis of elitism and pluralism in American society, an examination of the activities of political parties, a consideration of the nature of electoral campaigns and a discussion of the causes and the consequences of political corruption. This leads on to a description – in chapter 6 – of the role that the media have played in commenting upon and shaping America's political culture.

Some of the faultlines in contemporary American political life are then considered. Chapter 7 looks at the stratification of American society, particularly in terms of race, class and gender, and considers how these divisions have impacted upon the nation's politics. There may be no definitive answers to the problems raised, but the chapter conveys a sense of the energy and dynamism of political debate in the United States, which is essential to the democratic health of the nation. Chapter 8 traces American perspectives on the wider world and discusses the cultural underpinnings of the attitudes that have shaped and that continue to mould the nation's foreign policy. The concluding chapter of the book draws together some of the themes that have been discussed and suggests how the ideas of Jefferson and Madison, as they have been embodied within American political culture, may still be taken to inform the nature of politics and the political processes at the end of the 'American Century' and at the beginning of the new millennium.

What, then, of Huck Finn in all of this? According to Ernest Hemingway, '[a]ll modern American literature comes from one book by Mark Twain called *Huckleberry Finn*. . . . It's the best book we've had. All American writing comes from that. There was nothing before. There has been nothing as good since.' For Norman Mailer, moreover, '[i]t is always the hope of democracy that our wealth will be there to spend again, and the ongoing treasure of *Huckleberry Finn* is that it frees us to think of democracy and its sublime, terrifying premise: Let the passions and cupidities and dreams and kinks and ideals and greed and hopes and foul corruptions of all men and women have their day and the world will still be better off, for there is more good than bad in the sum of us and our workings.'[17] If Hemingway betrays a fellow novelist's reverence for Twain as a founding father of American literature, then Mailer's assessment hints too at the continuing relevance of Huck's decision to 'light out for the Territory': to escape into the limitless possibilities of the American Dream. For Huck's adventure may be a timeless metaphorical construction of the 'idea of America' itself; one that would have been as recognizable to the founders of America's republic as it is to their present-day descendants. It is, moreover, a vision steeped in a simple and enduring nostalgia for the political spirit of 1776.

# 2

# The Politics of Nostalgia

> In short, if the principle on which the cause is founded, the universal blessings that are to arise from it, the difficulties that accompanied it, the wisdom with which it has been debated, the fortitude by which it has been supported, the strength of the power which we had to oppose, and the condition in which we undertook it, be all taken in one view, we may justly style it the most virtuous and illustrious revolution that ever graced the history of mankind.
>
> *Thomas Paine*, Common Sense (*1778*)

Two years earlier in December 1776, Thomas Paine, the most influential propagandist of his generation, while remaining optimistic, had not been so sure. Then, in the first of his series of revolutionary pamphlets, *Common Sense*, he had vividly dramatized the situation as Britain's colonies in America fought for independence.

> These are the times that try men's souls. The summer soldier and the sunshine patriot will, in this crisis, shrink from the service of their country; but he that stands it now, deserves the love and thanks of man and woman . . . my secret opinion has ever been, and still is, that God Almighty will not give up a people to military destruction, or leave them unsupportedly to perish, who have so earnestly and so repeatedly sought to avoid the calamities of war, by every decent method which wisdom could invent.

Here, then, are the original elements of America's most prevalent and enduring sense of itself as a nation formed in the crucible of a revolution, fighting for independence, not simply against the tyranny of an imperial power, but for a fundamental principle of freedom. It was a war, moreover, in which the colonies were on the right side of the moral argument, peaceable until provoked, and so they had a powerful ally. God was on their side.

The political and religious values on which many Americans believe their country has been built were crystallized in a highly charged moment of history: the events of the last twenty-five years of the eighteenth century that resulted in the political transformation of Britain's American colonies into the United States of America. What is fascinating about this process, therefore, is the way in which its repercussions continue to ripple throughout America's contemporary political culture. This was the 'Big Bang' that created the universe of American politics. It also imbued the American political system with a profound sense of nostalgia: constantly looking backward – even as Thomas Paine did in 1778 – to an era in which revolutionary ideas became real, creating the framework within which political activity is structured even to this day.

Commenting on this political sentimentalism in the 1950s, the historian Daniel Boorstin observed in *The Genius of American Politics* that

> [b]iologists used to believe that if you could look at the seed of an apple under a strong enough microscope you would see in it a minute apple tree. Similarly, we still seem to believe that if we could understand the ideas of the earliest settlers – the Pilgrim Fathers or Founding Fathers – we would find in them no mere seventeenth- or eighteenth-century philosophy of government but the perfect embryo of the theory by which we now live. We believe, then, that the mature political ideals of the nation existed clearly conceived in the minds of our patriarchs. The notion is essentially static. It assumes that the values and theory of the nation were given once and for all in the very beginning.[1]

The twin sources of inspiration for this 'idea of America' became the Pilgrims and the Founders, one group religious, the other secular. In the beginning, then, were their words: the sermons of the puritan ministers as they spoke to their New England congregations, and later, with no less dramatic effect, those of Thomas Jefferson, the author, in 1776, of America's Declaration of Independence.

## The Rhetoric of Religion

Puritanism: the haunting fear that someone, somewhere, may be happy.

*H.L. Mencken*, A Book of Burlesques (*1916*)

The puritans occupy an ambiguous place in American cultural mythology. In *The Scarlet Letter* (1850), Nathaniel Hawthorne appears to foreshadow Mencken's famous definition, describing how the puritans lost the capacity for enjoyment: '[T]he generation next to the early emigrants, wore the blackest shade of Puritanism, and so darkened the national visage with it, that all the subsequent years have not sufficed to clear it up. We have yet to learn again the forgotten art of gayety.'[2] And yet no other group among America's early colonists have managed to exercise such a continuing hold upon the nation's political imagination.

The puritans, inspired by their faith not simply to settle in America but also to make a new world there, were firm in their religious and political convictions. They came with a plan. Yet inevitably the real world impinged upon their idealism. Sometimes things went wrong. When the community appeared to be failing in its task of building the 'city upon a hill', however, its leaders had a powerful weapon in their theological armoury. In the pulpits of New England, sermons took on a particular form – a rhetorical style that also helped to shape American political oratory: the jeremiad.

The puritan jeremiad was a form of spiritual stock-taking. It provided an analysis of misfortune: setbacks were due to the community's inability to live up to its ideals, to follow the blue-print that had been set out for it. To return to the path of righteousness, it was necessary for individuals to acknowledge their failings, repent for their misdemeanours and redouble their efforts to live according to the strict rules of puritan belief. As such, jeremiads are as useful for contemporary politicians as they were for puritan ministers.

The politics of nostalgia thus takes for granted that the ideals and ideas expressed by American patriarchs – be they Pilgrim or Founding Fathers – are both enduring and beyond debate. What is at issue is the capacity of the community at any given time to achieve these promises of American life. Hence America becomes the land of revivalism and evangelism: of religious, moral and political crusades. For this vision of a religious and secular utopia is both a burden and a hope. It may be difficult to achieve, but such is the mission that defines America not simply to itself but also to the wider world.

As Garry Wills points out in his analysis of religion and American politics, *Under God* (1990), during the 1988 presidential election campaign, both Pat Robertson and Jesse Jackson, from opposite ends of the religious-political spectrum in contemporary American public life, could nevertheless use virtually identical language in calling 'for a moral revival in America, a return to family values, a toughening of school discipline, a war on drugs'. Indeed, as Wills observes, '[p]reachers need devils. . . . The sinner needs to be rescued from the threat of an evil that breathes down on him. A crisis is always at hand.' Moreover, he suggests, '[t]his aspect of our political language is derived . . . from the jeremiads of New England meeting times.' The influence of puritan oratory thus imparts a high moral tone to much American political rhetoric, and the influence of religion in the nation's politics remains self-evident.

The significance of such highly charged religious language is that it provides a context within which Americans may be allowed to exercise their God-given rights: particularly liberty. Once more, the puritans are useful guides. Religious beliefs suggest codes of conduct, placing moral limits on an otherwise unabridged liberty to act according to individual choice. Here, then, the jeremiad becomes a way of policing the community's behaviour. It was, as Wills argues, 'less a genre of oratory than a style of thought, one used in the sermons of the Puritan calendar (especially the sermons preached on Election Days). As the name . . . would indicate, the preacher denounced like an ancient prophet the people's defection from its contract . . . with God, a defection that can free God from honoring his promises in the contract.'[3] Thus it is no accident that at the end of *The Scarlet Letter*, Hawthorne's Reverend Mr Dimmesdale confesses his secret relationship with Hester Prynne prior to his death on the scaffold, just after he has given an election day sermon: his own fate a symbolic microcosm of that which would befall the community if they too stray from the path of strict moral probity.

Tocqueville's observation was as accurate as it was acute: 'Liberty regards religion as its companion in all its battles and its triumphs, as the cradle of its infancy and the divine source of its claims. It considers religion as the safeguard of morality, and morality as the best security of law and the surest pledge of the duration of freedom.'[4] George Washington had expressed a similar view in his farewell address of 1796: 'Of all the dispensations and habits which lead to political prosperity, religion and morality are indispensable supports. . . . And let us with caution indulge the supposition that morality can be maintained without religion. . . . reason and experience both forbid us to expect that national morality can prevail in exclusion of religious principle.' This connection between religion, morality and the preservation of America's republican ideals is thus a continuing theme, shaping the nation's political culture.

Indeed as Neil Campbell and Alasdair Kean point out,

> [r]eligious traditions in America have always involved visions of America itself. America was where good and evil would struggle in a continuing

battle for supremacy in full view of the rest of the world. . . . The religious dimension to the story of America . . . has been a pervasive theme in the country's expressive culture, giving it a powerful resonance beyond the history of specific churches and often endowing its language with special meaning and force. From this perspective, religious imagery and religious themes have had a considerable influence on the way Americans have reflected and acted, not only in the literature they have produced, but also in political language and rhetoric.[5]

Patterns of religious thought have shaped, reinforced and influenced political ideas both directly and indirectly to produce a society in which spiritual convictions help to mould attitudes towards the nation and its place in the wider world.

This religious underpinning of political culture was something that Tocqueville too observed on his visit to America in the 1830s. So the 'character of Anglo-American civilization' was 'the result (and this should be constantly kept in mind) of two distinct elements, which in other places have been in frequent disagreement, but which the Americans have succeeded in incorporating to some extent one with the other and combining admirably. I allude to the *spirit of religion* and the *spirit of liberty*.'[6] In this sense, therefore, the ideals of the Pilgrim Fathers can be connected with those of the Founding Fathers, and indeed the nostalgic vision of America itself is firmly rooted in the fundamental charters of the nation: in the Constitution of 1787, but first, and perhaps even more significantly, in the Declaration of Independence of 1776.

## Life, Liberty and the Pursuit of Happiness

It will be a service to the Church of great Consequence to carry the Gospel into those parts of the world, and to raise a bullwark against the kingdom of Antichrist which the Jesuits labour to rear up in all places of the world.

*John Winthrop*, General Observations (*1629*)

When Winthrop was contemplating his 'errand into the wilderness' in the early years of the seventeenth century, one of the motivations to undertake the mission was to build a Protestant bridgehead in North America, since other European – and Catholic – powers were simultaneously staking their claims in the New World. Such religious antagonisms and rivalries were still present at the time of the American Revolution; indeed, British toleration of Catholicism in Canada after the Quebec Act of 1773 was a powerful source of resentment in the American colonies. By 1776, however, American hostility was focused not so much against 'the kingdom of Antichrist' as on the contemporary king of England: George III. And it was the Declaration of Independence that set out, eloquently, sincerely and dramatically, not simply the reasons for America's wish to become self-governing, but also the fundamental principles upon which the colonies would now seek to conduct their own political affairs.

> When in the Course of human events, it becomes necessary for one people to dissolve the political bands which have connected them with another, and to assume among the powers of the earth, the separate and equal station to which the Laws of Nature and Nature's God entitle them, a decent respect to the opinions of mankind requires that they should declare the causes which impel them to the separation.

Thomas Jefferson was thirty-three when he drafted this introduction to the document with which his name would be for ever associated. In it, he not only established the significance of his task: to provide a reasoned explanation as to why, instead of being a mere colonial rebellion, the American cause was of transcendent moral and political significance. The Declaration was, in essence, a self-justification of American actions flowing from a forensic analysis of the conduct of George III that had precipitated the colonial crisis, and including for good measure a more general attack on British imperial attitudes that had done little to avoid it. But Jefferson also provided the most concise – and often-quoted – articulation of the promise of American life, and in so doing not simply argued the case for independence, but also laid the foundations for what would become subsequently a new sense of political community within the United States.

> We hold these truths to be self-evident, that all men are created equal, that they are endowed by their Creator with certain unalienable Rights, that among these are Life, liberty and the pursuit of happiness. That to secure these rights, Governments are instituted among Men, deriving their just powers from the consent of the governed. That whenever any Form of Government becomes destructive of these ends, it is the Right of the people to alter or abolish it, and to institute new Government, laying its foundation on such principles and organizing its powers in such form, as to them shall seem most likely to effect their Safety and Happiness.

In framing the preamble of the Declaration in this way, Jefferson effectively asserted the principles of a democratic republic. That indeed is what makes the document a revolutionary charter. If it was taken seriously, it implied not simply that America should no longer be part of the British Empire, but that it should decide for itself a form of government that was different from that which it had rejected.

The Declaration reflected the cultural and social realities of its time. When Jefferson asserted that 'all men are created equal', it was self-evident that not only were African-Americans and indeed Native Americans excluded from the reckoning, but that women too were for the moment forgotten in this brave new political world. Nevertheless, Jefferson's argument, that those whom God creates as equals have been given 'unalienable rights' to life, liberty and the pursuit of happiness, is a vision of a community in which a sense of political – and social – hierarchy is absent. Moreover, the sole purpose of government is to guarantee those rights, and, furthermore, any political powers delegated to it are only exercised as long as the community continues to give its approval to its actions. This allows Jefferson to go on to make his revolutionary claim: that if government acts to deny people their unalienable rights, then they have the further right to 'alter or abolish it' and set up instead new structures that will better provide for their security and their happiness.

Jefferson wrote in a letter to John Adams in 1826 that the Declaration did not set out 'new principles, or new arguments, never before thought of', but instead put

> before mankind the common sense of the subject, in terms so plain and firm as to command their assent, and to justify ourselves in the independent stand we are compelled to take. Neither aiming at originality of principle or sentiment, nor yet copied from any particular or previous writing, it was intended to be an expression of the American mind, and to give to that expression the proper tone and spirit called for by the occasion.

Tom Paine's had been one of the most influential voices raised in favour of independence in the months before the Continental Congress unanimously endorsed the Declaration, and, indeed, *Common Sense* was influential in not only persuading Americans of the case for independence, but also convincing them to volunteer to fight for the cause. It was precisely because the British, along with their king, George III, lacked such common sense that Americans felt compelled to rebel.

The Declaration's indictment of George III also contributed to the rejection of the whole idea of monarchy in the newly independent states. In other words, the sub-text of Jefferson's arguments influenced the climate of opinion in favour of republicanism. Unelected and unaccountable, the king had abused his executive powers, had colluded with the British parliament to pass laws the colonists considered unconstitutional, and then had gone to war with them. Indeed, the Declaration's most powerful impact as a piece of political propaganda was to cast George III in the role of tyrant. His subjects, too, were little better in condoning his actions. They might have identified with the colonists' position: as the Declaration puts it, '[w]e have reminded them of the circumstances of our emigration and settlement here. We have appealed to their native justice and magnanimity.' But like their king, 'they too have been deaf to the voice of justice and consanguinity. We must, therefore, acquiesce in the necessity, which denounces our Separation, and hold them, as we hold the rest of mankind, Enemies in War, in Peace Friends.' In declaring their independence, moreover, Americans were throwing not simply their relationship with the British into a melting pot. The rhetoric that inspired rebellion would also provoke a political revolution. Independence destroyed the existing forms of governance in America, and ultimately led to the creation of something quite different: a democratic republic. Moreover, once established, this new political system has proved to be remarkably impervious to further radical change.

In the power of its argument and the eloquence of its rhetoric lies the enduring appeal of the Declaration as one of the most concise articulations of the 'idea of America'. It combines an appeal to general political principles together with a – necessarily – one-sided analysis of contemporary political reality to provide a justification not simply for independence but also for what was to follow. In sum, it revealed two significant facets of American thought as the colonies fought for independence: first, that if successful, Americans would be free to decide their own form of government; second, that they would not seek to re-create merely a less corrupt model of the monarchical system they had rejected. This much, then, was Jefferson's achievement in July 1776.

Yet the Declaration of Independence is also a manifesto for American expansionism. Although issued by the thirteen colonies that then clustered the eastern sea-board of the continent, there could be no doubt that its aims and aspirations implied that any new territories acquired or annexed would come within the orbit of what Jefferson later referred to as America's 'empire for liberty'. As his contemporary John Adams put it, '[t]hirteen governments thus founded on the natural authority of the people alone . . . and which are destined to spread over the northern part of that whole quarter of the globe, are a great point gained in favour of the rights of mankind.' In this sense, therefore, the Declaration is not simply an expression of the fundamental

values of American democracy. It offers the prospect for the growth
of an independent republic, eventually expanding 'from sea to shining
sea', in which the extension of Jefferson's ideal of an equal right to
liberty to all its inhabitants would prove to be a constant and continuing political struggle.

## Aftermath: The Westward Course of Empire

Go west, young man, go west.
*Saying attributed to Horace Greeley (1853)*

Following independence, expansion became an essential part of the
process of creating America's sense of national identity, such that even
after the territorial integrity of the nation was assured, the dynamism
of the principles that energized the republic endured. During the
nineteenth century, the preoccupation with building the 'empire for
liberty' limited expansion to the domestic sphere. Thereafter, however, the 'idea of America' was projected abroad, to an international
audience. The puritans' version of American history outlined the
plot. Their 'errand into the wilderness', which took place first in New
England, evolved into the national 'manifest destiny' to claim a continent in the name of the democratic and republican ideal. The heroes of
this later story, when the errand became more of an adventure, were
those who transformed, and who were themselves transformed by, the
frontier. As the religious roots of America's sense of mission became
secularized, the pioneer assumed responsibility for the successful pro-
jection of the 'idea of America' across the North American continent.
This was not necessarily the conscious motivation that inspired an
individual pioneering spirit. But for the historians who chronicled
it, the temptation was to see the westward migration as natural, and
even providentially designed.

   The puritans saw history as the enactment of God's will and
their future determined by providence. That belief, secularized and
universalized, structured the subsequent story of America's 'manifest
destiny'. The War of Independence separated the American colonies
from Britain. But as Thomas Paine appreciated, the real victory lay
in the philosophical and ideological triumph that inspired 'a revolution in the principles and practice of government'. The Jeffersonian
rhetoric of an equal right to liberty persuaded Americans not to re-
create European feudal institutions in their newly independent nation.
Indeed, the United States was a nation uniquely chosen to advance

the democratic cause. This version of American history, moreover, from its beginnings as an interpretation of both America's past and its purpose, removed the responsibility of historical causation from individuals, and placed it with the external agency of providence. In doing so it endorsed the ideology of a missionary and expansionary nationalism, since it was difficult to dissent from the dictates of a divine design.

For most of the nineteenth century the nation's missionary and expansionist impulse was directed towards internal concerns: the Louisiana Purchase, the annexation of Texas, disputing Oregon and fighting Mexico. It culminated in the cathartic crisis of the Civil War. This form of territorial expansionism within a self-ascribed sphere of influence was not quite the same as adventuring overseas – in European terms, imperialism. But it was a similar enterprise. If this imperialist persuasion initially can be seen purely in an American context, more-over, it necessarily affected the perspective of the United States on the wider world. Washington's farewell address (1796) and Monroe's Doctrine (1823), so often the cornerstones of an isolationist argument, can equally be viewed as part of a sustained effort to maintain an independent posture in foreign affairs, in order to preserve the con-tinental hinterland for America's own designs.

The assertion of independence thus involved territorial expan-sion. If Washington and Monroe argued rhetorically the need for an American sphere of influence that was free from foreign encroachment, then as new states joined the union, the assumption of sovereignty across the continent strengthened the political integrity of the nation. The movement westwards thus becomes a vital element in the process of building the nation. Yet at the same time as westward expansion was strengthening the union, so the argument over slavery – the 'peculiar institution' – drove the north and south apart. After Civil War had once threatened, and then in its outcome had preserved, the union, however, the desire to expand in order to consolidate once again proved difficult to resist. As the United States emerged intact from Civil War, it did so with an unreconstructed sense of national purpose. And the 'idea of America', endorsed domestically, would begin to be projected also abroad.

During the twentieth century, through two world wars, and par-ticularly during the Cold War, America seemed still to have, in Harold Evans' felicitous phrase, 'a franchise on the future'.[7] So George Bush, who was president at the symbolic moment when the fall of the Berlin Wall gave dramatic point to the collapse of communism as democracy's contemporary political adversary, could speak in his 1990 State of the Union address of 'America, not just the nation but an idea, alive in the minds of people everywhere. As this new world takes shape, America stands at the center of a widening circle of freedom – today, tomorrow and into the next century. . . . This nation, this idea called America, was and always will be a new world – our new world.' The politics of nostalgia once more connects Jefferson's vision with contemporary rhetoric: as history unfolds, America's destiny appears to be endorsed. It is not as simple as that. Within this celebratory version of America's past, there is another story to be told: the struggle of many to be included within the frame of Jefferson's reference, to press for the extension of the ideals of the Declaration of Independence so that it might fulfil its potential as a revolutionary document, relevant to all.


## 'What to the Slave is the Fourth of July?'


This Fourth of July is *yours*, not *mine*. *You* may rejoice, *I* must mourn.

> Frederick Douglass, 'What to the Slave
> is the Fourth of July?' (1852)

While white Americans might celebrate Jefferson's achievement in writing the Declaration of Independence, as the former slave and activist for black equality Frederick Douglass rightly pointed out in 1852, for those still enslaved, 4 July was a date that had no meaning. While slavery endured, the Declaration appeared to those who suffered under it as tantalizing rhetoric. Independence Day was a festival of exclusion – while some could participate in the annual ritual that reminded them of their achievement, for others the 'sounds of rejoicing are empty and heartless . . . your shouts of liberty and equality, hollow mockery'. For those who might only observe rather than participate in the political and cultural mainstream of American life, the politics of nostalgia did not mean merely a complacent faith in Jefferson's achievement. Rather, they saw the Declaration as a work in progress.

So, for Douglass, as for many other radicals, the Declaration of Independence remained both a promise and an inspiration. Until the outcome of the Civil War resolved the issue, the pernicious impact of slavery in its southern states did not simply define political debate in America, it also moulded the contours of the political system. Those, like Douglass, and other abolitionists, whose political views were often framed in the context of profound religious and moral conviction looked to the Declaration as a radical charter that endorsed their beliefs. In 1833, in Philadelphia, William Lloyd Garrison founded the American Anti-Slavery Society. In its *Declaration of Sentiments* it appealed to the political rhetoric of 1776 in order to make its case: 'With entire confidence in the overruling justice of God, we plant ourselves upon the Declaration of our Independence and the truths of Divine Revelation, as upon the everlasting Rock.' Seven years later, the society had over a quarter of a million members.

Moreover, abolitionism was not simply the preserve of ex-slaves and well-meaning enlightened white male liberals. Women too understood that slavery did not simply threaten the moral fabric of society, but had an impact too upon their status, notably in the south itself. Nineteenth-century radicalism would thus embrace not simply the cause of civil rights for African-Americans held in slavery, but also, by extension, the demand for increased political representation and participation for women. It was thus no accident that many leading abolitionists were women. In 1840, for example, Elizabeth Cady Stanton tried to attend the World's Anti-Slavery Convention in London, only to be refused entry to a meeting that British abolitionists, along with conservative American colleagues, wanted to keep – presumably without seeing the paradox – a male-only event. Eight years later, Stanton drafted the Declaration of Rights and Sentiments at the Seneca Falls convention, and, like Garrison before her, drew upon Jefferson's Declaration to make her case for women's rights.

If the Declaration of Independence was a promissory note for American expansionism, it was Native Americans who felt the full force of the territorial imperative that underpinned the rhetoric of the drive towards an 'empire for liberty'. Over time, the federal government consistently endorsed the policies that gave substance to the idea of 'manifest destiny' and that effectively determined how the west was won. And not simply the west of Hollywood's imagination. In appropriate and significant fashion, on 4 July 1803, twenty-seven years to the day after the Declaration had been signed, the *National Intelligencer* reported that President Jefferson had successfully concluded the Louisiana Purchase: one of the shrewdest real-estate deals ever made. This opened up the possibility of expansion beyond the Mississippi: one of the great themes in nineteenth-century American history.

Yet, as Clyde Milner observes,

[m]ilitary conquests, unfair treaties, and political inequities sustained government initiatives beyond the Mississippi. For example, in the first major effort to encourage settlement, the government forced the resettlement of American Indians in the trans-Mississippi by removing them

from lands east of the Mississippi. . . . After the War of 1812, the Monroe administration became more committed to the idea of exchanging Indian title, and thus changing Indian residency, to lands beyond the Mississippi. Proponents of Indian removal, from Thomas Jefferson to Andrew Jackson, justified this policy as a benefit to Native Americans.

This, then, was an early example of the idea of containment: keeping Native Americans away from the mainstream of American society. The policy of forced resettlement moved them to what was then thought to be 'worthless land', and 'the same logic that relegated eastern Indians' to such parts of the country 'would later be used to justify the creation of such diverse entities as national parks, nuclear bomb test sites, toxic waste dumps, and numerous Indian reservations.'[8] Whereas the winning of the west would be celebrated – not least by Hollywood – as an epic example of American achievement, for those who suffered as a result, for Native Americans in particular, the legacy of 'manifest destiny' is far more dubious, and the idealism of the Declaration a promise unfulfilled.

## Radicalism and Equality

Radical Chic . . . is only radical in Style; in its heart it is part of Society and its tradition – Politics, like Rock, Pop, and Camp, has its uses.

*Tom Wolfe*, Radical Chic and Mau-Mauing
the Flak Catchers (*1970*)

The mainstream politics of nostalgia, while celebrating Jefferson's rhetorical achievement, still leaves others room to question its contemporary reality as a description of American society. So to what extent do Americans still agree that all are 'created equal'? And what are the consequences of holding such a conviction? Jefferson's statement expresses an important principle. It becomes part of the broader spectrum of political values that form the basis of a political consensus within American society: the Declaration of Independence thus becomes the symbolic and enduring expression of those values and that consensus, of transcendent importance to any understanding of American political life.

Nevertheless, equality – whether defined in terms of equality of opportunity or equality of worth – may remain an ambition rather than an achievement in the United States. If this is the case, then the

Declaration indeed becomes a charter for radicalism, since Jefferson's assertion can be taken as a call for reform – nowhere better illustrated than in the campaign for civil rights. As Staughton Lynd observes, therefore, radicals in America 'have stubbornly refused to surrender the memory of the American Revolution to liberalism or reaction, insisting that only radicalism could make real the rhetoric of 1776. . . . Americans concerned to change the society around them have made appropriate use of the past as a source for forgotten alternatives, for encouragement to endure.'[9] Once again, Jefferson's articulation of an 'idea of America' is the fulcrum upon which such sentiment turns.

Yet the reality has been radically different from the Declaration's rhetoric. Equality has been the exclusive preserve of some rather than a right enjoyed by all. So at various stages in the nation's history, Native Americans, slaves and women have been denied the rights that flow from the Declaration's assertion of the principle. To a greater or lesser extent, each such disenfranchised group, if it seeks incorporation into America's political community, has had to battle with the politics of exclusion, some with greater success than others. This involves engaging in more than a semantic debate about the political implications of Jefferson's words. To the extent that its central animating ideal is thus compromised, the Declaration expresses an aspiration to achieve the ideal rather than reflecting the reality of American political life. Yet Jefferson's eloquence remains an inspiration for radicals in its expression of what was then, and can still be now, a revolutionary idea.

## Conclusion: 'The Secret of Paine'

The United States themselves are essentially the greatest poem.
*Walt Whitman*, Leaves of Grass (*1855*)

It was Louis Hartz who uncovered 'the secret of Paine'. 'The amazing success he had with his attack on monarchy in 1776 seems mysterious only because we overlook the fact that colonial history had long been preparing the nation for it. . . . What Paine did was to make this hostility explicit – the most powerful technique any propagandist can use.'[10] In similar fashion the influence of religion upon contemporary politics should come as no surprise, since it has been a feature of American political thinking since colonial times.

It should be equally unremarkable, then, that, while the Declaration of Independence became a charter for the creation of America's democratic republic, those who have agitated, protested and fought for the wider application of its ideals have often done so with a profound sense of religious conviction. In the 1830s, for example, as the contemporary historian George Bancroft noted, '[t]here is fast rising in New England a moral Democracy in harmony with Christianity . . . in harmony with the progress of Civilization. Democracy is practical Christianity.'[11] Indeed, an appeal to the higher law of a Christian conscience is at the core of transcendentalist ideas, which had their greatest impact in nineteenth-century New England. Ralph Waldo Emerson, and notably Henry David Thoreau, both from Massachusetts, were among the leading intellectuals and political theorists of their time. Both underpinned their philosophical ideas with a profound sense of Christian purpose. Thoreau's *Essay on Civil Disobedience* (1849) argued effectively that there were times when a sense of moral obligation outweighed the necessity to obey an unjust law: a philosophical position adopted subsequently not only by nineteenth-century abolitionists, but also by those who, a hundred years later, pressed the case for civil rights in America.

Religion and abolitionism were often inseparable. Indeed, to win support, abolitionists represented slavery as a Manichean battle between good and evil, a dramatic narrative being played out in a section of the United States, where every slave-owner was a tyrant, every slave a victim, and all were brutalized by an institution that remained at odds with the values of Christianity, democracy, civilization and social justice. It was a story that had to be told in stark terms; indeed the arguments were black and white. This, for example, was the climate of opinion in which Harriet Beecher Stowe produced *Uncle Tom's Cabin* (1852): a brilliant piece of political advocacy through literature. The Fugitive Slave Law, passed the previous year, was the catalyst for the work. In her 'concluding remarks' to the book, Stowe admitted that, after that legislation, when she heard 'Christian and humane people' debating whether they had a duty to return fugitives to slavery or to follow their more enlightened consciences, she concluded that such 'Christians cannot know what slavery is; if they did, such a question could never be open for discussion. And from this arose a desire to exhibit it in a *living dramatic reality*.'[12] The power and influence of the book represented an unprecedented achievement: *Uncle Tom's Cabin* presented an image of slavery that became established in popular imagination so forcefully that those who tried to defend the south's 'peculiar institution' could not dislodge it. As Abraham Lincoln exclaimed on meeting Stowe, after the political struggle between north and south had finally erupted into violent conflict, 'so you're the little woman who wrote the book that made this great war!'

The religious convictions that gave rise to abolitionism thus also helped to fuel the antagonisms that led to the Civil War. When, finally, it was over, William Lloyd Garrison went to Charleston, South Carolina, and on 14 April 1863 – the night of Abraham Lincoln's assassination – made a speech that once more connected his Christian beliefs with the idealism of 1776. He summed up the meaning of the long struggle against the 'peculiar institution'. 'Abolitionism, what is it? Liberty. What is liberty? Abolitionism. What are they both? Politically, one is the Declaration of Independence; religiously, the other is the Golden Rule of our Savior.'

Such faith in God is, as Billy Graham claimed in 1970, 'woven into the warp and woof of our nation'. For Garry Wills, 'nothing has been more stable in our history, nothing less budgeable, than religious belief and practice.' If such belief is an historical constant, contemporary manifestations of it in a political context are again nothing new; they point instead to the strength of religion as a dynamic force in the nation's life. Intensity of belief may fluctuate, but the core commitment remains. So as Wills observes, '[t]he revival has been the distinctively American religious experience (much as jazz is the most distinctive musical form).'[13] Yet revivalism is in itself a mixture of evangelical fervour and a belief that there is a need for new energies to be poured into an individual's or the community's religious commitment. As such it again draws a nostalgic inspiration from the sense of mission that imbued the Puritan's 'errand'. Indeed, the jeremiad, standing as a clarion call to renewed effort, is the dynamo of revivalism.

The pervasive influence of puritanism may also be found in unlikely places. In discussing television talk shows and the 'culture of confession' in contemporary America, Jeffrey Walsh argues that

> puritanism still exists in America, both as a cultural memory and as a stylistic mode which enables people to make sense of their society and their own lives. Talk shows, as do other cultural discourses, capitalise upon this legacy. . . . The talk show's sensibility, with its emphasis upon emotional self-disclosure, intimate revelations, confessions of guilt and the chastisement of wrongdoers, carries overtones of voyeurism alongside its implicit claims of instruction and moral guidance. The ubiquitousness of such a formula . . . has popularised a neo-Puritanical genre which has a tripartite structure: confession; trial by television; audience verdict. Inevitably, such media discourses have wider repercussions in cultural life'.[14]

Moreover, the most popular of America's recent presidents have been able to make political capital from the spirit of these times. So, as Garry Wills observes, 'President Reagan was constantly praised as "a great communicator" without giving enough emphasis to *what* he was communicating. He *communicated* religious attitudes. . . . He would pray at the drop of a hat – as when he prayed for a soap opera character's deliverance from the indignities imposed upon her by the show's writers.'[15] More significantly, Bill Clinton's ability to survive the political trauma of impeachment – itself often reminiscent of a puritan witch-hunt – with his popularity more or less unchanged owed much to his ability to cast himself in the role of puritan penitent. Jeffrey Walsh suggests that Hillary Clinton also used 'Puritan imagery' in her analysis of the impeachment verdict, and drew attention to the distinction in Christian belief between 'sins of weakness and sins of malice'. The president had committed 'a sin of weakness': behaviour that his national audience could judge and, steeped in the conventions of the talk show, upon which they could deliver their own verdict, depending upon their Christian capacity for forgiveness.[16]

Religion remains therefore one of the moral foundations of the American republic. Political movements in the United States often articulate their beliefs in religious terms. Thus, the 'Social Gospel' of the immediate post-Civil War period suggested that economic injustices caused by rapid industrialization and the excesses of capitalist development threatened the ideals of a Christian democratic republic. And the radical critique advanced by its proponents – in opposition to those who promoted the 'gospel of wealth' as the appropriate ideology for what Mark Twain dubbed 'the Gilded Age' – drew its secular inspiration once more from the values of the Declaration of Independence.

For black America, inspirational leadership has come from within its own religious community. The civil rights movement of the 1950s and 1960s was initially shaped by the values of the Southern Christian Leadership Conference, led by the Reverend Martin Luther King, Jr. In his famous speech at the end of the 'March on Washington for Jobs and Freedom' in August 1963, moreover, King gave an eloquent reminder of the continuing hope contained in the revolutionary vision of 1776.

> When the architects of our republic wrote the magnificent words . . . of the Declaration of Independence, they were signing a promissory note to which every American was to fall heir. This note was a promise that all men would be guaranteed the unalienable rights of life, liberty and the pursuit of happiness. . . . I still have a dream. It is a dream deeply rooted in the American dream. I have a dream that one day this nation will rise up and live out the true meaning of its creed: 'We hold these truths to be self-evident; that all men are created equal.'

For King, then, the Declaration of Independence becomes a source of political inspiration for a radical movement whose aims are rooted in his religious convictions. He used biblical imagery to end his dream 'that one day every valley shall be exalted, every hill and mountain shall be made low, the rough places will be made plain, and the crooked places will be made straight, and the glory of the Lord shall be revealed, and all flesh shall see it together.' The secular and religious rhetoric is fused together in an inspirational, compelling speech designed to galvanize the nation in the pursuit of racial justice and harmony.

To focus upon the significance of religion in American political life, and to point to the Declaration of Independence as the articulation of the core values of its republican democracy, is to emphasize the historical context within which the American political tradition has been framed. Just as the myth of exceptionalism and a sense of its providential mission map the contours of contemporary American politics, so an appreciation of the importance of the nation's historical experiences in shaping its political culture is critical to an understanding of the way in which America may be defined, both to itself and in terms of its sense of place in relation to the wider world. If the contours of American foreign policy can be traced through the pronouncements of its presidents, from George Washington's farewell address, and on to Monroe's or Truman's Doctrine, the idealism that also underpins the rhetoric of overseas adventurism is once more a product of the nation's history.

In an essay discussing the impact of the revolution upon the wider world, Richard Morris suggests that

> [f]rom its inception the American Revolution was pitched on a moral and even evangelical plane. The didactic character of the American Revolution has for better or worse permanently stamped itself upon American diplomacy. Stripped of its sense of mission the Revolution would have lost much of its world significance, while America's intervention in world affairs in the twentieth century would have assumed the character of a naked power grab. That America now ventures to shoulder global responsibilities of awesome dimension is attributable in no small part to the rearing of the American people during the infancy of the Republic.[17]

That sense of evangelical mission, expressed throughout the twentieth century in terms of Woodrow Wilson's desire that 'the world must be made safe for democracy', was the motor of overseas activism, which culminated in America's 'mission impossible' in Vietnam. And just as the Civil War stands as the most significant event in nineteenth-century American history, so the Cold War and America's defeat in Vietnam had profound political, social and cultural repercussions on the nation a century later. During and after Vietnam a sense of political consensus in the United States was shattered. With the country's political compass apparently awry, moreover, the moral certainties of religion once again became attractive: it is no accident that religious revivalism flourished in the aftermath of America's involvement in Vietnam, and that in a politically fractured society, fundamentalist religion has become a powerful political force.

As the American intervention in Vietnam unravelled into defeat, the rhetoric of mission that had initially sustained it was revealed as inadequate to its task. In an effort to rebuild its missionary morale, the nation embraced the politics of nostalgia, celebrating its former history of achievement – a talent best expressed during the 1980s in the speeches of its president, Ronald Reagan. The experience of Vietnam quarrelled with America's sense of history and of purpose. Reagan's approach was to attempt to bury memories of the recent past through rhetorical exhortations to remember the storybook truths that had, until then, served the nation so well. In so doing, he was honouring an established American tradition. As Daniel Boorstin points out, there are 'few nations whose oratory can bring the student so close to their history'. He also suggests, for example, that '[t]he famous Fourth of July oration is not simply an example of the dilution of American literature; it is actually an important institution, a touchstone of American political thought.' In many ways it is also the secular equivalent of the puritans' election day sermon. The most successful American politicians, be they presidents or not, have managed to connect a vision of the future with myths taken from a celebratory version of America's past, and have often spoken of it in quasi-religious terms. So for Boorstin,

> [t]he more popular and influential preachers of our national ideals have stood midway between politics and religion: Franklin, Washington, Jefferson, Lincoln, Bryan, Theodore Roosevelt, Wilson, and even Franklin Roosevelt. Much of our political articulation is in this religio-political realm and could be taken equally as an example of what we have called a generalized religion or as an affirmation of political ideals.[18]

To this list of political preachers might also be added, among others, Martin Luther King, Jr, and Ronald Reagan.

The politics of nostalgia moulds myth and history to create a powerful image of American national identity. Moreover, the 'idea of America' has acted as a spark not simply to ignite political rhetoric but also to fire literary imagination. In an essay discussing why, unlike

American playwrights and novelists, British writers are reluctant to 'map the state of the nation', Brian Appleyard suggests that '[i]n America, a fundamental patriotism is more than respectable, it is intrinsic; . . . its writers, though they may criticize, lampoon and abuse aspects of their national life, retain an underlying belief in the idea of America. The faults they find in it are faults of inauthenticity, of not being American enough.' He goes on to argue that

> [t]his produces a radically different view of history. To the British, the 18th century is just another historical era; to the Americans, it is the age of Washington and Jefferson, still sacred figures, when the greatest of all human experiments was launched. We appeal to other societies to show where we have gone wrong; Americans appeal to the greatness of their own past.[19]

The contemporary contours of American politics are thus defined in the context of an understanding of the importance of nostalgia: not simply a sentimental yearning for a lost past, but a sense that it is in the crucible of the founding period that the political ideas of the Declaration inspired the desire to design a democratic and republican system of government. The Founders – both religious and secular – gave the nation values and ideals, philosophical aspirations and political goals. From the Pilgrims came the hope that America might become what Ronald Reagan was fond of referring to as 'the shining city upon a hill'. From Thomas Jefferson came the radical political manifesto of the revolution: a demand for the equal right to life, liberty and the pursuit of happiness. What remained, however, was to create a political framework that would allow the 'first new nation' to realize such potential. That was the task of fifty-five white men who met in Philadelphia between 14 May and 17 September 1787, and who drafted the Constitution of the United States.

# The Challenge of the Constitution

> Fourscore and seven years ago our fathers brought forth, on this continent, a new nation, conceived in Liberty, and dedicated to the proposition that all men are created equal.
>
> *Abraham Lincoln, Gettysburg address (1863)*

In a memorable episode of the original series of *Star Trek*, the USS *Enterprise* encounters a planet on which a fierce feud is raging between two tribes: the Caps and the Coms. The Caps – with whom Captain Kirk and his crew ally – have a sacred document, handed down through generations, that contemporaries barely understand. Indeed, when their leader tries to read it aloud, he mangles the words: they seem strange and foreign. Kirk, though, can pronounce the familiar phrases: 'We the People of the United States. . . .' It is the preamble to the American Constitution. The Constitution has symbolic, mythological and even a quasi-religious status within America's political culture. Indeed, if the Declaration of Independence is the charter of American democracy, the Constitution is no less significant in historical terms. Although a confederation of the thirteen original states existed prior to it, it had proven a ramshackle attempt to build a Union. The Constitution thus in large measure created, and sustains, the nation. As such it has become an object of reverence, its fundamental principles beyond political debate. That was not always the case.

Lincoln's Gettysburg address came after the Union's critical victory over the Confederacy in the battle there had effectively decided the outcome of the Civil War. It has become one of the most celebrated speeches in American history. Yet in his opening statement, Lincoln deliberately appears to play with the historical record to make an important political point. 'Fourscore and seven years ago' from the time of his speech dates the founding of the 'new nation' to 1776, the year of the Declaration of Independence, which indeed was about liberty and 'dedicated to the proposition that all men are created equal'. The Continental Congress, under whose auspices the Declaration was issued, had first met the previous year, and was a step towards political union. But the Articles of Confederation, which it finally adopted in 1777 – and which did not come into effect until they were ratified by every state, a process that took another four years – committed the states only to 'a firm league of friendship with each other'. True, this confederacy was called the 'United States of America', but for many Americans it lacked a sufficient centre of political gravity to be regarded as a nation, and it was to survive only another six years. After Ben Franklin, John Adams and John Jay had successfully represented the American side at the negotiation of the Treaty of Paris, which ended the revolutionary war in 1783, the states regarded themselves not only as independent of Britain but also as largely independent of one another. However, individual state experiences with new and experimental forms of republican government created an atmosphere of confusion and instability. In 1786, Shay's rebellion in Massachusetts was the most visible and traumatic rejection of governmental authority, and seemed to many contemporaries as a prelude to anarchy. It was apparent that the existing national government lacked the power, prestige and authority to do much to help the situation. In such circumstances, the political will emerged to strengthen the Union. The outcome was the meeting in Philadelphia in 1787 that drew up the Constitution of the United States.

In 1863, Abraham Lincoln would have been aware that his audience would neither recall nor indeed care about such historical nuances. Yet by focusing on 1776 as the symbolic moment when the nation came into being – even if he was privileging one particular historical interpretation – he was politically astute. For if the Constitution of the United States of America established in 1787 was the document that, more than any other, embodied the idea of America as a 'nation', then subsequent interpretations of it had led to controversy, division and ultimately to the Civil War itself. Lincoln, who was to preserve the Union through the catharsis of that war, no doubt preferred his sense of when the nation began. Others would disagree. Indeed, when the pioneer film-maker D.W. Griffith made his historical epic about the reconstruction of the United States after the Civil War, he entitled it *Birth of a Nation* (1915). From this perspective, only after Gettysburg was there a resolution of the issue of individual state sovereignty versus the power and authority of the nation as embodied in its federal government.

Those who framed the American Constitution thus walked a tight-rope. On the one hand, the newly independent states were prepared to give up some of their autonomy to a national government, believing that the result would be greater political – and economic – security. On the other, they were jealous of their own powers and were reluctant to cede too much to a centralized authority. Evidence of that is suggested by the fact that on the day the Constitutional Convention was supposed to meet in Philadelphia, it was attended by representatives from only two states – Virginia and Pennsylvania (who, as hosts, could hardly be absent). It took a couple of months before the remaining delegates arrived, and even then, Rhode Island remained unrepresented. So, far from being a meeting that was attended with a sense of its subsequent historical importance, the Constitutional Convention was a gathering of politicians who mapped a plan for a Union of the states, but had no idea whether what they achieved was either workable or durable. And yet, amongst those who were in Philadelphia were Americans who not only had a profound vision of their future as a nation, but also had the ability to apply political theory, pragmatic common sense and a spirit of compromise to the problems that confronted them. Indeed, such qualities are evident in the work that rationalizes and explains the thinking behind the Constitution: the series of essays written by James Madison, Alexander Hamilton and John Jay as part of the attempt to persuade New York to ratify the Constitution, and subsequently collected as the *Federalist*.

## The *Federalist*

'Publius,' the man of the people, the public man.
  *Garry Wills*, Explaining America: The Federalist (*1981*)

The United States came into being as the result of fear of what would happen if some framework of national government could not be devised. Indeed, the first nine papers in the *Federalist* rationalize the move towards greater union by pointing out the military and political threats that the newly independent states faced: dangers from abroad, the prospect of war between the states, the possibility of continuing domestic divisions and insurrections. Whether such fears and threats were real is irrelevant: they had proved real enough to prompt the calling of the Constitutional Convention, and now they were played upon to encourage ratification of the new form of government that it had agreed. One example the Americans had before them was Great Britain: far more effective as a world power after England, Scotland and Wales had merged their sovereignties. As Alexander Hamilton suggested in *Federalist* 6,

> [a]lthough it seems obvious to common sense that the people of such an island should be but one nation, yet we find they were for ages divided into three, and that those three were almost constantly embroiled in quarrels and wars with one another. . . . Should the people of America divide themselves into three or four nations, would not the same thing happen?

Hamilton went on to argue that '[t]o look for a continuation of harmony between a number of independent, unconnected sovereignties in the same neighbourhood, would be to disregard the uniform course of human events, and to set at defiance the accumulated experience of ages.' This argument in favour of Union was thus much the same as would prompt closer European integration some two centuries later: commitment to a common cause would make it less likely that independent states would fight each other, and political as well as economic benefits would result from federation.

The world of the Founders was thus one in which political differences between nations and states caused conflicts that often resulted in war. The creation of the United States represented an opportunity to break with that cycle of violence that had historically characterized the human experience. More than that, in rejecting the idea of monarchy, Americans were venturing into new political territory. Experiments in republican government had a history of their own: it was one of failure. Remember Cromwell. So another underlying objective of those who framed the Constitution was to try to minimize, or at least to control, domestic political divisions, which were thought to be a breeding ground for the social instability that had traditionally defeated republican governments. As political conflict degenerated towards anarchy, the attractions of the strong ruler – Hobbes' Leviathan – had hitherto seemed the inevitable outcome of such experiments. Yet America would be different. Commitment to the idea of Union – embodied in the United States – meant that the privatized interests of individuals, groups and, indeed, states should be set aside to support a greater and common good: the idea of America itself. There is little doubt that its principal architects thought that their Constitution was a novel and ambitious attempt to solve some of the perennial political problems that had wrecked earlier experiments in republican government. It would indeed, as Madison observed, 'decide forever the fate of republican government'.

'Among the numerous advantages promised by a well-constructed Union, none deserves to be more accurately developed than its tendency to break and control the violence of faction.' The opening sentence of James Madison's first, and most famous, contribution to the *Federalist* – the tenth paper in the series – addressed another widespread contemporary fear. And his subsequent argument is one of the most concise and elegant justifications for the existence of the United States. Factions, according to Madison, were 'a number of citizens, whether amounting to a majority or minority of the whole, who are united and actuated by some common impulse of passion, or of interest, adverse to the rights of other citizens, or to the permanent and aggregate interests of the community'. In a free society, they were inevitable – '[t]he latent causes of faction are . . . sown in the nature of man' – and so the only way to deal with them was to lessen – if not remove – their ability to cause harm. If 'the *causes* of faction cannot be removed, . . . relief is only to be sought in the means of controlling its *effects*.'

If a faction is in a minority, it is controlled by the rules of the democratic game by which majorities gain real power while minorities can only protest and try to influence the political process. The problem for Madison, therefore, is to find a constitutional system that can best control a majority faction. His solution is simple:

> Extend the sphere, and you take in a greater variety of parties and interests; you make it less probable that a majority of the whole will have a common motive to invade the rights of other citizens; or if such a common motive exists, it will be more difficult for all who feel it to discover their own strength, and to act in unison with each other.

Madison's insight was to realize that the greater the variety of political interests represented in an extensive republic, the less likely it was that a majority faction would form that would be able to take control of the federal government. Yet there was still the possibility that government itself could act oppressively. The principle of federalism that animates the Constitution thus became part of an intricate framework of institutions designed to implement the theory that a separation of powers and checks and balances can effectively avoid abuses of power.

'A legislative, an executive and a judicial power comprehend the whole of what is meant and understood by government. It is by balancing each of these powers against the other two, that the efforts in human nature towards tyranny can alone be checked and restrained.'

The theory of a separation of powers, derived from the writings of the French theorist Montesquieu, is here expressed by John Adams in 1775 in the modified form by which it became the guiding light of American constitutional thought. For American government was not a reflection of a 'pure' separation of powers; instead each institution of government had a role in checking and balancing the others. In terms of the plan agreed in Philadelphia, this would mean that the federal government revolved around a legislature – the Congress – which passed the laws, an executive – the president – who made sure the laws were put into effect, and the judiciary – the Supreme Court – which would consider those disputes that arose as a result. Moreover, each institution was given residual powers to scrutinize and in certain instances either to ratify or to veto the decisions of the others. The price of preserving American liberty was to be eternal vigilance.

The political experience that had prompted the American revolution could be expressed in simple terms: arbitrary powers exercised by the British government threatened the liberties of the American people. Such tyranny presupposed the existence of a tyrant: the colonists had found one in George III, who, as monarch, represented the executive authority in the British system of government. It followed that in the aftermath of independence, the states remained suspicious of executive power, and had tended therefore to create systems of government in which legislatures – elected by the people – retained the greatest measure of governmental authority. With no effective political counterweight to their powers, state legislatures had proved vulnerable to the 'disease of faction', in which the majority of the moment – elections in some states took place every year – were able to pursue their exclusive political agenda against the interests of the community. Moreover, it seemed that whatever formal constitutional limitations were placed upon them, first the executive, now the legislative branches of government and potentially also perhaps the judiciary, were constantly probing the limits of their authority. As Madison asked in *Federalist 48*, '[w]ill it be sufficient to mark, with precision, the boundaries of these departments, in the constitution of the government, and to trust to these parchment barriers against the encroaching spirit of power?' Experience since independence had shown it was not: 'The legislative department is everywhere extending the sphere of its activity, and drawing all power into its impetuous vortex.' To 'extend the sphere' of the republic was fine; but for a legislature to attempt to do the same was a cause for concern.

The American Constitution introduced a new consideration into the political game. Not only were the institutions of government kept separate, but a system of checks and balances was established that allowed each of the actors in the ongoing drama of national politics to exist in a sphere of creative tension with one another. In other words, the American system of government becomes, in Richard Neustadt's phrase, one of 'separated institutions sharing powers',[1] so that no one predominates. For Madison, government is a battle between institutions for power, in which the strong will attack the weak unless each has some means 'of self-defence'. In a republic, the legislature remains, potentially, the strongest institution, and for that reason, Madison argues, it is right that it should be further subject to internal checks and balances, achieved through dividing it in two. So the Senate exists within the Congress as a counter-weight to the House of Representatives: the one giving political expression to the views of the states, the other to those of the people.

The Founders argued that they had achieved their objective. The Articles of Confederation had proved insufficient to their task. Now, as its preamble so elegantly and simply expresses it: 'We the people of the United States, in order to form a more perfect union, establish justice, insure domestic tranquility, provide for the common defence, promote the general welfare, and secure the blessings of liberty to ourselves and our posterity, do ordain and establish this Constitution for the United States of America.' As the *Federalist* shows, the architects of this brave new world were spurred on by fear of the consequences of their failure, but were inspired by the vision that if they could blend together the principles of federalism with the theory of a separation of powers, linking them together with a system of checks and balances, they could design a structure of government that would enshrine the fundamental values of their republican ideal. But not all Americans shared this optimism.

## The Bill of Rights

. . . a bill of rights is what the people are entitled to against every government on earth, general and particular; and what no just government should refuse, or rest on inference.
*Thomas Jefferson, letter to James Madison (1787)*

When Thomas Jefferson, then in Paris, was shown a copy of the Constitution, he saw its fundamental flaw: it did not incorporate a Bill of Rights. Jefferson's reaction, and indeed the existence of the Bill of Rights as the first ten amendments to the Constitution, suggests that there were still many Americans who thought that the new form of national government agreed in Philadelphia was a threat to individual liberties. This fear became the principal focus of opposition to the plan, and the debates in each state over whether to ratify the Constitution allowed anti-federalists to use such sentiment as a way of rallying support. The extent to which the whole idea of creating a 'more perfect Union' was contentious can be seen too in the process of ratification, which was by no means automatic. In order to increase their chances of success, the Founders agreed that ratification in nine out of the thirteen states would be sufficient to put the Constitution into effect. That was achieved within a year. But when New Hampshire, the ninth state to give its approval, voted in June 1788, New York and Virginia had still not decided. Without these two states endorsing it, the new national government would have remained a parchment plan. That they did so later that month owed much to the commitment from leading Federalists that the first task of the new Congress would be to propose the addition of a Bill of Rights to the original document.

Those in favour of the new plan of Union had made a considerable political concession. In *Federalist 84*, Hamilton argued strongly against the need for a Bill of Rights: it had 'no application to constitutions professedly founded upon the power of the people, and executed by their immediate representatives and servants. Here, in strictness, the people surrender nothing; and as they retain everything they have no need of particular reservations.' But the argument that it was unnecessary ignored the symbolic and even emotional attachment to the idea that an explicit stockade of individual rights should be constitutionally guaranteed, and no governmental power should be able to infringe them. Again, it was a matter of self-defence. Having accepted the need to frame such a Bill of Rights as the price of constitutional ratification, moreover, the Federalists assumed control of its design. Once more, it was Madison who was the architect, drafting a series of proposals that were eventually agreed by the new Congress, and that were ratified by the states as the first ten amendments to the Constitution in December 1791.

The Bill of Rights has become in many ways as significant as the Declaration and the Constitution: another fundamental document of American democracy. Its existence has given the courts tremendous scope and responsibility in arbitrating and interpreting what can and cannot be legitimately defended in terms of these guarantees of individual liberties. The first amendment, for example, prohibits Congress from making any law 'respecting the establishment of religion, or prohibiting the free exercise thereof; or abridging the freedom of speech, or of the press; or the right of the people peaceably to assemble, and to petition the government for a redress of grievances'. Probably the most famous of the amendments, it has been subject to constant contemporary reinterpretation. Does it preclude censorship of any kind? Does it mean that provocative, inflammatory or obscene forms of self-expression in any public forum or media are constitutionally protected? These and other equally problematic questions have been of perennial concern, for each generation has to stumble towards a consensus on such issues. For the Bill of Rights to have meaning, it has to exist in an ever-changing political and social context: rights may seem absolute, but they cannot so remain if values are relative.

The second amendment is the one that apparently enshrines the American right to carry weapons. This should not be confused with a right to use them. But the constitutional endorsement of gun ownership has undoubtedly contributed to the creation of a cultural climate in which the use of weapons is widespread, largely uncontrolled and, indeed, perhaps uncontrollable. Here again, what is often taken as an absolute right is in fact contingent. The amendment reads in full: 'A well regulated militia, being necessary to the security of a free state, the right of the people to keep and bear arms, shall not be infringed.' In the absence of a standing army, the people's militia was seen by the Founders as a necessary organization to allow the nation to defend itself if attacked. In that case, potential members of the militia had to 'keep and bear arms'. But the idea of such a 'well regulated militia' existing to protect the nation in times of war seems a long way from the disorganized mayhem that sometimes can erupt within a nation where many an individual's self-image is that of a gunfighter and when the gun itself becomes an instrument of casual violence.

While the third amendment, which prohibits the quartering of soldiers in private accommodation without the consent of the owner in times of peace, and which allows it in wartime only under a due process of law, is nowadays irrelevant – the US military has its own bases, and an unsuspecting householder is unlikely to answer the door to GIs demanding shelter – the fourth amendment is still significant. It protects the individual against 'unreasonable search and seizure', and requires that if either is necessary, each is conducted according to procedural rules and by the granting of specific warrants.

The most famous clause in the fifth amendment protects individuals from being 'compelled in any criminal case to be a witness against' themselves. In other words, it preserves the right to remain silent to avoid self-incrimination. This has been, on occasion, a vital constitutional protection of individual liberty. 'Taking the fifth' as a way of avoiding answers to the charges and accusations of Senator Joseph McCarthy's anti-communist investigating committee during the 1950s, for example, focused popular attention upon this right. In many cases, however, silence was taken to be a tacit admission of complicity or guilt. Nevertheless, as David Caute observes, among those subpoena'd, 'the Fifth Amendment became . . . the favorite resort of radicals called to account for their beliefs, affiliations and associations by grand juries and Congressional committees', as a constitutionally enshrined form of self-protection in such contentious times.[2]

The sixth and seventh amendments are procedural, and guarantee the right 'to a speedy and public trial' in criminal cases, with the additional right to a trial by jury in 'suits at common law' where 'the value in controversy shall exceed twenty dollars' – nowadays a sum so trivial as to be meaningless. The eighth amendment has more contemporary resonance, since it forbids 'cruel and unusual punishments' from being inflicted. Those who oppose the death penalty in the United States appeal to this amendment when pointing out the ingenious methods that are adopted in order to give effect to capital punishment. It is a matter of contemporary moral debate whether death by hanging, firing squad, electric chair, gas chamber or lethal injection might be interpreted as 'cruel and unusual'. But while popular sentiment continues to endorse the death penalty in most states, such methods of carrying out the sentence that fall short of torture or the deliberate prolonging of the process are seen as constitutionally permissible.

The final two amendments of the Bill of Rights are catch-alls: the ninth amendment points out that other rights exist, and that just because some rights are mentioned in the Constitution, it does not mean that these are either denied or disparaged; and the tenth emphasizes that '[t]he powers not delegated to the United States by the Constitution, nor prohibited by it to the states, are reserved to the states respectively, or to the people.' Taken together, then, the Bill of Rights defines the relationship between the citizen and the state. Its symbolic significance, as this survey of it outlines, is in the construction of that protective stockade that can be used in defence of the interests of individuals, and indeed the community, against the power of government. The Bill of Rights contributes to the climate of American democracy: if it did not exist, would freedom of speech be so firmly preserved, or would due processes of law have been so explicitly spelt out? Historically, its provisions may have been unevenly observed and partially applied, but like the Declaration, and indeed the Constitution itself, it maps out the values and the priorities of America's democratic ideal.

## Tinkering with the Mechanics

> Can one generation bind another, and all others, in succession
> forever? I think not. The Creator has made the earth for the
> living, not the dead. Rights and powers can only belong to
> persons, not to things, not to mere matter endowed with will. . . .
> Nothing is unchangeable but the inherent and unalienable rights
> of man.
>
> *Thomas Jefferson, letter to John Cartwright (1824)*

Since agreement was reached on the passage of the Bill of Rights, the
Constitution has been amended only a further seventeen times in a
little over two hundred years. On the one hand, this may show the
extent to which contemporaries have been reluctant to challenge what
has come to be seen as the wisdom of the Founders in their original
design. On the other, more prosaically, it reflects the difficulty of the
amendment process: two-thirds of both houses of Congress or two-
thirds of the state legislatures have to agree to propose an amendment,
and these have to be approved by three-quarters of the states. As the
United States has expanded – extending Madison's sphere – this process has become potentially more challenging. Nevertheless, following
the first ten amendments that defined the Bill of Rights, fine-tuning of
the Constitution continued, and despite the difficulties, more amendments were passed in the twentieth century than in the remainder of
the nineteenth.

Up until the Civil War, the Constitution was amended on only
two further occasions. Then, in 1865, slavery was finally abolished
by the thirteenth amendment, and in the Reconstruction period, the
two subsequent amendments guaranteed citizenship to 'all persons
born or naturalized in the United States' (amendment 14) and that
the right to vote 'shall not be denied or abridged . . . on account of
race, color, or previous condition of servitude' (amendment 15).

Amendments have thus often reflected the need to confront contemporary political problems, and to alter the Constitution as a response to them. Usually, the matters have been procedural, providing
for such things as the direct election of the Senate, votes for women
or the limitation of the president's term in office to a maximum of
eight years. On the one occasion when the amendment process was
used to try to influence the climate of moral behaviour in the nation,
the experiment proved less than convincing. The twenty-third amendment, agreed in 1919, ushered in prohibition, preventing the 'manu-
facture, sale, or transportation of intoxicating liquors within . . . the

United States' and also the import and export of alcohol. The ban lasted fourteen years, until, in the midst of the Great Depression – which was not caused by prohibition, but perhaps deepened by it – a further amendment lifted it.

Such an experience may have had an impact on other proposals that would imply profound social change. In 1972, for example, the Equal Rights Amendment was approved by Congress, but after a decade of trying, it had not been ratified by a sufficient number of states to be passed. Similarly, the proposal to amend the Constitution to require the federal government to balance the budget gained little support because of feelings that, like prohibition, it would prove practically impossible to implement and police. Tinkering with the mechanics of the Constitution has come to mean just that: a process that allows the document to continue to structure political life according to contemporary reality. More ambitious attempts at social or economic engineering would appear to be unnecessary extrusions on the nation's venerable political architecture.

## Party Time

> Every difference of opinion is not a difference of principle. We are all republicans – we are all federalists.
> *Thomas Jefferson, first inaugural address (1801)*

Jefferson's argument reflects the ambivalence with which political parties were regarded in the early years of the federal republic. Parties, after all, seemed similar to factions: political groupings that placed partisan considerations before the interests of the community as a whole. And yet, despite these suspicions, political parties eventually became accepted as both a legitimate and necessary part of the political process. Moreover, what is remarkable about American parties is their longevity: contemporary Democrats can trace their origins back to the early nineteenth century, and present-day Republicans to the period just before the Civil War. 'Republican' was also the name of the party formed by James Madison and Thomas Jefferson himself soon after President George Washington took office. If, however, the ideological divide between parties is small – more often a difference of emphasis rather than a matter of profound disagreement – it is a reflection of the fact that Jefferson was correct: so long as Americans remain in broad agreement upon the fundamental values and the animating principles of their nation, political parties, which function as the organized expression of such opinion, do not seek to redefine the dominant cultural consensus.

The party system is thus at once inclusive and exclusive. It is inclusive in the sense that the Democrats and the Republicans are the parties that routinely contest elections, both at the federal and the state level, for executive positions – president or governor – and for Congress and state legislatures. But it is exclusive in that those candidates who are not supported by one or other of these parties – apart from the odd maverick here and there – have little chance of achieving office. Further, the viable choice for voters is, in the main, restricted to supporting either a Democrat or a Republican; or else, as many do, to abstain from the electoral process altogether. But to the extent that the two major parties continue to dominate American political life, they do so out of a sense of history – a further example of the powerful hold of the politics of nostalgia upon the national imagination.

The Constitution created a federal republic, with an executive, a legislature and a judiciary as its institutions of government. From the moment the first Congress assembled in 1788, however, it was obvious that further forms of political organization were necessary if coherent public policies were to be devised and put into effect. Although the contemporary mood remained hostile to them, factions were quick to emerge: George Washington's cabinet would soon contain Alexander Hamilton, secretary of the Treasury, and leader of the Federalists, and Thomas Jefferson, secretary of state, who, with the support of James Madison, led the Republican opposition. When Washington, who, with John Adams as vice-president, identified with the Federalists, was re-elected for a second term as president in 1792, these factions were already evolving into the first American party system. In his farewell address, then, the president may have inveighed 'in the most solemn manner, against the baneful effects of the spirit of party generally', but his warning was too late. The contest to succeed him was between Adams and Jefferson: Federalist against Republican. Jefferson came second, and under the existing electoral rules became vice-president: an outcome made subsequently impossible as a result of the twelfth amendment in 1804. Then, in 1800, Jefferson, who was no longer on speaking terms with Adams, beat the incumbent to become president. It was a major achievement: the first time that power had passed peacefully between two political parties competing for office. In historical terms, it proved a legitimation of the electoral processes of American democracy. Politically, it signalled the end for the Federalists, who never again won national office. In the so-called 'era of good feelings' the first American party system largely fell apart.

So the original parties, organized by the Founders, reflected differing attitudes towards the government they had designed: philosophies that in turn depended upon economic priorities. Hamilton's Federalists were in favour of a stronger federal authority to promote commercial and manufacturing interests – principally located in the north. Madison's Republicans – led by Jefferson – supported a decentralized system under which the agrarian – and mainly southern – community might prosper. Jefferson's presidency ushered in a period of one-party ascendancy, during which the political elite from Virginia effectively controlled the White House for twenty-four years (Jefferson was succeeded first by James Madison and then by James Monroe, with all three serving two terms in office). The Federalist party disintegrated, and its remnants were absorbed by the Republicans (who added to the confusion of contemporary party identities by changing their name to Democrats).

The second American party system emerged as the Jeffersonian Republican/Democrat party began to lose control over elections to national office, particularly after the political manoeuvrings that appeared to deprive Andrew Jackson of the presidency in 1824. Four years later, Jackson was elected chief executive with the support of a new party organization, albeit one with a familiar name: Democrats. The party's candidates dominated presidential elections until 1860, winning six out of nine contests over a thirty-two-year period. Jackson thus became the figurehead for a new party organization, with a populist appeal. In keeping with their Jeffersonian heritage, however, the Democrats still maintained faith in the ideals of republican democracy, and although the party's roots may have been in predominantly rural – so still southern – areas, it also retained for a time a genuinely national appeal. Between 1836 and 1856, three of the five Democrat presidents elected – Martin Van Buren, Franklin Pierce and James Buchanan – came from northern states. Opposition organized in response, the Whigs – like the original Federalists – represented the commercial and industrial interests of the developing nation. The party was reasonably successful at the state level, and moderately so in the national legislature, but only captured the presidency twice, in 1840 and 1848.

There was another party realignment immediately before Abraham Lincoln's election in 1860. The Democrats had became increasingly identified with the sectional interests of the south: defending states' rights and thus the 'peculiar institution' of slavery. As the nation careened towards Civil War, a more effective opposition than the Whigs had emerged with its political centre of gravity in the north. The Republican party (once more the name chosen for the party reflected the politics of nostalgia at work) grew out of anti-slavery sentiment to a point where it could respectably contest the presidential election of 1856. Four years later, with Lincoln as its candidate, it won control of not only the executive but also the federal legislature, precipitating the secession of the south from the Union. The Republicans remained the dominant party in national politics for fourteen years, but its place in southern demonology as 'the party of Lincoln' meant that after the Civil War the former confederacy remained solidly Democrat for a hundred years.

Until America's war in Vietnam, indeed, confederates were the only Americans to have experienced wartime failure and defeat. But the outcome of Reconstruction – the attempt to reintegrate the Union – was ultimately to the benefit of those in the south whose political power had been formerly built upon slavery. Southern states still resisted federal authority. Immediately after the Civil War, ten held out against the ratification of the fourteenth amendment – which gave freed slaves the status of citizens. The result was that military rule was imposed throughout the south (except in Tennessee). Yet by the time that the confederate states had finally rejoined the Union, the framework of southern segregation was largely in place. In 1896, the Supreme Court's decision in *Plessy* v. *Ferguson* recognized the contemporary reality, and the south's 'Jim Crow' laws would maintain a system of racial apartheid for most of the twentieth century.

In turn, this reinforced the Democrats' political hegemony in the south. If radical Republicans had assumed that the freed slaves, once enfranchised, would support the 'party of Lincoln' in return, their optimism was self-evidently misplaced. As civil rights were ignored, few black citizens were able to vote. Southern Democrats were able to dominate state politics and exercise considerable influence at a national level, both in Congress and in nominating candidates for the presidency. Indeed, Franklin Roosevelt's ability to forge a winning coalition of northern and southern Democrats came at the cost of a tacit recognition that it was sustainable only while 'Jim Crow' was not under direct political attack. In 1948, when the Democrats adopted a policy in favour of civil rights in their platform for the presidency, the 'Dixiecrats' abandoned the party and Strom Thurmond of South Carolina ran as a States Rights candidate against Harry Truman. Again, in the 1968 presidential election, Governor George Wallace of Alabama became the southern Democrats choice after Lyndon Johnson's civil rights reforms had begun to redraw the map of party political allegiances across the south. For a century after the confederate surrender at Appomattox, therefore, the political repercussions of the Civil War resounded in national politics, with a stubborn minority in the south refusing to accept that racism should and could have no place within a democratic, multi-cultural republic. While that attitude persisted, those who embraced it remained in a place apart.

During Reconstruction, and in the early part of the twentieth century, party politics in the United States thus still revolved around the compass point: the industrial north, the defeated south and the emerging west of the country demonstrating that regional concerns, built still upon economic priorities, largely determined partisan allegiances. While Democrat candidates prevailed in the south, Republicans typically won in the north. Between 1860 and 1900, therefore, there was only one Democrat president: Grover Cleveland, who has the unique distinction of being thus far the only politician to have recaptured the White House after being voted out of office: a feat comparable to a heavy-weight boxing champion reclaiming the title after losing it. In the presidential election of 1896, Democrats almost managed to forge a national coalition capable of winning them the presidency. The populist insurgency in the south and west that captured the party's nomination might have carried its candidate, William Jennings Bryan, to the White House. But the radical wave was turned back by the Republican breakwater, built by the northern financial and business communities, which managed to elect William McKinley instead. The interests of corporate capitalism thus became firmly identified with the Republicans – a connection that has remained since then largely intact. In the early years of the twentieth century, Republican occupation of the White House continued, only disrupted by Woodrow Wilson's two terms in office.

The balance of party power changed in 1932. Franklin Roosevelt's New Deal coalition of northern and southern democrats – often implacably opposed on many political issues – shuffled the cards of party allegiance once more. During the Depression, the Democrats became the party identified with the expansion of federal government to try to remedy the deficiencies of unfettered capitalism, which had culminated in the Wall Street Crash. Just as FDR dominated national politics for twelve critical years in the mid-twentieth century, so the electoral alliance between conservative southern and progressive northern Democrats now became a fundamental feature of the American party system. With the exception of Eisenhower's elections in 1952 and 1956, Democrats captured the White House from 1932 until 1968. Lyndon Johnson was the last Democrat president to benefit from Roosevelt's political legacy, but his support for civil rights – along with his failure to win the war with Vietnam – effectively undermined the inheritance. Conservatives in the south found a new home amongst Republicans, ushering in a new era of more genuine two-party competition in the region.

Throughout the history of the republic, then, the dynamics of electoral competition have altered the landscape of American politics: within the context of a two-party structure, coalitions have either fragmented or re-formed, have evolved or reinvented themselves, at intervals of between thirty and forty years: 1800, 1828, 1860, 1896, 1932. Since Richard Nixon's success in 1968, politicians and academics alike have been arguing as to whether yet another – a sixth – party realignment has happened or is taking place. As their very names indicate, therefore, the principal American parties have never presented themselves as ideologically based; rather, they have changed their political identities in tune with perceived electoral priorities.

If, since the end of the Civil War, Republicans have spent more years in the White House than have Democrats, in terms of control of Congress, the picture is different. Between 1866 and 1900, Republicans and Democrats were in the majority in the House of Representatives for almost the same amount of time. In the twentieth century, however, Democrats dominated the House: the majority there for a total of sixty-eight years. From 1950 to the end of the century, moreover, the Republicans only managed eight years as the party in control. In the Senate, the Republican predominance that characterized the latter part of the nineteenth century was gradually eroded during the twentieth, and since 1950 Democrats again have been by far the more successful party there. So Republican success in presidential contests has been mirrored by relative failure in elections to the legislature. Why has this been so?

## The Rules of the Electoral Game

Hell, I never vote *for* anybody. I always vote against.
*W.C. Fields, quoted by Robert Lewis Taylor (1949)*

The electoral fortunes of political parties are determined by the rules of the electoral game. The fact that Republicans and Democrats have historically performed better or worse than one another in presidential and congressional elections confirms the influence of the electoral system in the political process. It also reflects, to a greater or lesser extent, the continuing influence of the federal principle in American electoral politics. Other factors – the tendency for voters to 'ticket-split' and support one party for the executive and the other for the legislature; the power of incumbency, particularly in the Senate; and the role of personality rather than party in influencing voters – are also significant. But the frequency and the method of election are undoubtedly of critical importance in deciding political outcomes.

There is both a logic and an elegance to the constitutional provisions for presidential and congressional elections. So, the House of Representatives, where legislators are directly chosen by the people, is elected every two years. Each state has a number of representatives, apportioned according to its population as determined by a census that takes place every decade. (In the original document the southern states were allowed to count slaves as three-fifths of a person for such purposes.) The president is elected every four years by a two-stage process. In each state voters mandate their representatives, whose votes in the Electoral College ultimately decide the winner. Senators serve for six-year terms, which are staggered such that in each two-year legislative electoral cycle, a third of their seats are contested. Originally, state legislatures chose senators, but now they are directly elected in state-wide contests. Again, therefore, there is an intricate system of interlocking elections designed so that a fixed majority is unlikely to dominate the two elected branches of the federal government, even after political parties became organized in the attempt to do just that.

In the House of Representatives, each legislator typically represents a district – in effect a single-member constituency similar to that which forms the basis of the contemporary British electoral system, with contests decided in the same way: a simple 'first past the post' wins. Historically, some states experimented with a state-wide 'general ticket' system of election, in which a party would win all the legislative seats contested if its slate of candidates won more votes than its opponents. In such instances, the state became a multi-member district; but this practice gradually fell from favour. Nowadays, the link between representative and district is the basis of the electoral and the political process. Once direct elections to the Senate were introduced, each senator – two from each state – had to win a state-wide election.

The Electoral College – constitutionally where the outcome of presidential elections should be decided – remains perhaps the least appreciated and most misunderstood institution within the American political system. It has taken centre-stage only when it has 'misfired', producing an unanticipated or contentious result, as it did most famously in November 2000. The Founders, however, were proud of their invention. In *Federalist 58* Hamilton described the Electoral College in glowing terms: 'If the manner of it be not perfect, it is at least excellent. It unites in an eminent degree all the advantages, the union of which was to be wished for.' The Founders' intention was that each state would elect representatives to the Electoral College (as many as they had representatives in the two houses of the Congress). They would meet and decide which presidential candidate was best qualified to become chief executive. The method of election to the Electoral College was left to the states to decide. In the early years of the republic, various options were explored. Some states voted for representatives in districts, others adopted the 'general ticket' system. Once parties became established, representatives were effectively mandated to support a particular candidate, and it followed that if the district system was used, a state's votes in the Electoral College might be divided between candidates, as one party might win some districts, and another would be successful in others. It is no accident, therefore, that the trend towards the general ticket method of election, which has been used more or less uniformly by the states since 1832, coincides with the evolution of the two-party system. Nowadays it means that if a party's candidate wins the majority of votes in a state, that candidate wins all the state's Electoral College votes. Presidential contests are thus about building a winning coalition of states in support of a candidate, rather than gaining a majority of the popular vote. Indeed, on one occasion, in 1876 – and amid some fairly blatant vote-rigging and fraud – the candidate who won the popular vote, Samuel Tilden, lost the Electoral College vote to Rutherford B. Hayes, who duly occupied the White House. Despite the potential for such anomalies, the Electoral College remains an important part of the political process, because it preserves the influence of the states within the system. If the president were directly elected by popular mandate, the role of the states in determining the outcome would be marginalized. The existing system preserves the federal principle: that the states still have a significant role to play in national political life.

How, then, do the rules of the electoral game impact upon the political process? Given that every member of the House of Representatives serves for only a two-year term, effectively political careers there are built on the basis of a permanent electoral campaign. For legislators, the interests of their districts become paramount, and although many become safe seats for their incumbents, the frequency with which they are held accountable by their electorates undoubtedly contributes to the sense of localism that can pervade politics in the House. Given too a straight choice between the policies of their party and the interests of their district, when such conflicts occur, members of the House of Representatives are usually persuaded by their sense of the impact of their decisions upon their electoral prospects. In the Senate, a six-year term opens the opportunity to take a broader political view: careers in the Senate have been one traditional route towards building the national reputation that may then be parlayed into a campaign to run for the presidency.

If the major electoral goal for political parties has become – certainly since the Roosevelt era – to win the presidency, then the electoral system undoubtedly effects both the choice of candidates and the strategies of the campaign. The need to win support from electoral majorities in a critical coalition of states in order to build a majority within the Electoral College means that a candidate has to be able to transcend sectional political divisions: a difficult task while the south remained in many ways both alienated from and isolated within the national political culture. As the dominant party in the south during most of the twentieth century, the Democrats traditionally nominated either their presidential or their vice-presidential candidate from one of the states of the former confederacy. Woodrow Wilson, indeed, epitomized the coalition of southern and northern influences that seemed necessary if the Democrats were to win the White House. Born in Virginia in 1856, Wilson was five when it seceded from the Union. His political career was, however, first forged in the north, where he was governor of New Jersey for two years before he became president. Of the other six Democrat presidents elected during the twentieth century, only two were not from the south. Harry Truman and Lyndon Johnson, who came to the White House following the deaths in office of the northerners Roosevelt and Kennedy, had, as vice-presidents, provided the southern balance to the Democrats' ticket: a reflection of the lasting strength of the coalition that Roosevelt forged between the northern and southern wings of the party. After the desegregation of the south in response to the civil rights movement of the 1960s, and as the north–south divide in national politics became less pronounced, in 1976 Jimmy Carter from Georgia ran with Walter Mondale from the midwest as his vice-president. Bill Clinton, like Carter, from a former confederate state, Arkansas, thus broke a traditional Democrat mould when he chose a fellow-southerner, Al Gore, then a senator from Tennessee, as his running-mate. But Tennessee had at least remained loyal to the Union in the Civil War, and Gore might be regarded as more a member of the Washington political establishment than a traditional southern politician.

As a party with its origins in the north, the Republicans have been less concerned about southern sensibilities; indeed, given the party's lack of an electoral base in the south for most of the twentieth century, it is no wonder that its presidential candidates did not come from that region. Rather, with the exceptions of Calvin Coolidge, born in

Vermont, and whose early political career was in Massachusetts state politics, and George Bush, born in Massachusetts, but who reinvented himself as a Texan, the other six twentieth-century Republican presidents came from either the midwest or the west. The discipline of the Electoral College thus imposed itself upon the parties. For many years, conventional political wisdom among Democrats was that their candidates for executive office – president and vice-president – should appeal at some level to the south. For Republicans, until the 'solid south' finally gave way, the basis of electoral support was to be found elsewhere: hence their preference for candidates from the heartland of the midwest, or, in the selection of Ronald Reagan, for a midwesterner whose acting and political career was forged in California. Herbert Hoover, a Republican, was the first president to be born west of the Mississippi. The only president to be born and raised in California was also a Republican: Richard Nixon.

If regional political allegiances have played their part in determining the outcome of presidential elections, broadly favouring the Republicans, a different factor helps to explain the dominance of Democrats in congressional contests. Historically, they have been better organized, particularly in the cities. Until comparatively recently, therefore, the efficiency of the party machine was integral to their electoral prospects.

## The Politics of the Machine

> Over the years, the son of an immigrant laborer might become a free-wheeling machine politician. His grandson might become a presidential advisor; his great-grandson might, as happened in 1960, become President of the United States.
>
> *Fred Greenstein*, The American Party System and the American People (*1963*)

In their heyday, the Democrat machines that dominated municipal politics in urban areas found their recruits among immigrants, often hitherto excluded from politics because of their religion. Many were Catholic. Take Tammany Hall, the famous Democrat machine in New York. In 1854 and 1860, Fernando Wood and then William Marcy 'Boss' Tweed became the first two leaders of Tammany – effectively the Democrat's organization in the city – to be elected mayors of the city. Both were Anglo-Saxon Protestants. But by the end of the nineteenth century, the Irish in New York had taken over Tammany, and ran the city until the 1920s, when other ethnic groups challenged their position. Tammany's leaders, from Aaron Burr onwards, also profited from politics, becoming – like George Washington Plunkitt, who gave a candid portrayal of the organization at the turn of the twentieth century – rich through what they regarded as 'honest graft', but which others saw as political corruption.

Republicans also had party machines. But the major industrial cities of the north and midwest were more typically Democrat fiefdoms. The machines' influence extended beyond the patronage of urban politics and into the national arena. Al Smith, the first Catholic to be nominated as a presidential candidate, began his political career in Tammany Hall. In Boston, P.J. Kennedy, a first-generation Irish American, rose through the ranks of the party machine and in 1888 was selected to deliver a speech seconding the nomination of Grover Cleveland at the Democratic National Convention. The same year, his son Joseph was born. By the mid-1950s, under Mayor Daley's machine, based in Cook County, Illinois, 'ethnic politics were to reach their classic triumph as an art form, as distinctively American as baseball', as Theodore White puts it. Daley was elected mayor in 1955, and for the next twenty-one years, until he died from a heart attack in 1976, remained a national influence in Democrat politics, such was his ability to 'deliver a power package' of votes in presidential elections.[3] Indeed, John F. Kennedy won the presidency in part because of the support he could count on from Catholic political machines in America's major cities, and not least in Chicago. Kennedy's opponent knew he could not counteract Daley's ability to influence the election's outcome. In his memoirs, Richard Nixon records how, as the ballots were being counted in 1960, '[t]he Daley machine was holding back the Chicago results until the downstate Republican counties had reported and it was known how many votes the Democrats would need to carry the state.'[4] As Nixon appreciated, political corruption is a fact of American political life.

## Conclusion: History, Myth and the Constitution

The question of the relations of the States to the federal government is the cardinal question of our constitutional system. At every turn of our national developments we have been brought face to face with it, and no definition either of statesmen or of judges has ever quieted or decided it. It cannot, indeed, be settled by one generation because it is a question of growth, and every

successive stage of our political and economic development gives
it a new aspect, makes it a new question.
    *Woodrow Wilson*, Congressional Government (*1885*)

The only academic thus far to become president was right. Whatever
the myths that have come to surround the Constitution, the fact remains that the elegant political theories that lie behind it have had
to confront the political realities that Wilson described. What, then,
of the historical record? The principle of federalism enshrined at the
heart of the Constitution led to immediate clashes between states
concerned to preserve their political rights, and a federal government
seeking to assert its political authority. The result was that less than
seventy-five years after the Constitution was ratified, the nation was
fighting a Civil War. And the separation of powers, along with the
checks and balances designed to prevent the abuse of power through
frustrating its use, has resulted in a contemporary situation of 'gridlock'
whenever the Congress and the executive are controlled by different
parties. Indeed, nowadays, on occasions the federal government is
reminiscent of an over-crowded stagecoach, with Congress arguing
in the back as to where it should be going, the president up front
driving, usually ignoring the babble behind, and the Supreme Court
riding alongside as a shotgun trying to arbitrate between the two.
The United States is saddled with a Constitution that symbolizes the
powerful mythology of a nation founded upon democratic, republican
values, but which, at the same time, has struggled to accommodate
the faultlines within the national political culture.
    Of these, the most significant and enduring is race. The fact that
slavery existed in the south when the delegates met in Philadelphia in
1787 meant that from the beginning an unsavoury compromise was
necessary to cajole the states into union. In trying to rationalize the
decision to allow southern states to count their slaves as three-fifths of
a person for the purposes of deciding their representation in Congress
– and by extension the Electoral College – even the *Federalist* was forced
to admit that the arguments in favour of this expedient 'may appear a
little strained on some points', while agreeing with the need to 'let the
case of the slaves be considered, as it is in truth, a peculiar one'. Thereafter, the issue of slavery continued to threaten the Union. In 1820,
north and south again found an accommodation necessary. The
Missouri Compromise, engineered by Henry Clay, mapped the border
between two sections of the United States. South of a line of latitude
slavery was allowed; north of that line, it was prohibited. But the politics
of the compass point still had to resolve whether, as the nation expanded
to the west, its 'peculiar institution' would be allowed to go with it.

For the first half of the nineteenth century, therefore, the south tried to preserve its political position within the United States, demanding that outsiders did not interfere in its social, economic and cultural traditions, and that the federal government respected its right to hold slaves. At the same time, however, another drama was being played out: the 'winning of the west'. Would slavery expand, or would it be encircled? If free-soil states outnumbered slave states, the south's influence in federal politics would be increasingly eroded. Ultimately, it could ignore moral pressure to abolish the 'peculiar institution' only as long as it retained the power within the federal government to resist any attempts to intervene in its internal politics. So the issue of states' rights – belief in the absolute autonomy of individual states in areas where the federal government threatened to expand its authority – became the fulcrum on which the south's constitutional defence of slavery turned. Equally, in order to preserve the Union, northerners were prepared to concede the argument up to the point where the south threatened secession. Thus it was that politicians from both sides spent their time trying to achieve political compromise, even though their efforts increasingly became strained as time went by.

Eventually, however, southern and northern interpretations of the Constitution, and indeed the 'idea of America' that it expressed, became irreconcilable. As early as 1798, Virginia and Kentucky unilaterally declared that the federal government had acted unconstitutionally in passing the Alien and Sedition Acts. In 1828, in protest against the perceived discrimination of the Tariff Act, a similar assertion of states' rights was revived when South Carolina adopted an Ordinance of Nullification, challenging the legitimacy of federal law. In response, President Andrew Jackson issued a proclamation to the people of the state, which argued that '[i]f this doctrine had been established at an earlier day, the Union would have been dissolved in its infancy.' He was right. To concede the principle of nullification would be to make federal authority rest upon the whim of a capricious state: 'You must perceive that the crisis your conduct presents at this day would recur whenever any law of the United States displeased any of the States, and that we should soon cease to be a nation.' For Jackson, South Carolina's action amounted to treason. He expressed his 'determination to execute the laws, to preserve the Union by all constitutional means, to arrest, if possible, by moderate measures the necessity of a recourse to force'. The Union came first. As the crisis escalated, he also threatened forcibly to collect the duties owed to the federal government from South Carolina, and to arrest and hang the nullification leaders, gaining authority from Congress in support of such violence in the so-called 'force act' passed in 1833. With the United

States government on the brink of going to war with a state, Henry Clay – again – negotiated the compromise on the tariff issue that brought about a gradual reduction in the burden of taxation. Yet South Carolina's defiance showed that the vigorous assertion of states' rights against federal authority, or conversely the determination of the national government to assert its power against the perceived interests of certain states, did not simply end in constitutional dead-lock. It threatened war.

In the midst of the tariff controversy, in a famous speech in defence of the Union in 1830, Daniel Webster, senator from Massachusetts, predicted where such defiance of federal authority would end: 'When my eyes shall be turned to behold for the last time the sun in heaven, may I not see him shining on the broken and dishonored fragments of a once glorious Union; on states dissevered, discordant, belligerent; on a land rend with civil feuds, or drenched, it may be, in fraternal blood!' Webster died in 1852: missing his apocalyptic vision by ten years. But he remained of that generation who tried to make sense of an increasingly untenable political situation and who lived through the cycles of crisis and compromise as the south stubbornly asserted the doctrine of states' rights in the face of federal measures it saw as calculated to undermine its economy, its 'peculiar institution' of slavery, and thus its social order.

In 1850 the proposed admission to the Union of California and New Mexico as free-soil states threatened the integrity of the United States once more. In the tortuous negotiation over the issue, the architect of agreement – inevitably – was Henry Clay. Yet whereas the Missouri Compromise had lasted for thirty years, this time the settlement would hold for a little over a decade, merely postponing what was, in many ways, the inevitable conflict between north and south. Following the election of Abraham Lincoln, southern states carried out what they had long threatened to do: they seceded from the Union. For Lincoln, like Jackson before him, this was an act of calculated rebellion. In his first inaugural address of 1861 he argued that secession was unlawful: '[N]o state upon its own mere motion can lawfully get out of the Union . . . resolves and ordinances to that effect are legally void.' The United States remained a constitutional given; secession a legal fiction: '[T]he central idea of secession is the essence of anarchy.' The Constitution remained the symbolic document that embodied the idea of the nation uniting the states, north and south, whatever their political differences. Lincoln concluded that

[w]e are not enemies, but friends. We must not be enemies. Though passion may be strained, it must not break our bonds of affection. The

mystic chords of memory, stretching from every battle-field, and patriot grave, to every living heart and hearthstone, all over this broad land, will yet swell the chorus of the Union, when again touched, as surely they will be, by the better angels of our nature.

The Confederacy ignored him. And so the Civil War was fought to keep the United States united: to reach, indeed, a political accommodation that Madison's Constitution had proved incapable of achieving.

Yet the cost of this settlement was not just the Civil War, but its aftermath. The defeated South remained culturally and economically largely unreconstructed, a victim of its history. The political repercussions of the war reverberated for over a century. Even after the abolition of slavery, the south was able to resist federal attempts to promote racial integration until the civil rights movement took to the streets in the 1960s. Here again, the constitutional system that separated and diffused powers through different institutions and layers of government worked in favour of those determined, it seemed, to keep fighting the 'lost cause' of the south, particularly in the federal Congress. The first national civil rights legislation since Reconstruction was passed in 1957, but it was only in 1964, cajoled by Lyndon Johnson, a Democrat president who was himself from Texas, that the legislature agreed to a more extensive Civil Rights Act. A year later, in 1965, and a century after the end of the Civil War, the Voting Rights Act effectively enforced the south to allow widespread black participation in the electoral process, a major step in ending the segregation of 'Jim Crow'. That it took this long is testament to the tenacity with which southerners stuck to their culturally ingrained beliefs, and to the fact that the 'one-party south' could become such an important element within the Democrat coalition at the national level that for many years it could resist attempts by northern Democrats and Republicans alike to make progress on such issues.

In many ways, indeed, the party system itself is a reflection not so much of ideological divisions in the European sense of the term, as of the historical polarization that resulted from differing interpretations of the Constitution, and that coalesced around the issue of slavery. If the Founders intended to create a Constitution that might avoid party rivalries, the need to give some organizational coherence to the multi-layered system of government led to their early development, and eventually to the contemporary duopoly of Democrats and Republicans. The Hamiltonian Federalists and the Jeffersonian Republicans were divided by their views on how much power the Constitution granted the federal government, and how much was reserved to the states. In the controversy over whether to charter a national bank in

1795, Hamilton had favoured a 'loose construction' of what was permissible, whereas Jefferson had adopted a 'strict constructionist' view that limited the capacity of the federal government to legislate in matters not expressly authorized in the Constitution.

As the problem of slavery took centre-stage, such disagreement developed into the southern advocacy of states' rights and the northern acceptance of the need to preserve, and if necessary extend, the federal power of the Union. The Democrats, true to their Jeffersonian heritage, sided with the south. Republicans disagreed. The Civil War was fought over this issue of constitutional interpretation, and its political repercussions, real or imagined. Since then, however, the attitudes of Democrats and Republicans to this problem at the heart of the Constitution have reversed themselves. The Democrats became the party that was, for much of the twentieth century, associated with the idea of 'big government', of using federal power as a means of bringing about economic reform, and eventually social progress: in Franklin Roosevelt's New Deal and Lyndon Johnson's Great Society, Democrats sponsored two major attempts to change the domestic landscape of American politics. On the other hand, it was the Republicans – the party of the Union that had espoused ultimately the cause of abolishing slavery – that, under President Reagan, declared that the states should be subject to less interference and regulation from the federal government.

So it is that the issue of states' rights versus federal authority remains the fulcrum upon which constitutional interpretation turns, although the only political controversy that has defeated compromise thus far has been that surrounding slavery. Since 1865, the United States has remained united. And indeed, the Confederate Constitution of 1861 only parted company with the 1787 original in two substantive matters: strengthening the institution of slavery, and weakening executive power by limiting the president to one six-year term in office. If it was merely a nuanced imitation of Madison's design, however, it still had a similar significance. It created a nation, another federal republic, contiguous with the older version, and on what was now its southern border. The commitment of many Americans to the ideal of union expressed in 1787, wrapped up in the idealism that saw slavery as a travesty of the sentiments expressed in the Declaration of Independence, meant that the south could not be allowed to maintain its idea of separate nationhood. Lincoln's Gettysburg address thus encapsulates the sense of cultural identity of America as a nation expressed through its founding documents. The outcome of the Civil War mapped the contours of American politics for a century and beyond. If the Union had been defeated, the idea of the United States would have crumbled, and Lincoln's oratory at Gettysburg would have become the throwaway lines of a failed president. But the United States endured through the most critical trauma in its history thus far. The survival of the nation endorsed the mythological significance of its founding documents, but the challenge of its Constitution remains.

# 4

# The Framework of Government

Jack Stanton also understood, intuitively, that the real challenge was far more difficult than simply meeting their expectations. It was about *exceeding* their expectations. It was about inspiring them. If you couldn't do that, you were Millard Fillmore. It was a *very* tough game. There were only two or three winners per century, and a fair number of losers were burned at the stake.

*Anonymous*, Primary Colors (*1996*)

The end-game of the presidential election of 2000 elevated the politics of spectacle to new heights. The campaign itself may have visited the familiar territory that now maps the political terrain in the land of 'infotainment'. To generate excitement, voters were offered guerilla politics (insurgent candidates attempting to ambush front-runners in the early primary season), entertainment politics (nominating conventions as Hollywood productions geared for prime-time), gesture politics (the vice-president who kissed his wife to appear more 'human') and symbolic politics (the carefully stage-managed debates). There was too the inevitable seasoning of dirty politics: negative advertisements and last-minute revelations (George W. Bush's arrest for driving while drunk). It was the outcome, however, that offered not only Americans but also a global audience a new, unfamiliar and fascinating political drama.

It was a tantalizing scenario mixing both spectacle and speculation. The first president of the twenty-first century would take office after a recount in a state – Florida – where his brother was governor. Al Gore's court battles would have been unnecessary had he managed to win the Electoral College votes of Tennessee, his home state, and

Arkansas, that of Bill Clinton. He won the popular vote, but George W. Bush won the White House as a result of the votes that mattered – not only in the Electoral College, but more crucially still in the federal Supreme Court, where six of the nine justices had been chosen by Republican presidents, including two nominated by his father, a former president himself. Had the court's ruling not resolved the issue (on a 5–4 vote), then Congress, split evenly between Democrats and Republicans, might have had to exercise its ultimate constitutional responsibility to choose the president when the outcome of an election is inconclusive. As it was, it fell to Al Gore himself, as presiding officer in the Senate, to announce his own defeat, as the outcome of the Electoral College votes was recorded there. So George W. Bush ensured at least that he would be remembered for one thing: the manner in which he achieved the office. Millard Fillmore, president between 1850 and 1853, could not even claim that distinction.[1]

Such a contemporary political drama demonstrates that the framework of government – the fixed and apparently arid constitutional procedures and processes – shapes political activity and outcomes in complex and sometimes unpredictable ways. The politics of nostalgia creates a reverence for the wisdom of the Founding Fathers, but their constitutional design has been preserved only as a result of determined efforts to accommodate it to such changing political realities and the dynamics of historical circumstance. It is, then, easy to discover the formal powers given to each of the principal contestants in the game of American politics: the president, the Congress and the Supreme Court. What is more difficult, but ultimately more rewarding, is to attempt to travel across the ever-changing political landscape of the relationships between these separate institutions, forced into creative tension by the Constitution and moulded by the politicians whose job it is to make them work.

# The Executive

> You can tell a lot about a fellow's character by his way of eating jellybeans.
>
> *Ronald Reagan, quoted in* The New York Times,
> *9 March 1981*

The powers of the executive are rehearsed in Article Two of the Constitution: itself an indication of the extent to which the Founders believed that the executive should defer to the legislature (the powers of Congress are found in Article One). Throughout the history of the American republic, however, sporadically at first, and then particularly since Franklin Roosevelt became the architect of the 'modern presidency', the executive has assumed its position of primacy as the focal point of the American political process. George W. Bush was the forty-third president to take office: all have been white, all have been male. In terms of reputation, among his predecessors, in the eighteenth century, George Washington stands apart from his peers; in the nineteenth century, Jefferson and Lincoln; and in the twentieth, Woodrow Wilson and Franklin Roosevelt have gained a similar political stature. This, at least, was the judgement of a 1962 survey among academics while John F. Kennedy occupied the White House. Since then, only two presidents – JFK himself and Ronald Reagan – may be remembered in positive terms for their outstanding ability to motivate their contemporaries through inspirational rhetoric. But their historical reputations may remain more mythic than real. It is indeed the case that of the forty-two (Grover Cleveland counts twice because he served two non-consecutive terms), thus far there have been many who have left office as 'losers' rather than 'winners' and only a handful have achieved the soubriquet of 'great'. In this sense, if most political careers culminate in failure or defeat, then the fate of contemporary American presidents characteristically has been to come to the office with high expectations, only to leave it with a shared history of disappointment.

It is, however, a testament to the significance of the office that comparisons and judgements of presidential achievements are so readily made and often so vehemently disputed. The stock of former presidents rises and falls as each generation interprets its history, often in the context of changing contemporary circumstances. Only four presidents – Washington, Jefferson, Lincoln and Theodore Roosevelt – have their reputations literally carved in stone: their heads sculptured from the granite of Mount Rushmore in the Black Hills of Dakota 'in commemoration of the foundation, preservation and continental expansion of the United States'. But most have left a less imposing legacy.

Unlike Jefferson, who had been vice-president, Washington and Lincoln had never held federal or even state elected offices prior to becoming chief executive. Theodore Roosevelt, president from 1901 to 1909, inaugurated a twentieth-century trend that the president normally comes to the White House after a political apprenticeship in either federal or state government. Of the seventeen presidents elected in the twentieth century, only three (Taft, Hoover and Eisenhower) had not run for any state executive or federal legislative office prior to campaigning for the presidency, although Taft had served as civilian governor of the Philippines. Seven (Theodore Roosevelt, Coolidge, Truman, Johnson, Nixon, Ford and George Bush) had served as vice-presidents. The first four succeeded presidents who had died in office and were then elected in their own right. Of the others, Nixon came to the presidency eight years after leaving office (defeated by Kennedy in 1960) and Ford inherited the White House on Nixon's resignation in 1974. Only George Bush served for a full eight years as vice-president and then was elected immediately to a term in the White House as chief executive. Harding and Kennedy were the only two senators to become president. The remaining five (Wilson, Franklin Roosevelt, Carter, Reagan and Clinton) came to the office having had political experience as state governors.

The 2000 election was thus a typical contest, between a vice-president and a state governor: now the two most popular spring-boards to the White House. Given the nature of his victory, however, it is difficult to conclude that George W. Bush's success demonstrates an increasing tendency for state governors to become presidents, implying that it is easier to run 'against Washington' than from within it. Since Kennedy – the last president to have been elected from the Senate – four former vice-presidents, and now four former state governors, have taken office as president. Had Al Gore's popular vote victory been translated into a winning margin in the Electoral College, that score would be five to three. So the best conclusion that may be reached is that nowadays there are two principal career paths to the White House: one is via the vice-president's official residence at the Naval Observatory in Washington; and the other is by way of a state governor's mansion. That is not to say that other routes – from the Senate, or even from outside the political establishment itself – are not still feasible; indeed, every primary season brings a fresh crop of hopeful senators to the presidential campaign carnival. But experience in the role of state executive or as understudy to the chief executive is a useful presidential qualification.

Self-evidently it has also helped to be white and male. Constitutionally, this is not a requirement for becoming president: the only stipulations nowadays relevant are that the holder of the office should be a natural-born citizen of the United States and over the age of thirty-five. Politically, however, there have been obvious barriers of race and gender that have hitherto maintained the exclusivity of the executive club. A contemporary statistical profile of the United States shows that even though the percentage of the white population relative to non-white has fallen since its mid-twentieth-century high-point, it still stands at over 80 per cent to 20 per cent, and is a similar differential to that which obtained at the birth of the republic. Given such demo-graphics, as well as the historical burden of racial discrimination in the United States, and despite the legitimate claims of multi-culturalists, it may still be difficult for a candidate from a non-white ethnic back-ground to gain enough electoral support to propel a successful bid for the White House. The liberal hope that this might happen has to confront and convince a conservative belief that it could not – and should not – occur. In the contemporary battleground of American politics, much is still possible, and much is still to be achieved; but a non-white president will have to be the product of a colour-blind polity.

Since the 1950s, the gender balance of the United States has changed: there are now more women than men in the country. The differential, 52 per cent female to 48 per cent male, is perhaps not as significant as the social and political advances that women in America have made over the last half century. Thus far, however, only one – Geraldine Ferraro – has ever been selected by a major political party to run for national executive office: as vice-president on the losing Democrat ticket headed by Walter Mondale in 1984. For a time, Elizabeth Dole was talked of as a contender for the Republican presidential nomina-tion in 2000, but her exploratory campaign failed to gain political momentum. Yet women have run successfully for executive office. Wyoming elected the first woman to become a state governor, Nellie Taylor Ross, in 1925.

Should speculation surrounding the ambition of Hillary Clinton be translated into political fact, the 'glass-ceiling' of the White House may be shattered sooner rather than later. As a former first lady – having had far more than a walk-on part in the drama of Bill Clinton's presidency – and having achieved a notable 'first' in moving from the White House to become senator from New York, she personifies the politics of spectacle at a time when political images are crucial to a candidate's success. If she does become the first woman elected to the presidency at some future date, she may also be the first senator to win the office since John F. Kennedy, but the symbolism of her victory would far surpass his famous handshake with her husband back in 1963. It would not simply connect two political generations, but rather resonate back once more to Jefferson's Declaration of Independence, showing finally that his promise of equality is no longer defined or circumscribed by gender. As a some-time resident of Arkansas, she would outdo indeed the achievement of Hattie Wyatt Caraway, the Democrat from that state who was the first woman elected to the Senate in 1932, the year Franklin Roosevelt came to the presidency.

Since Roosevelt's time, it has been the president's cabinet – the heads of all the executive departments together with those whom the president may wish to include as advisors – that has come to reflect the changing dynamics of American society in terms of both race and gender. George W. Bush, for example, selected a cabinet that was – particularly for a Republican administration – unusually self-conscious in its inclusion of women and representatives from ethnic minorities. Among the current fourteen executive departments, which have responsibilities ranging from agriculture to labour, and education to energy, four eclipse the rest: the Departments of State, Defense, the Treasury and the Office of Attorney General. Under Bill Clinton, Madeleine Albright became the first woman appointed as secretary of state. In Bush's cabinet, she was succeeded by the first African-American to hold that position: Colin Powell. At the same time, the achievement of such status need not bring with it real power and influence. Indeed, while diversity of cabinet membership has increased, its political significance as part of the 'modern presidency' shaped by FDR has declined.

Unlike its British counterpart, the American cabinet does not contain leading members of the political party in power, all of whom – with the exception of those from the House of Lords – have achieved their positions by being elected to the legislature. The American cabinet includes those whom the president wishes to be there. They may come from different walks of life: business, law and academia are favourite recruiting grounds. The president has remained secure in the knowledge that none can mount an effective political challenge to his authority and leadership during his term of office. Abraham Lincoln's famous – possibly apocryphal – remark sums it up. Faced with the unanimous opposition of his cabinet on a particular issue, he is reported to have summarized the vote: 'seven noes, one aye – the aye's have it'. If the political power of the cabinet has always been weak, however, its influence is determined by presidential style. Some presidents – Eisenhower, Reagan and George W. Bush – have been seen as more prepared to delegate authority than others, even though it is the chief executive who remains the ultimate arbiter of the administration's policies. Others – Kennedy, for example – may to all intents and purposes marginalize their cabinet subordinates from the political process. One, perhaps again apocryphally, managed to do both: Ronald Reagan's preferred method of delegation reportedly was accompanied by such a semi-detached attitude to his cabinet that on occasion he was unable to recall the identity of one of its less vociferous members.

George Washington would have been unlikely to forget the names of his secretary of state and secretary of the Treasury: Thomas Jefferson and Alexander Hamilton. Yet the contemporary decline in the status of the cabinet has to do with two major changes that have impacted upon the presidency since the seedtime of the republic. First, as part of the creation of the modern institution of the presidency, chief executives have been able to rely upon their own sources of advice and counsel within the White House. At the turn of the twentieth century, those employed to support the president in an administrative and clerical capacity could have travelled to Washington in a couple of stage-coaches: only thirteen were on the payroll. In 1937, however, the President's Committee on Administrative Management famously concluded that 'the president needs help'. Two years later, aid came to the Roosevelt party in the shape of the Executive Office of the President, to co-ordinate the staffing support for the institution, and within it the White House Office was established to provide personal assistance for its incumbent.

In effect, a parallel bureaucracy had been created, which, because it was more responsive to presidential control, and could provide the executive with independent resources to help in the processes of policy formation and decision-making, would rapidly eclipse the more venerable institution of the cabinet. At the same time as this structural alteration in the institution of the presidency took place, a second change also occurred. Roosevelt's political leadership during the economic depression of the 1930s, and the impact of the New Deal administration upon the legislative process, fundamentally – irreversibly – altered popular perceptions of the abilities and the capacities of the president. During a time of political crisis, presidential leadership had been exercised effectively to an extent perhaps unknown since the Civil War and the time of Abraham Lincoln. Thereafter, with America's involvement in the Second World War, and the nation's subsequent 'rise to globalism' in a world of super-power rivalries, the invention of nuclear weapons and the onset of the Cold War, attention was focused upon the president as never before. The culmination of such structural alterations and changing historical circumstances was seen in the growth of what the historian Arthur Schlesinger, Jr, styled 'the imperial presidency'.[2] This would dominate the American political scene until the curtain was brought crashing down upon it by the Vietnam war, together with the Watergate scandal and Richard Nixon's resignation to avoid what would have been his successful impeachment by Congress for 'high crimes and misdemeanors' while in office.

In this brave new world of presidential politics, therefore, the White House Office assumed a vital role in managing the president's popular image, and it is those who form his immediate entourage – the policy advisors, press secretaries, political consultants and 'spin doctors' – who influence popular perceptions of the administration's performance, and determine the president's ability to achieve his political agenda. Indeed, the award-winning television series *The West Wing* reflects the fact that the drama of the modern presidency is played out in corridors of power that now stretch from the Oval Office into all corners of the White House.

In terms of the creation of domestic policies and the design of the president's legislative programme, the Office of Management and the Budget, part of the 1939 reforms (and originally named the Bureau of the Budget), has assumed a key position, effectively challenging the authority of the Treasury. It gives the president fiscal control over the policy-making process: a critical political asset. In 1946, the status of the Treasury was further undermined when the Council of Economic Advisors was set up with a function made obvious by its title: to advise the president in the formulation of macro-economic policy.

Equally, if not more, significant in the context of Cold War America was the establishment of the National Security Council in 1947. This became the president's principal source of foreign policy advice, with the national security advisor proving a political competitor to the secretary of state, whose influence over the direction of foreign policy could be effectively undermined. Other sources of help have been established within the Executive Office of the President that reflect once more the need to confront contemporary circumstances and political priorities: the National Space Council, for example, or the Office of National Drug Control Policy. Of all the institutions of the federal government, therefore, it is the character of the presidency that has travelled the greatest distance from the Founders' original conception of it. The job description has fundamentally and irrevocably changed such that the range of responsibilities and initiatives assumed by presidents nowadays would be unrecognizable to their eighteenth- and nineteenth-century predecessors. Yet if the climate of expectations surrounding the presidency, and the political pressures on the president, have altered, the formal powers of the office remain broadly the same as those assumed by George Washington when he took the first presidential oath of office in 1789.

The Founders traced the boundaries of presidential power in Article 2 (sections 2 and 3) of the Constitution and the executive's brief was brief: the president is 'Commander in Chief of the Army and Navy of the United States'. The first formal power given to the office is 'to grant Reprieves and Pardons for Offenses against the United States, except in cases of Impeachment'. So President Ford could pardon former President Nixon for his actions during the Watergate scandal only because Nixon had resigned the office prior to impeachment. Had Nixon been removed from the presidency through a successful impeachment by Congress, his successor could not have pardoned him.

The president is, then, given the power of making treaties – subject to Senate approval – and – again, 'by and with the advice and consent of the Senate' – can 'appoint Ambassadors, other public Ministers and Consuls, Judges of the Supreme Court, and all other Officers of the United States'. Here, then, is a significant delegation of potential political influence and patronage, but the Senate still has to ratify presidential treaties and endorse nominations made at all levels of the federal institutional hierarchy. Finally, the president has the power to fill any vacancies that may occur during the recess of the Senate. This, then, together with the power of pardon, is the sum total of constitutionally granted autonomous presidential powers: limited, circumscribed and circumspect. So it is not in the formal exercise of such constitutional authority that presidential power is seen. Rather it is scripted in the roles that the chief executive has been called upon to play.

The Constitution thus requires the president to 'give to the Congress information of the State of the Union, and recommend to their consideration such measures as he shall judge necessary and expedient'. In terms of the direction of domestic policy, this has framed the context within which the modern presidency has come to operate. When Franklin Roosevelt became president in 1932, the State of the Union, as a result of economic collapse, was parlous. He used the potential for the executive to suggest a programme of action to Congress to seize a legislative initiative that has remained in the White House ever since his administration.

As Richard Neustadt put it, '[e]verybody now expects the man inside the White House to do something about everything.'[3] The president comes to office with a domestic legislative agenda that provides an immediate political context that structures the relationship between executive and legislature. The State of the Union address thus becomes a set-piece opportunity for the president to address the nation through Congress, pointing out policy priorities, taking credit for legislative achievements and setting goals for the future. To take command of the legislative agenda, however, means that successive presidents must enter into a battle with Congress for political supremacy. Some have been more successful than others. Following Franklin Roosevelt, only Lyndon Johnson stands out as having a similar ability to cajole the representatives and senators on Capitol Hill to support his legislative ambitions – indeed his Great Society was marked by a greater level of legislative activism than FDR's New Deal. But even those who have been less adept at congressional management may still have found comfort in another constitutional weapon: the power of veto. It may become the president's most effective way of shaping the legislation passed during his administration. Congress can override a presidential veto if it can muster a two-thirds majority in both the House of Representatives and the Senate, but even this option is not available if the chief executive uses the so-called 'pocket veto' to prevent the enactment of bills presented during the final ten days of a congressional session (when much legislation may finally emerge from the intricacies of congressional scrutiny and debate). So the president does not simply sponsor legislation, but also may block measures that are passed by the legislature but that do not accord with the political goals of the administration. In effect, then, once the president decides to become involved in the legislative process, there is no ignoring the power and the influence that may be wielded from the White House.

From the Constitution comes the designation of the president as Commander in Chief – a reflection of the extent to which the Founders thought of the position, consciously or unconsciously, with George Washington in mind. In the nineteenth century, presidents such as Andrew Jackson, William Henry Harrison and Zachary Taylor parlayed their military careers into successful campaigns for the White House. Following the Civil War, four generals – Ulysses S. Grant, Rutherford B. Hayes, James A. Garfield and Benjamin Harrison – became chief executives, while William McKinley too had achieved the rank of major in the war between the states. In 1898, Theodore Roosevelt founded the 1st US Voluntary Cavalry and took part in the Battle of San Juan Hill in Cuba during the Spanish–American war. During the twentieth century, Eisenhower moved to the White House after an outstanding military career – not least as supreme commander of allied forces during the invasion of Europe – while Kennedy's political image was enhanced by his service during the Second World War, and his heroism after his torpedo boat – *PT 109* – had been sunk by a Japanese warship. So throughout the history of the republic, from time to time, it may have helped the civilian Commander in Chief to have had military experience. And there is no doubt that after the president assumed responsibility for ultimate control of America's arsenal of nuclear weapons, and also of the nation's international security agencies – as head of, among others, the Central Intelligence Agency (CIA, founded 1947), which was added to the White House's existing oversight of domestic security agencies such as the Federal Bureau of Investigation (FBI, founded 1908) – then the potential of the office to define military and foreign policy priorities, along with guarding the domestic security of the nation, was magnified far beyond the vision of the Founders.

As early as 1790, there had been those who had glimpsed the prospect that the president would direct the foreign affairs of the new republic. For Thomas Jefferson, '[t]he transaction of business with foreign nations is Executive altogether. It belongs, then, to the head of that department except as to such portions of it as are specially submitted to the senate. Exceptions are to be construed strictly.' Most modern presidents, when frustrated by congressional attempts to sabotage their domestic legislative programmes, have turned to foreign policy as an arena in which they may demonstrate untrammelled political leadership. That is not to say that they are guaranteed success in this role. Lyndon Johnson, as Commander in Chief, and blamed for committing the nation to war in Vietnam, saw the political capital of his Great Society squandered as a result. Yet to the extent that America's standing in the world has a direct impact on the president's own prestige, few can resist the temptations of at the least a little international diplomacy: even Bill Clinton, whose election campaign in 1992 focused almost completely on domestic issues – 'It's the economy, stupid' – spent his final days in the White House trying to broker an elusive peace settlement between Israel and the Palestinian authority in the Middle East.

The office thus offers opportunities to direct the domestic and foreign policy priorities of the most powerful nation in the world. It tempts its occupants into an often elusive quest for a political stature that may place them in the company of those like Washington, Jefferson, Lincoln and Franklin Roosevelt – the most honoured and remembered members of the most exclusive political club. In the end, however, for all the power, the influence and the accompanying responsibilities that define the modern presidency, it remains the political talent for persuasion that is the fundamental skill necessary for the communication of a vision, and the successful realization of the president's agenda. Whether seen in Theodore Roosevelt's use of the 'bully pulpit' of the office to influence public opinion in support of his policies, or in Franklin Roosevelt's 'fireside chats' to reassure a nation traumatized by economic depression, or in the soaring rhetoric of John F. Kennedy's inaugural address as he outlined his idea of the 'new frontier', or in Ronald Reagan's use of mythic images from America's past to support his optimistic view of its present and future prospects, it is this ability to inspire confidence and motivate the nation that may determine a president's historic reputation. At the same time, however, presidential leadership is but one facet of the

American process of government. The exercise of political power takes place within a constitutional framework in which Congress, divided into the House of Representatives and the Senate, each with its complex network of committees, and also the Supreme Court, cannot be ignored.

# Congress

It could probably be shown by facts and figures that there is no distinctly native American criminal class except Congress.
*Mark Twain*, Pudd'n head Wilson's New Calendar (*1897*)

If, following Franklin Roosevelt, presidents have seized the initiative to set a domestic policy agenda, they have still had to face up to the constitutional reality that it is Congress that has ultimate responsibility for making laws within the framework of the national government. The Founders' intent was plain. The legislature would have the central role within the political process: the president was there to execute the laws it passed. As the Constitution phrases it, '[a]ll legislative Powers herein granted shall be vested in a Congress of the United States, which shall consist of a Senate and a House of Representatives.' Then, with its characteristic suspicion of governmental power, the document proceeds to define specific powers of Congress: an indication of the importance attached to the institution, which is further demonstrated by the fact that the description of its structure and sphere of authority takes up roughly half of the entire text of the Constitution itself. The most significant power is fiscal: 'to lay and collect taxes' (although it was only in 1913 that the sixteenth amendment allowed the federal government to 'lay and collect taxes on incomes'), as well as 'to borrow money on the credit of the United States', and 'to coin money'. It also has responsibility for the regulation of commerce, 'with foreign nations, and among the several states, and with the Indian tribes'. Scarcely less important, however, is Congress's power to declare war, and also 'to raise and support armies', 'to provide and maintain a navy' and 'to provide for calling forth the militia to execute the laws of the Union, suppress insurrections and repel invasions'.

There is no doubting the intent. Control over matters such as the declaration of war and military preparations gave Congress a central role in providing for the common defence of the new Union, and with its powers of taxing and regulating commerce came the responsibility for spending, while also encouraging the dynamic of further economic activity within a common market in order to promote the general welfare. In other words, if the rhetoric of the Constitution's preamble was to have any meaning in practice, the Founders looked to the legislature to provide the necessary political leadership. It is no accident, therefore, that when Congress was unable to prevent the nation sliding into Civil War, and when it seemed powerless in the face of the economic recession of the 1930s, two presidents, Lincoln and Roosevelt, were able to establish their historical reputations through acting to resolve the crises that threatened the future of the republic. Political circumstances have thus impacted upon Congress's capacity to fulfil its constitutional potential: during the Cold War, the quickening of institutional trends leading to the growth of the 'imperial presidency' were in part the result of the legislature's deference to executive leadership at a time of high anxiety over the perceived threats of international communism and nuclear war.

From the early days of the republic, however, the precise role of Congress within the federal political system has been disputed, discussed and debated. The argument that was to dominate Congressional debate until the Civil War – over the abolition, retention or extension of slavery within the United States – illustrates the political reality that within a federal system the most controversial matters are fought out on the borders drawn between state sovereignty and federal power. So Congress has had to define – and redefine – its priorities in terms of the changing political dynamics that may occur not simply in relation to the other institutions of the federal government, but also in terms of contemporary attitudes towards the idea of federalism itself. If that is not enough, the legislature itself is a fascinating and complex microcosm of American political life: its very structure impacting upon its capacity to fulfil the ambitions set for it by its eighteenth-century Founders.

## The House of Representatives

The grand depository of the democratic principle of the Government. It was, so to speak, to be our House of Commons.
*James Madison,* Debates in the Federal Convention of 1787

With the exclusive power of originating 'all bills for raising revenue', the House of Representatives is, in many ways, the engine room of federal politics. The number of members of the House from each state is determined according to population (and revised according to the decennial census). Each state's delegation is elected nowadays in single-member districts, giving the representative an affiliation not simply to a political party, but also – and primarily – to a particular geographical constituency. The House of Representatives is the closest political interface between the public and the federal legislature; it epitomizes local – parochial – concerns and priorities.

It is elected every two years. This can turn the political life of its members into a perpetual campaign for re-election; and yet, increasingly, turnover of membership is low. Typically, over 90 per cent of House members who run for re-election can expect to be successful. One reason for this, however, may be the encouragement that the combination of localism and the short time between elections gives to the politics of the 'pork-barrel' – that vivid metaphor to describe the practice of spending government money for political benefits. For Robert Stein and Kenneth Bickers, therefore, the fundamental elements of politics in the United States can be seen as 'the utilization of domestic spending programs to address the needs of specific constituency groups, legislators seeking to use domestic programs to bolster their electoral fortunes, interest groups working in concert with bureaucrats to influence elected officials, the demands on policy makers to support individual policy objectives despite the need to reduce federal spending in the aggregate'.[4] To the extent that there is such a low turnover among incumbents, the use of the federal pork-barrel is evidently successful.

Constitutionally, leadership of the House of Representatives is vested in the speaker. Though his political influence has varied from time to time (there have been thus far no women speakers), the potential of the office arises from the fact that its power is derived from a number of sources. There is the institutional role, which combines the functions of acting as presiding officer and administrative head of the House. The speaker is also the leader of the party that controls a majority of the seats in the House, and retains his representative role as one among its 435 elected members. Among the notable speakers of the House in the nineteenth century were Henry Clay from Kentucky – who in 1825 used the authority of the position to seal the so-called 'corrupt bargain' that delivered the White House to John Quincy Adams, the son of a former president. (Andrew Jackson had beaten him in the popular vote, but did not have a majority in the Electoral College, so the House was called upon to decide the issue.) Clay became secretary of state in Adams' administration before returning to Congress, where he played a leading role in the various political compromises that postponed the Civil War. James Polk from Tennessee is the only speaker of the House to go on to become president in his own right.

During the twentieth century, from the Republican party, Joseph Cannon and Newt Gingrich, and, from the Democrats, Sam Rayburn and Thomas ('Tip') O'Neill, dominated the House to a degree achieved by few other speakers. If Cannon's style was – in keeping with his name – both bombastic and autocratic, Rayburn's was essentially pragmatic, as his advice to new members demonstrates: 'Don't try to go too fast. Learn your job. Don't ever talk until you know what you're talking about. If you want to get along, go along.' O'Neill – whose Massachusetts district was that represented by John F. Kennedy before he ran successfully for the Senate – held the office for eight years (1977–85), during the presidential terms of both Jimmy Carter and Ronald Reagan, when Congress began to reassert itself in the aftermath of the collapse of the imperial presidency. And in the 1990s came Gingrich, possibly the most partisan among contemporary speakers, who, after the 1994 mid-term elections delivered control of both Houses of Congress to the Republicans for the first time in forty years, became the focus of opposition to President Clinton's policy agenda. His four year tenure (1995–9) encompassed the shutdown of the national government after legislature and executive were unable to agree a federal budget, and the drama of the decision – constitutionally reserved to the House – to impeach the president.

Political leadership in the House of Representatives is also exercised by the leader of the majority party, who, along with the speaker, helps to formulate the legislative agenda, and attempts to ensure its enactment. In an institution where party loyalties may be weak, and where representatives value their political autonomy, however, such leadership can be a difficult task. For George Stephanopoulos – later, for a time, one of Bill Clinton's closest advisors – working as executive floor assistant to Richard Gephardt, the Democrat's majority leader, in the late 1980s afforded an insight into how the House works.

> [I]t wasn't enough to know the rules,or the fine points of policy. In the House, the personal is political and the political is personal. To know the House you have to know the members – their home districts, their pet projects, their big contributors. You have to know what votes they'll throw away and which lines they'll never cross. You have to listen to a message in a throwaway line and laugh at a joke you've heard a thousand times. A personal feud might persist for decades, or an alliance could shift in a moment. The most fascinating part of the job was following those patterns, figuring out who held the key votes or which amendment would lock in a majority, watching the coalitions form, crack apart, and come together again.[5]

Unable to rely upon the strict discipline of party allegiance, guiding legislation through the House of Representatives requires both political sensitivity and skill. And the same is true for the Senate.

## Senate

> I am convinced that the decline – if there has been a decline – has been less in the Senate than in the public's appreciation for the art of politics, of the nature and necessity for compromise and balance, and of the nature of the Senate as a legislative chamber.
> *John F. Kennedy*, Profiles in Courage (*1955*)

Two senators represent each state. With a hundred members, and a constitutional role that encompasses legislative initiative and scrutiny as well confirmation – or rejection – of presidential nominations for positions in the executive branch and vacancies in the Supreme Court, and the ratification – or not – of treaties, the Senate is not only a powerful but also an exclusive institution. It also acts as a tribunal in cases of impeachment: when the president is on trial, the chief justice of the Supreme Court is the presiding officer. Originally chosen by the state legislatures for six-year terms, since the passage of the seventeenth amendment in 1913, senators have been directly elected. Terms of office are staggered such that one-third of the Senate is eligible for election every two years.

Power does not mean pomposity: the Senate is a less structured, more informal institution than the House of Representatives. Nevertheless, it does have its own distinctive traditions. Using the prerogative of unlimited debate – the filibuster – individual senators can obstruct legislative initiatives merely by being prepared to make speeches of an inordinate length. The vice-president is nominally the presiding officer, but is by no means the Senate equivalent of the speaker of the House, having a vote only when the Senate divides equally on a particular issue. Historically, then, the president's understudy appears infrequently in the legislature, and the Constitution provides for the Senate to appoint a 'president pro tempore' in the absence of its formal official. Again, an honorary role, it is traditionally taken by the senior member of the majority party, who in that position has no political influence over the Senate's business. During Bill Clinton's presidency, when Al Gore was away, Senator Strom Thurmond took on that role.

It follows, therefore, that effective leadership within the Senate is in the hands of those elected by the majority and minority parties, respectively. In keeping with the collegial character of the institution, moreover, there can be a high degree of co-operation between the majority and minority leaders in order to make things work. The most effective majority leader of the twentieth century was Lyndon Johnson, who held the position for five years (1955–60) while his fellow Texan, Sam Rayburn, was speaker of the House. In Congress, both were political virtuosi.

Johnson used his position as majority leader to launch a bid for the presidency in 1960, only to lose the Democrats' nomination to his fellow senator, John F. Kennedy. Johnson became JFK's vice-president. In so doing, he was following an established career path. During the twentieth century, prior to Johnson, five other senators had become vice-president (Charles Fairbanks, Charles Curtis, Harry Truman, Alben Barkley and Richard Nixon). Two – Truman and Nixon – like Johnson himself, ultimately became president. Following LBJ, a further five senators have served as vice-president: Hubert Humphrey, Spiro Agnew, Walter Mondale, Dan Quayle and Al Gore. In what would seem to be a more definite trend, since 1960, and with the exception of Gerald Ford and Nelson Rockefeller (both nominated as a result of resignations), only George Bush and Dick Cheney have held the office without prior service in the Senate. Whereas in 1832 John Calhoun resigned as vice-president to return to the Senate, nowadays, it is seen very much as a platform for establishing a national political career. It follows, therefore, that while all senators must necessarily speak for the interests of their states, during their minimum period of six years there, they have the opportunity build a public profile, and so some at least have one eye fixed upon other political prizes. The Senate, although far smaller, is more expansive than the House: its perspectives are longer-term, and its political horizons are broader. Yet, like the House, its real political agenda is set not so much through debate as in committee.

## Committees

I know not how better to describe our form of government in a single phrase than by calling it a government by the chairmen of the Standing Committees of Congress.
*Woodrow Wilson*, Congressional Government (*1885*)

Think Congress, think committee. The corridors of legislative power lead to a labyrinth of committees where the daily business of Congress is orchestrated. Almost fifty different committees have given rise to over three times as many sub-committees. A distinction is made between standing committees, which, as the name implies, are integral to the work of the legislature, and which continue from one congressional session to the next, and select committees, which are set up in response to *ad hoc* situations, and which then meet for the duration of the congressional session, but which may be reinstituted at the start of a subsequent session. All committees are powerful, but some may be more powerful than others. In the House of Representatives, three committees between them effectively determine the fiscal and legislative priorities of the institution: the Appropriations Committee sets the level of spending that will underpin legislative initiatives; the Ways and Means Committee establishes the tax rates and fiscal policies that produce the revenue that government can spend; and the Rules Committee decides which legislation will finally emerge from the shadows into the full glare of discussion on the floor of the House – and when – thus in effect controlling the political agenda through prioritizing the measures that will then stand a chance of being enacted. Similarly in the Senate, the Appropriations Committee, the Armed Services Committee, the Foreign Relations Committee and the Judiciary Committee are high-profile players in the game of congressional politics.

While the tasks of framing legislation, scrutinizing it, debating it, as well as holding members of the executive to account, investigating issues of public concern and acting as the vital cogs in the congressional machine are no doubt important, the recondite steps by which legislation passes through the institution's committees are enough to confuse all but the most committed observers of American politics. They are easily found elsewhere. On the principle that it is not always necessary to understand how a jet-engine works in order to enjoy the sensation of flight, it may be more interesting to consider how the structure of Congress impacts upon those whom John F. Kennedy once described as suffering from 'Potomac fever', and who build their political careers upon time spent in the federal legislature.

To them, committees mean power. To chair a congressional committee is a way to accrue political capital, which may be spent to good purpose, or in – sometimes literally – an orgy of self-indulgence. Certainly for the three decades between 1940 and 1970, congressional committees could appear to be extensions of the political personalities of those who chaired them. Holding their positions of authority through seniority, and during a time when one party – the Democrats – dominated Congress, power flowed to them and through them. While some, like Senator William Fulbright, chair of the Senate Committee on Foreign Relations, could use the position to take a stand on a particular issue – opposition to America's war in Vietnam – and have a profound influence upon vital areas of national policy, others were less concerned with affairs of state. In 1973, the newly elected woman member of Congress from Colorado, Pat Schroeder, became a member of the House Armed Services Committee, along with Ron Dellums, an African-American. The chair was seventy-two-year-old F. Edward Hébert from Louisiana – a member of the same party, but with different political sensibilities. Schroeder wrote:

> Hébert didn't appreciate the idea of a girl and a black forced on him. He was outraged that for the first time a chairman's veto of potential members was ignored. He announced that while he might not be able to control the makeup of the committee, he could damn well control the number of chairs in his hearing room, where he was enthroned on a carpet of stars, surrounded by military flags. He said that women and blacks were worth only half of one 'regular' member, so he added only one seat to the committee room and made Ron and me share it. Nobody else objected, and nobody offered to scrounge up another chair. Armed Services was the most powerful committee in Congress during the Vietnam War, and Hébert ran it like a personal fiefdom.[6]

'Potomac fever' is a political virus that infects in different ways – historically, committee chairs have been as vulnerable to its contagion as other members of Washington's political establishment.

Given such abuses of power in the legislature, and at a time when the political power of the executive was also under scrutiny, it is not surprising that from the 1970s onwards there have been attempts within Congress to change traditional structures, with the committee system a natural target for reform. The system collapsed whereby seniority of service in Congress brought its entitlements to chair committees – which had worked to the advantage of southern Democrats, whose security of tenure in the 'one-party south' had lasted for many years. With 'Tip' O'Neill as speaker, efforts were made to decentralize power and authority in the House of Representatives. When Republicans became a majority there in 1994, Newt Gingrich exercised strong party leadership in the House, and the influence of committees – and their chairs – was further undermined. Although such change may have seemed necessary in the context of the times, it could be argued that Congress is now less able effectively to oversee, scrutinize and criticize legislation: functions traditionally facilitated by the powerful and independent committee system. Reforms may carry costs as well as benefits.

Power in Congress thus flows through the House and the Senate into the arteries of their committees, which, by the 1960s, had undoubtedly become blocked due to the seniority system. This gave incumbents a large amount of autonomy simply because of their longevity. The Republican party's political advances in southern states – symbolized in the career of Newt Gingrich from Georgia – together with the reforms in the 1970s and in the post-Watergate period, have meant that although there is still the potential for political capital to accrue to committee chairs, the security of tenure enjoyed by those occupying such positions has been eroded. F. Edward Hébert eventually lost his autocratic control of the Armed Services Committee following a rule change requiring chairs to be elected at the beginning of each congressional session. In 1992, Ron Dellums became chair: itself testimony to changing political dynamics in a Congress that has begun to reflect – however imperfectly – contemporary America's multi-cutural society. Nor should the historical reputation of Congress be judged entirely by the behaviour of some of its more ancient – and idiosyncratic – personalities. Within the framework of the Constitution, Congress still makes its own rules. It remains a legislature that has enormous political powers, and a national authority quite independent from that of the executive. A president who ignores it, or who challenges its prerogatives in the belief that public opinion will support such a move, is frequently and abruptly reminded of that. The executive and the legislature have a symbiotic relationship: each may be diminished to the extent that the other is perceived as politically weak. That said, the balance of power between the two is a political dynamic that changes over time, and that may be affected too by the role played within the framework of American government by the third actor in the triumvirate of federal institutions: the Supreme Court.

## The Supreme Court

It is confidence in the men and women who administer the judicial system that is the true backbone of the rule of law.

*Supreme Court Justice John Paul Stevens in*
Bush v. Gore (*2000*)

If the presidency is about character and the Congress is about personality, then the Supreme Court is about style. During its history it has sometimes entered periods of judicial activism as opposed to exercising judicial self-restraint. As an institution that may claim merely to occupy the abstract space of legal debate and objective argument, it nevertheless plays a crucial role in the American political process. Its structure and powers are, like those of the executive and the legislature, written in the Constitution; its status is derived from the fact that its interpretation of that document is meant to be final. The politics of nostalgia becomes its everyday concern: its apparently exhaustive and forensic examination of the Founders' intent becomes the authoritative basis of its reconciliation of law and constitutional propriety – even if, on occasion, its legal reasoning has been more creative than deductive. In sum, then, the Supreme Court treads a tight-rope stretched between political purposes and judicial impartiality. And sometimes it misses a step.

For an institution that has established itself as the custodian of the Constitution, the Supreme Court can derive little of its power from the document itself, which details only that '[t]he judicial power of the United States shall be vested in one supreme court. . . . The judges . . . shall hold their offices during good behavior.' Neither the size of the court nor its exact role within the constitutional system of separated institutions sharing powers is closely defined. Supreme Court justices are to be nominated by the president and confirmed by the Senate. After that, they can leave office voluntarily through retirement, or involuntarily through impeachment or death. It follows that the average age of members of the Supreme Court tends to be higher than that of the president or those elected to Congress. Since the Court was established in 1790, there have been only sixteen chief justices, and barely a hundred associate judges appointed; the average tenure is fifteen years.

Originally the membership was fixed at six: George Washington appointed them under the terms of the Judiciary Act of 1789, passed by the first Congress. This act created a framework in which the country was divided into thirteen judicial districts, organized into three circuits. The Supreme Court, based in the national capital, was nevertheless required to 'ride circuit'- two justices were to visit each judicial district twice a year. This practice, which dominated the life of the Court for just over a century, detracted from the appeal of becoming a justice at a time when communications were poor and travel difficult.

It took time, then, for the Supreme Court to establish itself as a significant force in American political life. It decided its first cases in 1792, and thereafter started to establish legal precedents that might govern its future conduct. The first chief justice, John Jay, who had collaborated with James Madison and Alexander Hamilton in the writing of the *Federalist*, resigned in 1795, becoming governor of New York: an early example of a judge with political ambitions. He refused to return to the Court when the position of chief justice again became vacant in 1800, contrary to the wishes of the then president, John Adams. But by the time his son, and by then former president, John Quincy Adams appeared before it to argue the *Amistad* case in 1841, the status and the reputation of the Court had changed dramatically. There were two reasons for this: the role played in the Court's development by the chief justice Adams appointed instead of Jay – John Marshall from Virginia – and the assertion of the principle of judicial review. Marshall was chief justice for thirty-four years, and provided the necessary leadership to establish the Court as a vital element within the framework of American government. His decision, taken early in his tenure, to assert the idea that it was the Court that should act as the ultimate interpreter of the Constitution equipped it with its most formidable political power – the source of its subsequent authority.

In *Federalist 78*, Hamilton famously outlined the contemporary perspective upon the limits of judicial power within the context of a separation of powers.

> Whoever attentively considers the different departments of power must perceive that, in a government in which they are separated from each other, the judiciary, from the nature of its functions, will always be the least dangerous to the political rights of the Constitution; because it will be least in a capacity to annoy or injure them. The executive not only dispenses the honours, but holds the sword of the community. The legislature not only commands the purse, but prescribes the rules by which the duties and rights of every citizen are to be regulated. The judiciary, on the contrary, has no influence over either the sword or the purse; no direction either of the strengths or of the wealth of the society; and can take no active resolution whatever. It may truly be said to have neither *force* nor *will*, but merely judgment; and must ultimately depend upon the aid of the executive arm even for the efficacy of its judgments.

Having effectively, and at considerable length, set out the arguments that relegate the judiciary to a walk-on part in the American political process, Hamilton then admits that it must still be given one essential duty: 'to declare all acts contrary to the manifest tenor of the Constitution void'. It is this principle, indeed, which enshrines the Constitution as a permanent feature of the political landscape: if a law is passed that is contrary to constitutional principles, then the document is open to constant change. It follows, therefore, that '[n]o legislative act . . . contrary to the Constitution can be valid.' Hamilton concludes.

The interpretation of the law is the proper and peculiar province of the courts. A constitution is, in fact, and must be regarded by the judges, as a fundamental law. It therefore belongs to them to ascertain its meaning, as well as the meaning of any particular act proceeding from the legislative body. If there should happen to be an irreconcilable variance between the two, that which has the superior obligation and validity ought, of course, to be preferred; or, in other words, the Constitution ought to be preferred to the statute, the intention of the people to the intention of their agents.

It remained, therefore, for the Court itself to translate that potential into power.

Between 1787 and 1857 the Supreme Court only declared one federal law unconstitutional. But in its decision that did so – the case of *Marbury* v. *Madison* (1803) – it established the single most important precedent that would determine its future direction: asserting its power of judicial review. John Marshall, delivering the unanimous opinion of the Court, echoed Hamilton's analysis:

It is, emphatically, the province and duty of the judicial department, to say what the law is. . . . If two laws conflict with each other the courts must decide on the operation of each. So, if a law be in opposition to the constitution; if both the law and the constitution apply to a particular case, so that the court must either decide that case conformably to the law, disregarding the constitution; or conformably to the constitution, disregarding the law; the court must determine which of these conflicting rules governs the case. This is of the very essence of judicial responsibility. . . . The judicial power of the United States is extended to all cases arising under the constitution.

It was an annexation of authority that was as politically bold as it was legally suspect. As Max Lerner put it,

[f]rom a legalistic point of view alone, *Marbury v. Madison* has a nightmarish fascination. If ever the history of the Court is written with the proper cosmic irony here will be the cream of the jest. Upon this case, as precedent, rests the power of judicial review. Yet every part of its reasoning has been repudiated by commentators and decisions of later courts which none the less continue to exercise the power it established. . . . Ultimately, the whole of the theory is in No. 78 of the Federalist Papers; in fact, much of Marshall's career may be viewed as a process of reading Hamilton's state papers into the Constitution. And yet having translated these ideas into judicial action is Marshall's decisive achievement.[7]

If asserting the right of judicial review gave the Supreme Court the final say in American political debate, however, in the nineteenth century it tended to remain silent on the constitutionality of federal laws. During that time, and including that first earth-shaking pronouncement of its prerogative in 1803, the Court only asserted its power on twenty-two occasions. When it did so, the effect could be seismic. On the second occasion when it ruled on a constitutional issue in *Dred Scott* v. *Sandford* (1857), it made its own contribution to the political crisis that accelerated the nation towards Civil War.

Since the end of that conflict, however, the Supreme Court has struck down an increasing number of federal laws, and in the twentieth century it has exercised the power of judicial review in over a hundred separate cases. At the same time, after the Civil War emphatically altered the balance of power on the borders of federal authority versus state autonomy, the Court also intervened more frequently in extending the process of judicial review to state laws. Again, it was building upon a precedent set by the Marshall Court in its decision in the case of *McCulloch* v. *Maryland* (1819). The state government of Maryland, opposed to the establishment of the second National Bank, had tried to tax it out of existence in the state. Was this a constitutional action? In Marshall's opinion, the constitutionality of the bank itself was not an issue. The Constitution had framed a national government with implied as well as explicit powers to pass legislation 'necessary and proper' for the welfare of the nation. The ghost of the first secretary of the Treasury had reappeared. Just as Hamilton had argued for a broad interpretation of the Constitution when the creation of the first National Bank was at issue, so now the chief justice reiterated that idea. For Lerner, indeed, 'Marshall made it the occasion of his most resounding opinion, building a doctrine of implied national powers on the "necessary and proper" clause.'[8] In so doing, he removed obstacles to progress that might result from a strictly constructionist conception of federal power: the Constitution should be interpreted in the light of contemporary needs and circumstances. In *McCulloch* v. *Maryland*, therefore, Marshall argued that the Founders had written

> a constitution intended to endure for ages to come, and consequently, to be adapted to the various crises of human affairs. To have pre-scribed the means by which government should, in all future time, execute its powers, would have been to change, entirely, the character of the instrument, and give it the properties of a legal code. It would have been unwise to provide by immutable rules, for exigencies, which, if foreseen at all, must have been seen dimly, and which can best be provided for as they occur.

Marshall's Constitution was designed not to inhibit the growth of the nation but to facilitate it.

Moreover, 'a power to create implies a power to preserve' and 'a power to destroy, if wielded by a different hand, is hostile to, and incompatible with, these powers to create and preserve . . . where this repugnancy exists, that authority which is supreme must control, not yield to that over which it is supreme.' In other words, if the federal government acted constitutionally to create a National Bank, and a state government tried to destroy it, then it was, by definition, acting unconstitutionally. 'The states have no power, by taxation or otherwise, to retard, impede, burden, or in any manner control, the operations of the constitutional laws enacted by Congress to carry into execution the powers vested in the general government.' And once more, the final judgement in such matters would rest with the Court.

As Thomas Jefferson pointed out in 1819, the assumption of judicial review gave the Supreme Court a controversial power. 'The constitution, on this hypothesis, is a mere thing of wax in the hands of the judiciary, which they may twist, and shape into any form they please.' At the same time, however, the remark attributed to Andrew Jackson when disagreeing with the interpretation of the Court is an accurate assessment of the realities of political power within the framework of American government. When the Court ruled that the president had acted unconstitutionally in forcing the removal of Cherokee Indians in the state of Georgia, Jackson is said to have responded: 'John Marshall has made his decision, now let him enforce it.' The Supreme Court has enormous influence. However, though its opinions may be respected, they are not necessarily acted upon unless the other institutions of government agree with them. It cannot consistently set itself against the grain of either executive policies or legislative priorities without squandering its most valuable asset: its prestige. Yet the implications of Jefferson's analysis, irrespective of the truth of Jackson's remark, remain clear. During his thirty-four years as chief justice, Marshall shaped the Court as a political institution of the federal government, and it has remained so ever since.

# Conclusion: 'A Republic, if you can keep it'

In matters of style, swim with the current; in matters of principle, stand like a rock.
*Thomas Jefferson*, Notes on the State of Virginia (*1787*)

What emerges from an analysis of the Founders' achievement – the American framework of government – is an understanding of the subtlety of political thought that underlies the Constitution itself. The principles of federalism and a separation of powers are woven together in an intricate pattern, creating a political system in which institutions and layers of government are held together in a constantly evolving process of creative tension.

There are, then, two sets of interlocking relationships that continue to define the nature of America's republican ideal. Federalism seeks to establish the dividing line between the scope of national government and the autonomy of individual states. That border is, by its nature, ill defined and has occupied a contentious space in American politics; indeed, the Civil War was the product in part of a failure to agree upon the legitimate spheres of state and federal authority. At the end of that conflict, the focus of political attention shifted decisively towards the federal government. That trend has continued, helped by industrialization and urbanization – in 1870, a quarter of the nation's population lived in cities, and three quarters in rural areas, whereas a century later those proportions were almost exactly the reverse – together with increasing globalization and the emergence of the United States as the pre-eminent world power.

Yet federalism remains a force in American politics. State governments matter. And so does the principle of federalism itself. It is most visible within Congress, where the Senate, giving equal representation to each state, acts as a political counterweight to the House of Representatives. When Thomas Jefferson discussed the new Constitution with George Washington over a cup of coffee, he asked him the reasoning behind having the Senate as part of the legislature. As he did so, in keeping with the manners of the time, Jefferson poured his coffee from cup to saucer. Washington asked him why. 'To cool it.' Washington's rejoinder is worth remembering: 'So,' he said, 'we will pour legislation into the Senatorial saucer to cool it.' And not just legislation. The fact that the House may vote to impeach the president, but the Senate tries the case, has had a similar impact upon the political process. In the two cases where Congress has exercised this power – the impeachments of Andrew Johnson and Bill Clinton – the Senate has failed to muster sufficient majorities for the effort to succeed. As Jefferson later commented, in a letter he wrote to James Madison in 1794, '[t]he Senate . . . was intended as a check on the will of the Representatives when too hasty.' So the animating idea of federalism has a direct impact not simply upon the structure but also upon the manner in which Congress conducts its business.

The idea of federalism also underlies the institution of the Electoral College. It has served, indeed, often to magnify margins of victory in close elections. In 1960, Kennedy won the Electoral College vote more convincingly than he defeated Nixon in the popular vote. John Quincy Adams enters the record books as the most badly defeated presidential candidate from a major political party by virtue of the fact that in 1820 he received only a single Electoral College vote. Ignored when it works, it is maligned on the occasions when it 'misfires', producing, on occasion, an anomalous result that may undermine the popular mandate of the president who benefits from it. In the nineteenth century it happened three times – in 1824 (John Quincy Adams), 1876 (Rutherford Hayes) and 1888 (Benjamin Harrison). Each time the eventual winner of the election did not receive the greatest number of votes in the election. Throughout the twentieth century, however, the Electoral College effectively endorsed the winner of the popular vote. But in the first election of the new century, it allowed one state – Florida – to have a decisive impact on the result.

Just as the national government has become the dominant player within the framework of the federal republic, however, so the executive has become the principal actor within the constitutional system that separates, checks and balances powers. It may have been the Founders' original intention that the legislature should be the creative motor of American federal politics, but the modern president is no longer subservient to Congress. From economic depression, through the Second World War, to the Cold War and beyond, the president has become, in Alfred de Grazia's phrase, 'the focus of the anxious crowd of the age'.[9] And yet, the transition from legislative to executive supremacy has been anything but smooth. As the 'imperial presidency' crashed in flames over Vietnam, and was further wounded by Watergate, the dynamics of the relationship between president and Congress have provided much of the drama of contemporary American politics.

But so too has the Supreme Court. From its decision in *Brown* v. *Board of Education* (1954), which helped to shape the character of the civil rights movement, to its judgement in *Roe* v. *Wade* (1973), which provides the context for the enduring struggle between 'pro-choice' and 'pro-life' campaigners, to its determination in *Bush* v. *Gore* (2000), which effectively determined the outcome of the presidential election, the Court has been at the confluence of contemporary controversies. More and more it is seen as a political institution in the purest sense of the term, and to the extent that it enters the partisan world inhabited by the executive and the legislature it is diminished as a result. Indeed, when the Supreme Court, by a single vote, awarded the White House to George W. Bush, by bringing to an end the recounting of votes in Florida, that much was evident. As Justice John Paul Stevens put it in his dissenting opinion, '[a]lthough we may never know with complete certainty the identity of the winner of this year's Presidential election, the identity of the loser is perfectly clear. It is the nation's confidence in the judge as an impartial guardian of the rule of law.' Admiration of the Constitution, influenced by the politics of nostalgia, remains undimmed. But the politics of spectacle still fascinates. The character, personality and style of those whose strengths and weaknesses, foibles and fallibility, shape the process of national politics in turn breathe life into the institutions that structure the framework of American government. So it was that the election of 2000 demonstrated a combination of constitutional propriety and political venality that at times brought to mind Ben Franklin's comment in 1787 when asked what the Constitutional Convention in Philadelphia had achieved. 'A Republic, if you can keep it', was his reply. In the twenty-first century, that challenge remains.

# 5

# Playing the Political Game

When President Nixon took up residence on Pennsylvania
Avenue, Coke vending machines disappeared. When President
Carter arrived, the Pepsi machines went out. . . . Coke was a
company whose roots were in the South. Its executives were true
Southern gentlemen. Pepsi was a two-fisted, self-made Repub-
lican corporation in the East.
                    *John Sculley*, Odyssey: Pepsi to Apple (*1988*)

Power, in the United States as in other countries, is not constrained
by a constitution within the framework of a system of government.
If political power is a resource – capital that may be accrued or spent
in pursuit of particular objectives – then it follows that the ability
to accumulate it determines both its distribution and its expenditure.
It is necessary to have power in order to use it. The 'idea of America'
is itself powerful at a rhetorical and emotional level: a democratic
republic founded on the principles of liberty and equality for all. But
that idea must confront a different reality. In contemporary American
society, power is not distributed equally among individuals, groups
or minorities. The idea of democracy rests upon concepts such as the
'sovereignty of the people', with the organizing principle of 'majority
rule' as its operative mechanism in deciding courses of action. Yet
even majorities rule in a very limited political context: they may determine who wins elected office in certain circumstances. But does the
majority decide the political agenda and the policies that are imple-
mented in the name of the people?

Clearly the issue of power is central to any discussion of the nature
of American politics. Traditionally, two descriptions of its distribution

have been used to explain the dynamics of the political process: the elitist model and the pluralist model. Both reveal something of the way in which power flows through the American polity. Yet there are other ways of looking at the issue: linking economics and politics, money and power. Imagine American political parties – Democrats and Republicans – as investment banks. They use their political capital to support candidates, who, if they win election, gain resources of power and patronage: the political return, or interest, on the original investment. Indeed, translating metaphor into fact, it is possible to trace a symbiotic relationship between American political parties and the evolution of banks as their financial counterparts. In politics, however, cash – although predominant – is not the only source of power; ideas and organization are also significant. In this context it is worth considering again how religion, and notably Protestant fundamentalism, has impacted upon the framework of American politics and party structures. None of these approaches may give the whole picture, but each illuminates facets of a complex, dynamic – and sometimes corrupt – political system. Power exists, so where does it lie?

## Elitism: The Monopoly Game

> The panic of 1907 and the death of Harriman, his great opponent in railroad financing, in 1909, had left him the undisputed ruler of Wall Street, most powerful private citizen in the world. . . . So admirably was his empire built that his death in 1913 hardly caused a ripple in the exchanges of the world: the purple descended to his son, J.P. Morgan, who had been trained at Groton and Harvard and by associating with the British ruling class to be a more constitutional monarch.
>
> *John Dos Passos*, USA (*1938*)

During the Civil War, John Pierpoint Morgan had underwritten a scheme whereby five thousand obsolete rifles were bought inexpensively, refurbished and then resold to the Union Army for a considerable profit. He was a remarkable businessman. By 1912, the year before he died, Morgan, who had inherited a fortune from his father, and had increased it tenfold, and who, in 1901, had made US Steel the first billion-dollar industrial conglomerate, held seventy-two directorships in forty-seven corporations. Morgan once confessed that 'America is good enough for me.' And as William Jennings Bryan observed, '[w]henever he doesn't like it, he can give it back to us.'[1] His son,

J.P. Morgan, Jr, known more familiarly as Jack, was born in 1867. On his father's death, he took over the family business. J.P. Morgan & Co. was and remained one of the most powerful financial institutions in the United States – and indeed the world. In 1935, however, it was forced to separate its deposit and investment banking activities as a result of legislation under the Glass–Steagall Act, passed by Congress two years earlier. Morgan Stanley & Co., the new treasurer of which was Jack Morgan's son Harry – elder brother Junius stayed with the orginal company – took on the securities and brokering role, but its activities were still largely underwritten by the financial power of the original company. With further changes in the post-war financial environment, family control of the companies weakened. Indeed, when Jack Morgan died in 1943 – thirty years after his father – the reality that the financial world he had inherited was being remade was symbolized in the fate of his personal possessions: his houses and yachts were sold not to individuals but to institutions. But just as had happened when his father had died, news of Jack Morgan's death was not made public until after the stock market had closed in case it had an adverse impact on the prices of shares. Subsequently, however, the transition from family-run business to institutionally directed public corporation was accelerated by a number of mergers and acquisitions during the remainder of the twentieth century.

In 1799, Aaron Burr – who later fought a duel with Alexander Hamilton, and fatally wounded him – became a co-founder of the Manhattan Company, which was chartered to set up a bank. After the Civil War – from which J.P. Morgan had profited so handsomely – the Chase National Bank, named after Salmon P. Chase, secretary of the Treasury in Lincoln's wartime administration, and subsequently chief justice of the Supreme Court, was established. During the first half of the twentieth century, the Bank of the Manhattan Company took over more than twenty of its competitors, but in 1955 it was bought by Chase National, to form the Chase Manhattan Bank. By 1996, as a result of further mergers in the financial industry, Chase formed the largest bank holding company in the United States. In 2000, one further merger took place: between Chase and J.P. Morgan. In January 2001, J.P. Morgan Chase & Co. opened for business.

As Ron Chernow suggests, then, in the case of J.P. Morgan it may well be, as Ralph Waldo Emerson observed, that 'an institution is the lengthened shadow of a man'. Moreover such explorations of the historical and dynastic links that have forged the character of the contemporary corporate life of American finance may be repeated in other contexts. Sometimes the networks uncovered are labyrinths, and provide a useful quarry for those who see in the connections that can be made evidence of sinister, deliberate purposes at work. For Chernow, '[t]he old House of Morgan spawned a thousand conspiracy theories and busied generations of muckrakers. As the most mandarin of banks, it catered to many prominent families, including the Astors, Guggenheims, du Ponts, and Vanderbilts. It shunned dealings with lesser mortals, thus breeding popular suspicion.'[2] More often than not, however, the links are merely indicative of the ways in which wealth, once it has become concentrated, is preserved as it flows through the economic, political and indeed cultural arteries of American society.

Elites, then, may be encountered anywhere and everywhere. But do they give rise to elitism: the dominance of several groups in society that effectively shape and direct not only public philosophy but also public policy for their own purposes and benefit? It may indeed be the case that a small number of people monopolize positions of power and authority in the realms of politics, business, communications, the law and the military, and that those who come from a wealthy background and a privileged education assume positions of leadership within society as a matter more of right than because of their talents. Elitism is the antithesis of the American Dream. Yet for this model of power in American society to work, elites have to co-operate: consensus, along with monopoly, is the name of their political game. If they squabble, then such disagreement may threaten their survival. It follows, then, that the consolidation of power among elites is most visible at times of maximum consensus, and the 1950s remains as a case in point.

In 1956, the sociologist C. Wright Mills published *The Power Elite*, an analysis of contemporary American political, economic and military institutions that emphasized the extent to which they were dominated by individuals from a common – but privileged – educational, social and family background. 'They occupy the strategic command posts of the social structure, in which are now centered the effective means of the power and the wealth and the celebrity which they enjoy.'[3] Using the media as an effective conduit to shape public opinion, the power elite effectively governs what Mills termed an emerging 'mass society', which quietly and generally without question defers to its judgement.

There appeared to be corroborative empirical evidence for Mills' observations. Philip Burch's analysis in *Elites in American History* (1980), for example, showed that 83.5 per cent of elite cabinet and diplomatic appointees in the Eisenhower administration were drawn from those who had occupied a prior position of corporate or professional responsibility. This was the highest percentage since the pre-First World War period. What Mills and Burch drew attention to, therefore, was the small and relatively homogenous strata of economic, political and military society from which such leaders were drawn. If John F. Kennedy recruited – in David Halberstam's famous phrase – the 'best and the brightest' for his administration (although over half his appointees also came from elitist backgrounds), Eisenhower's White House was home to the 'great and the good'. The president himself had been supreme commander of Nato forces in Europe. His first secretary of defense, Charles E. Wilson, had been president of General Motors. The secretary of state was John Foster Dulles, who had served briefly in the Senate, but whose profession was the law: he was a senior partner in a prestigious New York firm of corporate lawyers. His younger brother, Allen Dulles, would become Eisenhower's director of the CIA. George Humphrey, the secretary of the Treasury, was a leading figure in the corporate community. The administration, then, was undoubtedly one in which connections and a background in business were qualifications for preferment. American business liked Eisenhower. In 1949, the future president attended a dinner with, as Peter Lyon observes, 'such other guests as the chairman of Standard Oil of New Jersey, the president of six other big oil corporations (Standard of California, Texaco, Socony-Vacuum, and the like), the executive vice president of J.P. Morgan & Company, the presidents of another ten assorted corporations, and a stray Vanderbilt'. It was, according to Eisenhower himself, 'a great success'.[4]

The critical question, of course, is how much influence such elite groups have had over the formation and execution of public policy in the United States. Here, Eisenhower also provided an insight. In his 'farewell address' to the nation at the end of his second term in office, he noted that by then the nation was spending more on its military security than the 'net income of all United States corporations'. As the president observed,

> [t]his conjunction of an immense military establishment and a large arms industry is new in the American experience. The total influence – economic, political, even spiritual – is felt in every city, every States house, every office of the federal government. We recognize the imperative need for this development. Yet we must not fail to comprehend its grave implications. Our toil, resources and livelihood are all involved; so is the very structure of our society. In the councils of government, we must guard against the acquisition of unwarranted influence, whether sought or unsought, by the military-industrial complex. The potential for the disastrous rise of misplaced power exists and will persist.

Eisenhower had coined an enduring phrase. His warning of the
dangers inherent in the creation of a 'military-industrial complex' is
a remarkable one, coming as it did from a member of Mills' power
elite; albeit one about to retire from active service.

## Pluralism: Like Mind Games

> Americans of all ages, all conditions and all dispositions con-
> stantly form associations. They have not only commercial and
> manufacturing companies, in which all take part, but associ-
> ations of a thousand other kinds, religious, moral, serious, futile,
> general or restricted, enormous or diminutive.
>     *Alexis de Tocqueville*, Democracy in America, *vol. 2 (1840)*

The Founders had also wrestled with the problem of power. They
clearly thought that they had devised a system of government
that would avoid the problems that, less than two centuries later,
Eisenhower warned against. In *Federalist 51*, Madison outlines the
fundamental issue: 'Ambition must be made to counteract ambition.'
Moreover, this could be achieved in the United States, because, '[w]hilst
all authority in it will be derived from and dependent on the society,
the society itself will be broken into so many parts, interests, and
classes of citizens, that the rights of individuals, or of the minority,
will be in little danger from interested combinations of the majority.'
This, then, is a classic articulation of an alternative analysis of the
nature of power in America – the idea of pluralism.

The Madisonian model of republican democracy, where a separation of powers and federalism gives protection against government
encroachments on individual rights, need not deny the existence of
economic, political and social elites. It suggests instead that their influence is moderated not simply because their interests are both fluid
and sometimes overlapping, but more crucially because they are forced
to compete within the marketplace of American ideas, where no one
group predominates. Pluralism can thus operate as a functional analysis
of American democracy in action, but beyond that it also becomes a
prescriptive idea of how, in practice, it should work. It is no accident
that pluralist views of American politics were expressed as trenchant
critiques of elitist ideas at a critical time in the nation's history. The
Cold War was not least a battleground of ideas and ideologies. Pluralism, which maintained the individual and the group as key actors
in the political process, offers a more democratic perspective on the

nature of American politics than elitism, which is redolent of the ideas of oligarchy and state control that appear the antithesis of core American values and principles.

Whereas the natural focus for elitism lies in its characterizations of the cultural milieu from which America recruits its ruling political class, and in particular, during the era when the 'imperial presidency' appeared to dominate the political process, in the composition of the executive, pluralism directs its attention elsewhere. The proliferation of interest groups, political associations and lobbyists seems to be tangible evidence that public policy in the United States is the product of heated debate in the cacophony of the political marketplace. Indeed to the extent that the nation now recognizes itself as a multi-cultural society, pluralism might seem to reflect contemporary political realities more accurately today than it did fifty years ago, when pluralist theories were first advanced to explain the distribution of power in America. An elite is concerned with maintaining the status quo in support of the defined interests of those who are its exclusive members. Yet the issue of civil rights started to gain its momentum as a mass movement during the Eisenhower administration, a period in which the conservative mood was meant to predominate. The dynamic for social and cultural change in America that marked the subsequent decade of the 1960s, then, was generated by those outside the political establishment. That those who were on the wrong side of the political barricades stormed the citadels of power, and gained access to them, such that racial and gender diversity in positions of responsibility is now accepted is a remarkable, if not revolutionary, achievement. Yet for pluralism to move from a prescriptive to a descriptive model of how power meshes with political processes in America, more needs to be done. For at core, power is still structured around one main resource: money.

## The Money Game

Brother can you spare a dime?
*E. Y. Harburg (1932) – song title*

In the United Kingdom, candidates stand for election; in the United States, they run for office. But before they can run, they need to find sponsors willing to donate money to the cause: backers prepared to bet on the outcome of the race. George W. Bush's campaign for the presidency in 2000 raised almost $200 million, most of which it spent.

Al Gore was funded to the tune of $132 million. Even Ralph Nader managed to find almost $8 million in campaign finance. Contrast Harry Browne, the candidate for the Libertarian party, who also ran for the presidency in 2000, with a campaign budget of just over $2 million. Few people knew of his attempt to win the White House: only 382,000 voted for him, while Bush and Gore between them gathered almost 100 million votes.

Money doesn't just talk in American elections. It is the cheerleader of the political system. Without the power of money, there is silence. In politics, though, money may also nudge and whisper. Bill Clinton, as one of his last acts in office, issued a pardon to the appropriately named Marc Rich. Had money's voice been heard? Rich had left America in 1983, rather than face charges of tax evasion, rigging oil prices and trading with Iran illegally during the hostage crisis of 1979; if convicted, he might have been sentenced to 300 years in prison. He still ran a $30 billion a year business from his new base in Switzerland. He made donations to numerous charitable causes, mostly in Israel, whose then prime minister, Ehud Barak, telephoned Clinton to press for a pardon. His ex-wife – a celebrity fund-raiser for the Democrats, who donated $70,000 to Hillary Clinton's campaign for the Senate and money to support Clinton's presidential library – signed a petition in his support. Rich retained Jack Quinn, a former counsel to Clinton, and a chief of staff for Al Gore, to promote the idea of a pardon. 'Quinn made a strong case,' said Clinton, 'and I was convinced he was right on the merits.' But as his former labor secretary, Robert Reich, observed, after the pardon had been announced: 'This has all the appearances of a payoff. They make a [political] contribution because they want something back. This is the sort of thing that makes democracy look like a sham.' Yet as the scandal of this and some of Clinton's other pardons demonstrated, it is also part of contemporary American political culture. Money rarely comes without strings attached.

Madison wrote in *Federalist 10*,

> the most common and durable source of factions has been the various and unequal distribution of property. Those who hold and those who are without property have ever formed distinct interests in society. Those who are creditors, and those who are debtors, fall under like discrimination. A landed interest, a manufacturing interest, a mercantile interest, a moneyed interest, and many lesser interests, grow up of necessity in civilised nations, and divide them into different classes, actuated by different sentiments and views. The regulation of these various and interfering interests forms the principal task of modern legislation, and involves the spirit of party and faction in the necessary and ordinary operations of government.

The idealistic view of American democracy assumes that government arbitrates fairly between these groups, on the basis of justice and equity. The reality, however, may be somewhat different.

It is in the electoral process itself that Madison's ideal seems most distorted. For Randy Kehler and Martin Jezer, '[t]he contours of American history have been shaped by the corrupting and undemocratic influence of money in politics. Indeed, corporations owe their current powerful position in American society in large degree to their dominant role in American elections.'[5] The Madison model of a republican democracy could not accommodate to historical change and the development of an industrial economy. After the Civil War, therefore, industrialization, with capitalist enterprise as the dynamic motor of the economy, impacted with significant political consequences upon a political process framed originally in the context of a comparatively small and rural society. Nowhere was this better dramatized than in the election campaign of 1896, which was fought out between William Jennings Bryan, the populist Democrat candidate, and William McKinley for the Republicans.

The rampaging capitalist ethic that captured the American imagination after the Civil War ushered in the era that Mark Twain would satirize in *The Gilded Age* (1873). Yet in the early 1890s, economic confidence collapsed, undermined by a loss of faith in the federal government's capacity to maintain the gold standard: the pledge that dollars could be redeemed for gold, thus insuring the currency's value. In the 1890s, owing to movements in international capital, gold began to be transferred from America to Europe. The federal government had always appreciated the need to keep gold. In the early years of the republic, George Washington's administration had established gold reserves worth at least $100 million. They fell below that psychological safety-net in 1894 and a year later stood at $68 million. It was only through the financial manipulations of J.P. Morgan – who for a time was able to regulate exclusively America's international gold trade – that the country remained on the gold standard. Here the economic imperatives of finance capitalism meshed directly – and publicly – with the political priorities of President Cleveland: a Democrat who was committed to the defence of the gold standard. Morgan marketed an issue of government bonds on Wall Street and in London, to be paid for in gold, and profited hugely from the deal. In 1896, he pressed for a commitment to maintain the gold standard to be included in the Republican party platform.

The economy, however, remained in a state of depression. If keeping faith in the gold standard became the financial mantra of industrial capitalism, for ordinary people it was the reason for hardship. The

Democrats under Cleveland split between those who agreed that the currency should be based upon gold, and the Populists, principally from the agrarian west and south, who believed that economic prosperity would return if a certain amount of the currency was also convertible into silver – the policy of bimetallism. In July 1896 the thirty-six-year-old William Jennings Bryan won the party's nomination for the presidency with a speech that entered American political folklore: 'The Cross of Gold', named for its concluding phrase. He argued that, despite industrialization and urbanization, the democratic pulse of American republicanism remained in the land itself:

> You come to us and tell us that the great cities are in favor of the gold standard; we reply that the great cities rest upon our broad and fertile prairies. Burn down your cities and leave our farms, and your cities will spring up again as if by magic; but destroy our farms and the grass will grow in the streets of every city in the country.

The fight over the gold standard was a battle between capital and wealth, on the one hand, and farmers, tradespeople, wage-earners and workers, on the other; between Madison's creditors and debtors. For Bryan,

> [h]aving behind us the producing masses of this nation and the world, supported by the commercial interests, the laboring interests, and the toilers everywhere, we will answer their demand for a gold standard by saying to them: 'You shall not press down upon the brow of labor this crown of thorns, you shall not crucify mankind upon a cross of gold.'

Yet in the election of 1896, it was the power of money that prevailed.

For the historian Richard Hofstadter, 'The Cross of Gold' speech was testimony to the fact that after a century of American republicanism, the core values of Jefferson and Jackson still formed the basis of the nation's political thought. But to others that idealism was threatening. As a contemporary issue of the *Nation* put it, '[p]robably no man in civil life has succeeded in inspiring so much terror, without taking life, as Bryan.' In response, McKinley's Republican supporters injected money into presidential politics in unprecedented amounts, in effect ensuring that in contemporary presidential politics, cash and campaigns are now inseparable. The chief strategist in this was McKinley's ally from Ohio, Mark Hanna, who, as C. Wright Mills observes, 'raised money from among the rich for political use out of the fright caused by William Jennings Bryan and the Populist nightmare'.[6] The wealthy rallied to McKinley – J.P. Morgan was one contributor – enabling him to outspend his rival ten times over. Even though the eventual result was close, Hanna had demonstrated conclusively that a well-financed campaign was the route to electoral success.

Bryan became secretary of state in Woodrow Wilson's administration, which created the federal reserve system: an attempt to reduce the power of Wall Street financiers to influence the political process directly. The government would become at last a major player in the American economy – indeed, during the Clinton administration the chairman of the Federal Reserve Board, Alan Greenspan, was widely seen as the architect of national economic policy and the guardian of its success. Yet the importance of money, demonstrated in that last presidential election campaign of the nineteenth century, grew in the twentieth century, such that it is impossible for any candidate – Republican or Democrat – to win the White House without having either a personal fortune or, more realistically, substantial corporate sponsorship to draw upon. On the other hand, it is also true that the battle against the influence of money has also persisted: campaign finance reform is an enduring political issue in America, partly, perhaps, because it has remained a perennial lost cause.

The most prominent effort to curb the excessive role played by money in the electoral process came after a history of corrupt practices finally eroded popular confidence in the core values of the political system itself. The Watergate scandal, among other things, focused on the activities of Nixon's infamous Committee to Re-Elect the President (CREEP) in raising funds for the 1972 presidential campaign. Congress acted to help sweep away the wreckage of that débâcle by passing legislation that aimed to restrict campaign contributions and expenditure, and to encourage more public financing for presidential campaigns. Yet money is like water: it will always find a way through anything but the most impermeable barriers, and the post-Watergate reform soon seemed to be a well-intentioned but inadequate effort at plumbing; like water too, it became evident that money could be 'hard' or 'soft'.

'Hard money' can be regulated under federal election law, which now limits the amount that individuals and organizations can contribute to a campaign for election to a federal office. In effect, however, the regulatory framework has simply encouraged the development of new – legitimate – ways of raising money. Political Action Committees (PACs), first organized by labour unions in the 1940s, and then later by business groups as well, were revolutionized by the 1974 reforms. Their contemporary high-profile influence in the fund-raising process is suggested by the dramatic increase in their number – by the mid-1980s, they were numbered in their thousands as they became the major way in which interest groups – notably corporations – could donate to campaigns.

In the State Department's official guide to the presidential and congressional elections of 2000, Danny McDonald, one of the three Democrat members of the Federal Election Commission – there are also three Republicans – was interviewed. The Commission is responsible for enforcing campaign finance laws, and McDonald's response to a question on the role of PACs in the political process was revealing.

> Let's take the pro and the con. The con is that PACs represent special interests and special interests dominate Washington politics. On the other hand, you can certainly take just as strong a position that PACs represent nothing more than a group of individuals with like interests pooling their resources to try and have an impact on the political process. It seems pretty natural that most people get together with people who have like interests to support candidates.

In December 2000 McDonald was elected chair of the Federal Election Commission. His interpretation suggests that PACs are now regarded as legitimate players in the political game: they may represent special interests, but that is a fact of life, and to prohibit them would be to inhibit natural political activity.

What McDonald left unsaid is, however, just as illuminating. As a result of Supreme Court rulings, notably in the case of *Buckley* v. *Valeo* (1976), there are no limits on what PACs may spend in support of a candidate, if that is done without collusion with the official campaign. So 'negative advertising', which is profitably financed through this mechanism, established itself as a flourishing industry in electoral politics. Campaign finance reform has thus impacted upon the character and style of American politics in unforeseen ways.

'Soft money', however, is now an entirely predictable – if sometimes less visible – fact of political life. Under the 1974 reforms, it could still be given to political parties, ostensibly to support such causes as 'voter registration' or 'party building'. Indirectly it is filtered into a candidate's campaign. According to the public interest group Common Cause, '[s]oft money is a scandal. This loophole has given a rebirth to the kinds of huge individual and corporate contributions in the political process that have not been seen since Watergate.' In the 1999–2000 presidential election season, the Democrat and Republican national party committees raised a record $457.1 million in 'soft money', almost double that of the previous presidential election cycle of 1995–6. This source of funding has acquired a quasi-official status, tracked by such groups as Common Cause, and even included in press releases from the Federal Election Commission. On the eve of the 2000 presidential election, according to the Commission, soft money represented '42% of all National Republican Party financial activity and 53% of Democratic National Party fundraising.'

'There's no such thing as a free lunch' is a saying associated with the apostle of monetarism, the economist Milton Friedman. In American politics today, other meals may be expensive as well. Kehler and Jezer note that in 1996

> [f]or the Republicans, breakfasts got very expensive, with $45,000 netting a shared croissant with Speaker Newt Gingrich. Black tie dinners are perhaps the most common fundraising technique; tables with prominent officeholders can cost over $100,000 a plate. At two Washington black tie dinners held by the Republicans and Democrats in early 1996, more soft money was raised than in the entire 1988 election cycle – nearly $28 million in one night.[7]

The Clinton White House, to some of its critics, was a luxury hotel for wealthy supporters of the president and his party. To be a dinner guest of the president – and to spend the night in the Lincoln bedroom – could cost anywhere between $50,000 and $100,000, but for some it might be preferable to an evening in 'honest Abe's' log cabin.

In an article in the *Journal of Political Economy*, Hugh Rockoff analysed Frank Baum's enduring classic *The Wizard of Oz*, first published in 1900, as a 'monetary allegory' of the battle over whether to maintain the gold standard, which framed the presidential election of 1896. Who, then, was the Wizard? For Rockoff, '[t]o a Populist at the turn of the century, there is only one answer: Marcus Alonzo Hanna. A close adviser of McKinley and the chairman of the Republican National Committee, he was, in populist mythology, the brains behind McKinley and his campaigns. It was the money that Hanna raised from giant corporations, according to Populists, that defeated Bryan.'[8] Hanna did not have to pay attention to the distinction between 'hard' and 'soft' money; and from then on, the power of money remained as a tangible reminder of the impact of the growth of capitalism and its influence upon American political life. At the same time, however, the major political parties in the United States have never been slow to realize that politics is itself a business.

## Betting on Banks

The almighty dollar is the only object of worship.
                                        Philadelphia Public Ledger (*1836*)

The American party system can be seen, as Jefferson saw it in 1801, as one in which competition is about means rather than ends, and in which two broad-based coalitions provide simple choices for the electorate. From this perspective, then, a basic two-party structure has dominated politics at national – and state – level, and, despite political realignments, has changed little over time except in name. There is, however, another view of the party politics that introduces the realities of economic power into the equation. So politics is an expensive business, and once more an understanding of American politics begins – and ends – with an appreciation that money is power. Further, it is worth exploring the connections between political institutions and economic institutions, between party realignments and developments in American finance, between political parties and banks.

If the history of party alignment and realignment in the United States is juxtaposed with an examination of the development of an integrated financial system to facilitate the nation's economic development – in other words the establishment of banks and a national currency – then some interesting coincidences and connections appear. For example, the political divide between Hamiltonian Federalists and Jeffersonian Republicans was no more clearly dramatized than in their respective attitudes towards the creation of a National Bank. Hamilton's and Jefferson's opinions on its constitutionality have become textbook arguments illustrative of the debate over the nature and scope of the federal government's authority. After George Washington had sided with Hamilton, Jefferson resigned from his cabinet. When the Republicans took over the government, however, there were elements of the party who looked favourably on banks as institutions that could act as engines of economic growth. Moreover, banks themselves had become politically partisan. So, as Bray Hammond suggests,

> [t]he Jeffersonian impetus in banking may well have begun in reaction to the Federalist character of the first banks, all of which were conceived and defended as monopolies. The surest procedure for any new group that wished to obtain a bank charter from a Jeffersonian state legislature was to cry out against monopoly in general and in particular against that of the Federalist bankers who would lend nothing, it was alleged, to good Republicans.[9]

The Bank of the Manhattan Company was set up because Aaron Burr wanted a Republican institution to rival the (Federalist) Bank of New York, which had been sponsored by Alexander Hamilton himself. There were thus political as well as economic motives behind the creation of the first American banks.

The National Bank remained a political football. Its first charter (1790) was not renewed by Congress in 1811. In January 1815, James Madison, as president, vetoed a bill to recharter it only to recommend, at the end of the same year, the creation of its successor. The Second National Bank was given a twenty-year charter in 1816, and figured in John Marshall's famous judgement in the *McCulloch* v. *Maryland* case (1819), which set significant precedents for the growth of federal authority. However, the party realignment of 1828, which brought Andrew Jackson to the White House, foreshadowed its abolition. The president indicated in his first State of the Union message that he regarded the Bank as an unconstitutional monopoly, and vetoed the bill rechartering it in 1832. The Bank's director, Nicholas Riddle, called Jackson's veto message 'a manifesto of anarchy, such as Marat or Robespierre might have issued'. And in a sense he was right: the American banking system, decentralized in the states, remained in a chaotic condition until the Civil War.

As Tocqueville observed, '[t]he contest between the bank and its opponents was only an incident in the great struggle which is going on in America between the states and the central power, between the spirit of democratic independence and that of a proper distribution and subordination of power.'[10] In the absence of a central monetary authority, however, banking operated more or less autonomously in a laissez-faire environment within most states. While the commercial operations of banks could fuel expansion, during economic downturns they contributed to economic instability. Banks had to keep some reserves – usually between 10 and 20 per cent of money deposited in them – in gold and silver coin, which was available on demand in exchange for the notes they issued. In times of crisis, demand for coin would increase, and banks would have trouble fulfilling it. Moreover, as Paul Trescott points out, prior to the Civil War,

> [v]irtually every bank issued its own notes; there was no standardization of size or design. Amid the confusion of more than one thousand valid types of notes, counterfeiting and fraud also flourished. Notes of defunct banks were also frequently kept in circulation. . . . There was no national paper currency. . . . Newspapers carried lists of good and bad notes, and periodicals devoted entirely to evaluating notes came into existence.[11]

American banks – many of which failed – were not places where money could be safely kept.

The 'wildcat' banks dramatized the problem. If paper currency could be kept in circulation without being redeemed against reserves of coin, then it followed that more assets were available for speculative purposes. So if notes circulated at a distance from the bank's location, it would be easier to escape demands for redemption: the inexorable logic was to hide the bank's headquarters, 'out among the wildcats', where it was difficult to find. Such was the demand for credit in the country that these practices, although condoned neither by government nor by the older established banks, could flourish. If the American banking system was a mess, it was the Civil War that provided the stimulus for reform. The party realignment that foreshadowed the conflict thus had profound financial and economic, as well as political, consequences for the nation.

The problem of financing the war suggested the necessity of an improved system of banking and a better currency. Hammond, again, points out the essence of the Lincoln administration's problem: it was faced with 'the anomaly of a sovereign authority waging a war in defense of its sovereignty without possessing that most ancient and elementary attribute of sovereignty – control of the monetary system'.[12] In 1862 Congress passed an act that established the first national currency – legal-tender notes known as 'greenbacks'. The following year, a system of national banks was established to permit the circulation of a uniform national currency, and subsequently a tax levied on state banknotes led to their extinction. However, the inflationary impact of the federal government printing money lasted beyond the war, as did controversy over whether 'greenbacks' were to be preferred to the national currency, and whether notes should be convertible to gold. Post-war cycles of boom and bust became the economic context within which the supporters of the gold standard and the advocates of bimetallism defined the political landscape during the remainder of the nineteenth century. The intricacies of monetary policy were as relevant to political argument then as the merits of tax cuts are today.

If the economic history of the United States is seen in terms of cyclical eras of growth and depression, banks have had a constant role throughout: praised for facilitating the former, and traditionally blamed for the latter. In 1932, the shockwaves of the Wall Street Crash resonated in the panic that resulted from the collapse of banks. As president, Roosevelt's first fireside chat – the radio broadcast on 12 March 1933, which revolutionized the presidency – aimed to restore confidence in the nation's financial institutions. So in simple language, he explained the principles of banking: '[w]hen you deposit money in a bank the bank does not put the money into a safety deposit vault. . . . It puts your money to work to keep the wheels of industry and agriculture turning around. . . . In other words, the total amount of all the currency in the country is only a small fraction of the total deposits in all of the banks.' In the aftermath of the crash, people did not trust banks: they wanted their money back. The president analysed the situation:

> [B]ecause of undermined confidence on the part of the public, there was a general rush by a large proportion of our population to turn bank deposits into currency or gold – a rush so great that the soundest banks could not get enough currency to meet the demand. . . . By the afternoon of 3d March scarcely a bank in the country was open to do business.

Roosevelt had declared a bank holiday – which subsequently had been extended – as 'the first step in the Government's reconstruction of our financial and economic fabric'. Congress had passed measures 'to develop a program of rehabilitation of our banking facilities'. This involved the Federal Reserve Banks issuing 'additional currency . . . sound currency because it is backed by good assets', and then cautiously and gradually reopening banks across the country. FDR insisted that people should regain confidence in the system, and assured his listeners that it was safer to keep their money in a 're-opened bank than under the mattress'. Nevertheless, he admitted that 'we had a bad banking situation. Some of our bankers had shown themselves incompetent or dishonest in their handling of people's funds. They had used the money entrusted to them in speculations and unwise loans. . . . It was the Government's job to straighten out this situation and do it as quickly as possible.' Roosevelt had done enough. When banks started reopening the following day, queues formed not to take more money out of them, but to put it back in.

The Democrats had also come full circle. From the party that had historically been suspicious of a central banking authority, they now became the advocates of increased federal control of national financial and economic activity and policy. Although they gained widespread support through this change in their outlook, they also, inevitably, alienated others, who, in another party realignment, ultimately moved to the Republicans. As his biographer Edmund Morris writes, 'Ronald Reagan has been mocked for protesting, "I didn't leave the Democratic Party – it left me", but he was correct in stating that in 1932 Roosevelt advertised himself as a stalwart of individualism, states' rights, rural values, and reduced government.' The Depression and the New Deal – economic and political realities – changed that.

It also changed the Republicans, who, particularly since the collapse of Roosevelt's electoral coalition in the late 1960s, and subsequently under the leadership of Ronald Reagan in the 1980s, became Jeffersonian in their advocacy of limited government and the virtues of unfettered economic liberty. Indeed, Reagan himself engineered a change in the public philosophy as radical as that achieved by FDR, through his advocacy of tax cuts and reductions in the government's role in the promotion of public welfare. Instead, there would be major increases in defence spending – no doubt to the delight of members of Eisenhower's military-industrial complex. The result, as Morris observes, was that the president 'committed the American economy to eight years of self-compounding deficits, and a trillion dollar short-fall, greater than the entire debt of the past two centuries. Yet – such is the mad logic of economics, he also initiated the greatest sustained peacetime boom since the founding of the Republic.'[13] Apart from the blip that proved sufficient to help eject George Bush from the White House in 1992, that economic boom continued for the remainder of the twentieth century. Democrats could tolerate the problem of debt when they regained political power, but their opponents recognized the political capital that could be made from a problem that they too had been prepared to live with while in office. When Republicans gained control of Congress in 1994, therefore, President Clinton was forced to focus upon the problem of the deficit. Two years later, he proclaimed 'the era of Big Government is over', and by the end of his time in office, political debate centred on how best to spend the federal surplus.

From the early days of the Republic, therefore, politics and eco-nomics have been intertwined and political parties have become acutely aware that economic issues determine electoral success, such that they have reinvented themselves and their philosophies to suit the mood of the moment. This, then, helps to explain the modern map of party politics in the United States. Following the fragmentation of the political system in the post-Vietnam, post-Watergate period, in the battleground of ideas that influence political outlooks the balance of power has shifted from the philosophy of New Deal liberalism towards those – notably in the contemporary Republican party – who remain intensely suspicious of all centralizing, and globalizing, polit-ical and economic institutions. The influence of contemporary religion in this should not be underestimated.

## Fundamentalism and the Conspiracy Game

There is a great difference between locating conspiracies *in* his-tory and saying that history *is*, in effect, a conspiracy.
                    *Richard Hofstadter, 'The Paranoid Style in*
                    *American Politics' (1965)*

In his essay, Hofstadter points out that 'style has to do with the way in which ideas are believed and advocated rather than with the truth or falsity of their content.' As an example, he tells the story of three men who, in 1964, drove from their home state of Arizona to Washington DC to testify against a bill introduced in the Senate, following the assassination of President Kennedy, that would have introduced stricter controls over the sale of mail-order firearms. One of them argued that this was ' "a further attempt by a subversive power to make us part of one world socialistic government" and that it threatened to "create chaos" that would help "our enemies" to seize power.' Barry Goldwater represented Arizona in the Senate; in the same year he would capture the Republican presidential nomination, and would campaign as an ideological right-winger against Kennedy's successor, Lyndon Johnson, losing by a record margin. The 'paranoid style' of his constituents has been a recurrent feature of America's political landscape. Hofstadter's essay traces its influence from the origins of the republic to the time of Goldwater's Republican adventure. Since that time, moreover, the Republican party has become home for activists among the Christian fundamentalist right, who have at times acquired influence within the party that is disproportionate to their numbers, but which nevertheless has had a profound effect upon its attitudes and policies.

In 1988, Pat Robertson, fundamentalist preacher and religious entrepreneur, with business and media interests centred on the Christian Broadcasting Network, defeated George Bush in the Iowa caucuses that were the preliminary skirmishes in the battle to win the Republican presidential nomination. When Bush, as president, proclaimed the need to build a New World Order, after the collapse of communism and on the eve of the Gulf War, Robertson responded with a best-selling book of the same name. It is a classic statement of the paranoid style, the 'plausibility' of which, 'for those who find it plausible', Hofstadter suggests, 'lies, in good measure, in . . . [the] appearance of the most careful, conscientious, and seemingly coherent application to detail, the laborious accumulation of what can be taken as convincing evidence for the most fantastic conclusions, the careful preparation for the big leap from the undeniable to the unbelievable'.[14]

Consider, then, Robertson's argument about the role of money in politics. He starts from the premise that '[t]he power to create money and to regulate its quantity and value is the power to control the life of the nation.' Moreover, '[i]f the power to create money is taken away from those whom the nation has elected to guide its destiny – the president and the Congress – then the people will have lost their democratic control.' And that is what has happened in America. When the Federal Reserve was established, this 'new central bank could not be called a central bank because America did not want one, so it had to be given a deceptive name'. Nominally, it was to be under congressional control, but the cartel of financiers and bankers whom Robertson suggests designed the new institution had one objective in mind: 'The power over the creation of money was to be taken from the people and placed in the hands of private bankers who could expand or contract credit as they felt best suited their needs.'

What were – and are – their needs? Following 'the money barons of Europe', they loan money to governments that must be repaid through taxes, so '[t]he object of the lenders was to stimulate government deficit spending and subsequent borrowing' and '[f]rom 1945 to 1990 the full mobilization for the Cold War and the resulting massive national borrowings accomplished the result.'[15] The conspiracy is unmasked: once again, unscrupulous bankers – among them J.P. Morgan – accumulate political power and manipulate economies in the pursuit of private gain. Jefferson, whose own religious views were privately heterodox, is nevertheless pressed into service as a political guide for fundamentalists: they endorse his commitment to individualism and his suspicion of centralized authority, whether in the shape of a National Bank – the Federal Reserve – the federal government, the World Bank or the United Nations.

In the looking-glass world that fundamentalism inhabits, it is perhaps appropriate that at the turn of the twenty-first century Robertson's arguments from the right echo the propaganda put forward by the Populists a century before. In 1895, a populist manifesto claimed that

> [a]s early as 1865–66 a conspiracy was entered into between the gold gamblers of Europe and America. . . . For nearly thirty years these conspirators have kept the people quarreling over less important matters, while they have pursued with unrelenting zeal their one central purpose. . . . Every device of treachery, every resource of statecraft, and every artifice known to the secret cabals of the international gold ring are being made use of to deal a blow to the prosperity of the people and the financial and commercial independence of the country.

The New World Order of contemporary fundamentalists in the post-Vietnam era seems much like the old world order as it was defined by radicals of the post-Civil War generation. And the bridge between the two is one first crossed by the standard-bearer of Populism in 1896: William Jennings Bryan.

If the financiers, industrialists and entrepreneurs of the 'Gilded Age' paused from their pursuit of wealth long enough to reflect upon their social philosophy, they would have discovered it in the intellectual revolution in the natural sciences that occurred after the publication of *On the Origin of Species* in 1859. Charles Darwin's idea that in the 'struggle for existence' those who could best adapt to changing environments would have an evolutionary advantage over those who could not – the 'survival of the fittest' – seemed to correspond to the competitive reality of contemporary capitalism. But to those like William Jennings Bryan, such 'social Darwinism' ran counter to faith in individual rights and the concept of community. By 1920, then, and convinced that Darwin's theories had helped provoke German militarism and the First World War, although, as Karen Armstrong points out, he was 'not a typical fundamentalist', Bryan had become certain 'that evolutionary theory was incompatible with morality, decency, and the survival of civilization.'[16] He started a new crusade opposing the teaching of the doctrine of evolution in schools. His political and religious convictions thus persuaded him to take centre-stage at a defining moment in the history of twentieth-century fundamentalist debate: the Scopes trial in Tennessee in 1925.

The American Civil Liberties Union brought a test case to challenge a Tennessee state law forbidding the teaching of evolution in school biology courses. The trial took its name from the defendant, John Scopes, a teacher who became a bit-part player in a trial that pitted Bryan for the prosecution against Clarence Darrow, a famous contemporary lawyer, for the defence. Indeed, according to Armstrong, 'once Darrow and Bryan became involved, the trial ceased to be simply about civil liberties, and became a contest between God and science.' If God won the legal verdict – Scopes was convicted and his fine was paid by the ACLU – Darrow's humiliation of Bryan during the trial (Bryan died a few days later) led the supporters of science to believe their arguments had been proven right and that '[f]undamentalists belonged to the past; they were enemies of science and intellectual liberty, and could take no legitimate part in the modern world.'[17] In fact, fundamentalists had only retreated into the securities of their religious convictions.

The political reconfiguration represented by the New Deal led many of them away from Bryan and the Democrats and towards the Republicans, such that their emergence as a political force in the 1980s forged an alliance within that party that mirrored FDR's strategic coalition of northern and southern Democrats. Nowadays religious social conservatism and economic radicalism – in terms of a rejection of Roosevelt's New Deal economic nostrums – are characteristic elements of Republican political life. Party activists in many states are fundamentalists. Their strength should not be underestimated: they are committed, and represent the militant tendency within the party.

In 1980, Pat Robertson claimed that fundamentalists would control the government if they all turned out to vote. The election of Ronald Reagan that year, and again in 1984, together with the Republican success in the congressional elections of 1994, and indeed in the disputed presidential election of 2000, demonstrates that for the last twenty years, right-wing fundamentalism – of the kind that William Jennings Bryan would have undoubtedly opposed – has become part of the fabric of American political life. In many ways, however, the fundamentalist strain within the Republican party resembles nothing so much as a mirror-image of the old-style organization of Democrat party machines. Protestant fundamentalists grab at the levers of party control in order to promote a specific policy agenda.

## Conclusion: A Game of Paradox

Politician: An eel in the fundamental mud upon which the superstructure of organized society is reared. When he wriggles he mistakes the agitation of his tail for the trembling of the edifice. As compared with the statesman, he suffers the disadvantage of being alive.
*Ambrose Bierce*, The Devil's Dictionary (*1911*)

Political power in America is at once fascinating and repulsive. The power of individuals, elites, groups, money, religion or political parties to influence or control the formation of public policies, the electoral process and the passage of laws is a topic of continual debate and scrutiny. At the same time, the roots of 'the idea of America' itself lie in a deep suspicion of power, a pessimistic view of human nature and the expression of it in government, and a belief that politics is, in essence, an invitation to abuse the exercise of power. The Declaration of Independence was framed as part of the rejection of the authority and the perceived arbitrary use of executive power by King George III. If Jefferson's appeal was to natural rights and fundamental values, and animated the idealism of the revolutionary war, then those who established the constitutional framework of the American republic remained aware of the capacity for politics to subvert that vision. As Madison put it in *Federalist 51*, '[i]f men were angels, no government would be necessary. If angels were to govern men, neither external nor internal controls on government would be necessary.' But human nature was less than angelic: hence the separation of powers, and checks and balances designed to prevent political tyranny. Even that, though, might not avoid the corrosive impact of corruption. Jefferson made the point in his first inaugural address in 1801: 'Sometimes it is said that man can not be trusted with the government of himself. Can he, then, be trusted with the government of others? Or have we found angels in the forms of kings to govern him? Let history answer this question.'

In the two centuries since Jefferson asked it, history has wrestled with its response. The problem of power has been discussed as part of a continuous critical commentary upon the practices of American politics. The dynamics of territorial expansion, economic development and the growth of international influence have cast doubt on the capacity of a constitution written in a very different era to accommodate to new realities. Yet here, in essence, lies the fundamental paradox of political power in America. A nation that prides itself upon its suspicion of power has demonstrated a pragmatic sense of purpose in adapting its political structures and institutions to changing circumstances. So while realizing that concentrations of power – whether exercised in the political, economic, social or even cultural spheres – may run counter to the rhetoric of America as 'the last best hope for mankind', nevertheless it has been sufficient to recognize the problem and advocate change, but only within the boundaries of existing constitutional and institutional structures.

So reform takes place within defined parameters. When capitalism suffered its greatest set-back in 1932 with the Wall Street Crash, it still remained the favoured design as the engine of the American economy. Franklin Roosevelt's New Deal merely shuffled the deck of capitalist cards and invited the nation to continue the capitalist game that until then they had enjoyed so much. Similarly, in the political life of the nation, gerrymandering may have been curbed, but it continues to exist. The impact of money upon electoral fortunes may be observed, but thus far campaign finance reform has proved an elusive goal.

Imagine, then, during the century after his first appearance, that the Wizard of Oz had, from time to time, surveyed the American political landscape from the balloon in which he was last seen drifting away from the Emerald City. Much would have remained familiar. The power of money in politics, the basis of the strategic alliance between corporate wealth and electoral campaigns first forged by Mark Hanna – his political alter ego – if anything, would have become more pronounced. The Wizard would have observed aspects of elitism in American society. Indeed, if he had witnessed the swearing in of Eisenhower's cabinet in 1953, he would have seen George Humphrey, who in 1929 had become president of M.A. Hanna Co., in Cleveland, taking up his position as secretary of the Treasury. Across the nation as the century progressed, he would also have seen groups in American society organizing themselves and competing in the hope that they too could achieve positions of power, influence and status within the economic and political community, creating a more recognizably pluralistic republican democracy. He would have observed too the power of religion to influence outlooks and attitudes and continue to shape political life in America. Though he would have seen the decline in the power of political machines, throughout the century he would have witnessed 'political families' – the Roosevelts from New York, the Tafts from Ohio, the Kennedys from Massachusetts, the Gores from Tennessee and the Bushes from Texas via Connecticut – competing for national office in the federal Congress and for the presidency. And he would have recognized too the corrosive influence of power, as political scandals repeatedly exploded across the nation, sometimes with as devastating effects as a tornado in Kansas.

The Wizard would also become a character in the movie that bears his name. That would have been unimaginable in 1900, when the industrial revolution in popular culture – Hollywood – had yet to occur. Over the century, however, newspapers would be joined by radio, television and the internet as forms of political communication, and the power of these media, and indeed the influence of Hollywood itself, would impact upon the character and the style of American politics. So to understand how to play the political game in the United States it is necessary to know how the media too may determine its rules.

# Making Headlines

The journalists of the United States are generally in a very humble position, with a scanty education and a vulgar turn of mind.
*Alexis de Tocqueville*, Democracy in America, *vol. 1 (1835)*

While many American politicians might, on occasion, agree with Tocqueville's assessment of the character of those who work in the media, they would also admit that the status of the profession has changed dramatically since the 1830s. At that time – the hey-day of Jacksonian democracy – newspapers were either overtly partisan, funded by political parties as a means of direct communication with the electorate, or the forerunners of the modern tabloids: cheap, sensationalist and aimed at entertaining as much as informing their readership. Using new technology – the steam press, which enabled more copies to be printed more quickly, and the telegraph, which allowed information to be communicated across greater distances – the newspaper industry in America expanded rapidly. By 1850, there were ten times as many newspapers in circulation as there had been at the beginning of the century. The Associated Press was established in 1848 by six newspapers in New York, and this provided a mechanism for efficient gathering and distribution of news. Such developments were mirrored abroad: in Britain the Reuters news agency carried the first reports of Abraham Lincoln's assassination in 1865.

In 1872, Joseph Pulitzer started publishing the *St Louis Post-Despatch*, and, having established it as an important newspaper in the midwest, he switched his attention to the east coast. In 1883 he bought the *New York World.* Once again, increased circulation was built upon a combination of news, sensationalist stories and an agenda of reform politics: Pulitzer's newspapers supported ordinary individuals – his readers – in crusades against the excesses and abuses of corporate wealth and political power. On the west coast, William Randolph Hearst applied a similar strategy to the business of selling newspapers, with sensationalism very much the key ingredient in the success of the *San Francisco Daily Examiner*, of which he took control in 1887. When, in 1895, Hearst bought the *New York Morning Journal*, he and Pulitzer battled for supremacy in what was then the nation's biggest, and potentially most profitable, media market. Hearst's world was one of excesses, where anything that was good for the sales of his newspapers was worth pursuing. So in 1898 when the artist Frederic Remington, whom he had sent to Havana to draw the rumoured atrocities taking place in the Cuban revolution, suggested that there was nothing happening worth either reporting or sketching, Hearst allegedly sent him a telegram: 'You furnish the pictures, and I'll furnish the war.' McKinley's subsequent decision to involve the country in the conflict with Spain was to a large extent the result of pressure from the media.

As Tocqueville had observed, '[w]hen many organs of the press adopt the same line of conduct, their influence in the long run becomes irresistible, and public opinion, perpetually assailed from the same side, eventually yields to the attack. In the United States . . . the power of the periodical press is second only to that of the people.'[1] By the end of the nineteenth century, that power was being used in investigations of political and corporate corruption. Writers for monthly magazines like Lincoln Steffens, Ida Tarbell and Sinclair Lewis were 'muckrakers' – so called by Theodore Roosevelt, after the man whom John Bunyan had characterized in *Pilgrim's Progress* as one who 'could look no way but downwards, with a muckrake in his hand'. But these investigative journalists – and novelists – highlighted the abuses that prompted the progressive reforms of the period.

Daily newspapers were willing accomplices to such exposés. Indeed, Hearst, who had supported William Jennings Bryan in the 1896 presidential campaign, had a clear political agenda. As the novelist John Dos Passos described it, 'his editorials hammered at malefactors of great wealth, trusts, the G.O.P. [Republicans], Mark Hanna and McKinley so shrilly that when McKinley was assassinated most Republicans in some way considered Hearst responsible for his death.'[2] What should be the responsibility of a free press in a democratic society? As McKinley's successor, Theodore Roosevelt, reminded an audience in 1906, '[t]he men with the muck-rakes are often indispensable to the well-being of society; but only if they know when to stop raking the muck.' Two years later, Pulitzer's *New York World* revealed that

$40 million that the president said that the US government had paid to the French government as part of the project to build the Panama Canal in fact had been given to an American syndicate set up by J.P. Morgan and William Cromwell. Cromwell was a New York corporate lawyer who had lobbied Mark Hanna, then senator from Ohio, to set up a Congressional Commission to establish the best route across the Panamanian isthmus. He had been involved in the complicated and underhand politics that led eventually to a revolution in Panama and the United States gaining sovereignty over the land through which the canal ran. Roosevelt alleged criminal libel by the newspaper. He sued Pulitzer and lost. In calling the powerful to account, therefore, newspapers established an investigative role that continues to define the relationship between media and politics.

Joseph Pulitzer gave up managing newspapers, and, following an American tradition whereby the wealthy give back to the society from which they have profited, became a philanthropist: giving Columbia University $2 million as an endowment for a School of Journalism, and establishing the prizes for journalistic and literary achievement that have been subsequently associated with his name. William Randolph Hearst, however, tried to use his influence as a publisher as leverage for a political career. He was elected to the House of Representatives, and campaigned at various times for the Democrat's presidential nomination and to become mayor of New York. In the end, he became the model for Orson Welles' film *Citizen Kane* (1941). As the modern media industry developed in the United States, then, it too became part of the structure of the nation's corporate life. So if the media do have influence in the political process, whether through their support for particular candidates, or through criticism of public policies, or by exposing abuses of power, they are also subject to the demands of the capitalist market economy: commercialism, balance sheets and profit. Above all, the media need stories that sell.

People, power and politics are thus the essential ingredients of the modern media's news agenda. Politicians and the media are locked together in a mutually exploitative but sometimes fatal embrace.

## Setting the Political Agenda

Franklin Roosevelt . . . was the greatest newsmaker that Washington had ever seen. . . . Before his arrival, the federal government was small and timid; by the time he died it reached everywhere, and as the government was everywhere, so Washington became

the great dateline; as it was the source of power, so it was the
source of news.

*David Halberstam*, The Powers That Be (*1979*)

Few presidents have had as instinctive and intuitive a grasp of the
mechanics of political communication as Franklin Roosevelt. His predecessor, Herbert Hoover, held twelve press conferences during his last
year in office. Roosevelt averaged over one a week during each of his
first three terms. The president made news, and in so doing controlled
the political agenda. According to David Halberstam, '[t]hirty and
forty years later, politicians like John Kennedy and Lyndon Johnson
would study how Franklin Roosevelt had handled the press, it was a
textbook course in manipulation.'[3] Fully aware of the significance of
his performance in the role of president – he reportedly told Orson
Welles that there were two great actors in America at that time, and
Welles was the other one – he understood the power of not simply
print journalism, but also the new medium of radio. This had already
established itself as a popular form of entertainment – even drawing
audiences away from the silent cinema of the 1920s – but FDR was
the first president to use it as an effective tool of political communication. The 'fireside chats' connected him with his audience – on average some fifty million people listened to his speeches – and collapsed
the space between the president and his constituents: 'my friends', as
he would refer to them. For the first time, Americans could hear the
voice of their president as a guest on the radio in their homes. Politics
became personalized. The president took the public into his confidence, talking about himself, his family, even his dog, named Fala.
Before Roosevelt, the White House had needed only one person to
deal with letters received from the public. Hoover might have read
personally the forty or so letters delivered daily, but after Roosevelt
started to broadcast, an average of four thousand letters arrived each
day at his house on Pennsylvania Avenue.

If radio allowed politicians to claim a new intimacy with the public,
the development of television added a further dimension to the politics of media communication. Now the audience could see as well
as hear their political leaders, and style became as important as substance, if not more so. In 1952, Eisenhower's presidential campaign
broke new ground in using television as a medium for political advertising. Television was also crucial in the career of Eisenhower's choice
as vice-president – Richard Nixon. During the campaign Nixon was
beset by newspaper allegations that he had personally benefited from
a 'secret fund' set up by Californian businessmen to support his political
activities. He appeared on television. In his account of the broadcast

in *Six Crises*, Nixon explained why he included the anecdote that gave the 'Checkers' speech its name: 'Thinking back to Franklin Roosevelt's devastating remark in the 1944 campaign – "and now they are attacking poor Fala" – I decided to mention my own dog Checkers. Using the same ploy as FDR would irritate my opponents and delight my friends, I thought.' It is an indication of how a professional politician planned to manipulate his audience: just as Roosevelt had made his dog famous on radio, now Nixon's pet would achieve canine immortality on television.

Having revealed details of his 'financial history', the candidate talked about a gift his family had received as the campaign began. 'It was a little cocker spaniel dog . . . and our little girl Tricia, the six-year-old, named it Checkers. And you know, the kids, like all kids, loved the dog, and I just want to say this, right now, that regardless of what they say about it, we are going to keep it.' Again, Nixon was able to use a new medium to communicate with his audience in such a way that they would identify with him. The story of 'Checkers' is critical to his success. How could anyone – particularly families with children – blame him for accepting this gift of a pet for his daughters? The Nixons will keep the dog even if criticized for doing so, despite 'what they say about it'. Who are 'they'? Political opponents, the newspapers who had attacked him, all those with power who do not understand the realities of how ordinary people and their families live.

As Nixon observed, '[a]pproximately sixty million Americans saw or heard the radio–television speech, it was estimated, making it the largest audience in television history. That record lasted until 1960, when I appeared on radio–television again, in my "first debate" with John F. Kennedy.' Although criticized as 'a carefully rehearsed soap-opera', the 'Checkers' speech remains a landmark in political communication.[4] It confirmed the power of television and radio in allowing politicians to appeal directly to the public, with their words unmediated by newspaper reporting and analysis. Nixon, then, embraced the electronic media. In so doing, he set a new style for political campaigning. And yet, he learned to his cost in the debates with Kennedy that television can create new political stars while established performers look on. Nixon's pride in his audience ratings from 1952, his conviction of his ability to win over a television audience, and his appreciation of the medium as a way of communicating directly with voters may all have influenced his decision to debate John Kennedy in the presidential campaign of 1960. It then become part of political folklore that Nixon lost the critical first encounter, not as a result of anything he said, but because of the way he appeared on television: pale, nervous and ill shaven in contrast to the tanned, relaxed, well-groomed JFK. As Nixon himself reflected in his memoirs, '[i]t is a devastating commentary on the nature of television as a political medium that what hurt me the most in the first debate was not the substance of the encounter between Kennedy and me, but the disadvantageous contrast in our physical appearances.'[5] Looking good on television became part of a successful political career.

Television, therefore, has played a key role in politics from the 1950s onwards. Edward R. Murrow, the CBS correspondent whose radio reports from London during the Second World War had influenced the opinions of the millions of Americans listening to him even before their country joined the conflict, became one of the most influential television journalists of the decade. On 9 March 1954 the CBS documentary series *See It Now* broadcast 'A Report on Senator Joseph R. McCarthy', introduced by Murrow, which highlighted the abuses of investigative power that fuelled the anti-communist witch-hunt of the times. As Murrow's biographer, Ann Sperber, puts it, '[a] nationally known figure, non-partisan and no polemicist, with a high factor of trust, had spoken up on national TV to say he didn't like McCarthy. And tens of thousands were suddenly replying, in letters, calls, and cables, that they didn't like him either.' Again, the capacity of the medium to unleash the power of public opinion had a critical impact upon the political process. McCarthy's political decline was not caused by one television broadcast. But it helped.

In a speech made in 1957, Murrow observed that in the television age, it was probable that neither Lincoln nor Jefferson would ever have become president. 'Jefferson had a most abrasive voice and did not suffer fools gladly. . . . Mr. Lincoln did not move gracefully, was not a handsome man, had a wife who was not a political asset, and . . . was a solitary man.'[6] Television made image vital to political success. It followed that politicians had to learn the art of controlling their image. Nixon, again, is a case in point. By 1968, and learning from his experience in the debates with Kennedy, Nixon's campaign used live but carefully scripted television appearances to create an appealing image of the candidate, which, combined with astute political advertising, helped Nixon to the presidency. Indeed, in his memoirs, Nixon credits his election eve appearances on television as critical to his victory: 'It was my best campaign decision. Had we not had that last telethon, I believe Humphrey would have squeaked through with a close win on Election Day.'[7] What his television image could not affect, however, was his relationship with the media – in particular the newspapers – and the historical framework within which his presidency was set.

So, like FDR, Kennedy had enjoyed a close and very effective relationship with the media, such that his celebrity transcended his presidency (not least because of his assassination) and he became a powerful political icon. In the decade following his death, however, the contemporary relationship between politicians and the media was framed by events that between them demonstrated that manipulation of the media was becoming an inherently more complex challenge than it had hitherto been. The Vietnam war and the Watergate scandal confirmed the power of TV and newspapers in their turn to mould the national political agenda so as ultimately to cost two presidents – not only Richard Nixon but also Lyndon Johnson – not simply their careers but also their political reputations.

## The Powers That Be

We have in this country two big television networks, NBC and CBS. We have two news magazines, *Newsweek* and *Time*. We have two wire services, AP and UPI. We have two pollsters, Gallup and Harris. We have two big newspapers, the Washington *Post* and *The New York Times*. They're all so damned big they think they own the country. But . . . don't get any ideas about fighting.

*Lyndon Johnson to Spiro Agnew (1969)*

It became 'Lyndon Johnson's war' and he lost it. Vietnam was a conflict fought not only in Southeast Asia, but also, crucially, on television in the United States. At stake was the president's credibility in having to sustain a policy that, to his critics, was inherently flawed and manifestly a failure. When the administration finally lost control of the story in 1968, during the Tet offensive in Vietnam, the so-called 'credibility gap' between what officials said about Vietnam, and what the media presented as the reality there became politically unbridgeable. Even though military the Tet offensive failed, the psychological impact in the United States, where audiences, recently reassured by their government that there was 'light at the end of the tunnel', saw television footage of the US Embassy in Saigon beseiged by its Vietnamese enemies, provided the backdrop against which Lyndon Johnson effectively resigned from the presidency. On 31 March 1968, he announced he would not run again in that year's presidential election.

Walter Cronkite, whom Ed Murrow had hired to cover the Korean War for CBS television, and who had become, by 1968, the most respected news 'anchorman' in America, went to Vietnam during the Tet offensive. Cronkite had told the news – both good and bad – to his television audience since the 1950s. It was he, who, wiping a tear from his eye, had made the first public announcement of the death of John F. Kennedy: a moment of television news history. Now, having seen the war, and talked with other journalists, such as Jack Laurence, then a CBS correspondent based in Vietnam, he delivered his verdict. In a broadcast reminiscent in style if not in tone to Murrow's exposé of McCarthy, Cronkite editorialized: 'To say we are closer to victory today is to believe, in the face of the evidence, the optimists who have been wrong in the past. To suggest we are on the edge of defeat is to yield to unreasonable pessimism. To say that we are mired in stale-mate seems the only realistic, yet unsatisfactory, conclusion.' If it had been a 'television war', it was perhaps appropriate, in David Halberstam's words, that 'it was the first time in American history a war had been declared over by an anchorman.'[8] The president, having watched the programme, reportedly said that if he'd lost Cronkite, he'd lost the average American citizen who had voted for him in 1964, when he had run on an anti-war platform. America's military involve-ment in the Vietnam war would last another five years, yet Johnson's presidency was effectively over a month later.

Whether the media actually had the power to influence American foreign policy in such a profound way is not as important to consider as the fact that politicians believed that newspapers, radio and televi-sion had come to hold the key to the formation of national public opinion. So when the Vietnam war unravelled the political, social and cultural consensus in America, the 'best and the brightest' blamed the media. As Halberstam observes,

> when the public and the Congress, annoyed at being manipulated, soured on the war, then the architects had been aggrieved. They had turned on those very symbols of the democratic society they had once manipu-lated, criticizing them for their lack of fiber, stamina and lack of belief. Why weren't the journalists more supportive? How could you make public policy with cameras everywhere?

Vietnam – which after Kennedy's presidency and the campaign for civil rights became the biggest and most dramatic story of the 1960s, focused attention on the fundamentals of the relationship between politicians and the media.

In this context the politician's perspective is plain. The day after he had announced his decision not to run for re-election, Lyndon Johnson addressed the National Association of Broadcasters in Chicago. He revealed his sense of betrayal, and his belief that the media had misrepresented him. Television had 'the power to clarify and . . . the power to confuse', and if its intepretation of events was wrong, then its errors were compounded. For, '[u]nlike the printed media, television writes on the wind.' In a war like that in Vietnam, television images undoubtedly had an impact upon audiences, but '[n]o one can say exactly what effect those vivid scenes have on American opinion.' Johnson suggested that the media preferred to report dramatic war stories rather than focus upon the search for peace. 'Peace, in the news sense, is a "condition". War is an "event".' In moulding public opinion against the war, moreover, television news had become subjective in its judgements. Instead, the president warned,

> you must defend your media against the spirit of faction, against the works of divisiveness and bigotry, against the evils of partisanship in any guise. For America's press, as for the American Presidency, the integrity and the responsibility and the freedom – the freedom to know the truth and let the truth make us free – must never be compromised or diluted or destroyed.

As Halberstam points out, the president's speech to the broadcasters 'placed the blame for the failure squarely on their shoulders, their fault being that the cameras had revealed just how empty it all was. A good war televises well; a bad war televises poorly.'[9] And Vietnam was a bad war. The 'credibility gap' – the distance between Johnson's defence of the war and the media's assessment of events in Southeast Asia – was the result of a process of mutual recrimination. The president could argue for consensus but it no longer existed. He could urge the media to be objective but the criteria for objectivity had been lost. The president no longer controlled his message, and his political career was thus at an end.

If Lyndon Johnson left the presidency suspicious of the power of the media, Richard Nixon succeeded him with a well-documented history of antagonism towards it. Though he had used television to be elected, he still felt abused by it. Indeed, in his memoirs, he quotes approvingly from a book called *The News Twisters*, which concluded that the three major networks had consistently attacked him during the election. Edith Efron, the book's author, suggested that '[t]ogether they broadcast the equivalent of a New York *Times* lead editorial against him every day – for five days a week for the seven weeks of his campaign.'[10] In contemporary American politics, however, it was becoming increasingly evident that the president needed to nurture a good relationship with the media. Instead, Nixon gave them a story that, during the early 1970s, surpassed even Vietnam as one of historic importance: Watergate.

# Richard Nixon's 'True Crime'

> In one meeting Jacob Javits leaned over to me reassuringly and
> said, 'Lincoln was called a lot worse things than you, remember
> that.' 'I'm catching up,' was all I could reply.
> *Richard Nixon*, RN: The Memoirs of Richard Nixon (*1978*)

The political game in the United States has always been played with
a sense that in order to make things work it is perhaps necessary to
treat ideas with respect but ideals with scepticism. So democracy and
republicanism may be shaped by the principles of liberty and equality,
yet the Constitution itself remains a framework that structures political activity, and that frustrates as much as it facilitates. In such a
situation, certain political practices may be tolerated to the point
where they appear to make a mockery of the Founders' intent. Lines
are drawn, however, in those instances where political conduct, whether
institutional or personal, is deemed unacceptable. In such situations,
the Constitution becomes sacrosanct: the ideals it embodies are not
impossible, impractical standards; rather, sharp practices are evidence
of corruption. Politicians so accused are charged with disrespect for
the fundamental values of American political life. If the allegations
are proven, they are held in contempt of the Constitution itself and
may face its ultimate penalty of impeachment. For it is one thing to
exploit loopholes in the fabric of American constitutionalism; it is
entirely another to be exposed as a cheat.

In *Federalist 55*, Madison argued that '[a]s there is a degree of
depravity in mankind which requires a certain degree of circumspec-
tion and distrust, so there are other qualities in human nature which
justify a certain portion of esteem and confidence. Republican government presupposes the existence of these qualities in a higher degree
than any other form.' So politicians in the United States are expected
to be 'public servants', and many are. But those who put personal
gain before the public good, or who attempt to free themselves from
constitutional restraints upon political conduct, are, in Madison's
terms, corrupt. And such corruption, once exposed, becomes the script
of scandal.

Corruption scandals stain American political history. They may
involve abuses of power, money or sex; and sometimes all three.
Yet until the collapse of the post-war political consensus in the late
1960s and early 1970s, the media were generally reticent about expos-
ing presidential misdemeanours. With Nixon in the White House, it
did not hold back. Franklin Roosevelt, John F. Kennedy and even

Lyndon Johnson had been protected by the culture of self-denying ordinances followed by the media. Watergate changed that. Following Nixon, two of the last five elected presidents – Reagan and Clinton – have been involved in major political scandals. Iran–Contra and the repeated investigations of Bill Clinton's affairs (which in the end focused on the one with Monica Lewinsky) show that misbehaviour takes on different guises, but that an assumption of corruption – political, institutional or moral – is now the basis upon which investigation proceeds.

In these terms, the aftershocks of Watergate continue to impact upon contemporary American politics. Richard Nixon's 'true crime', as Theodore White described it, was that he 'destroyed the myth that binds America together, and for this he was driven from power' . . . 'The myth he broke was critical – that somewhere in American life there is at least one man who stands for law, the President.'[11] As the scandal engulfed his administration, the president was forced to protest his innocence. In 1973, Americans heard him insist that '[p]eople have got to know whether or not their President is a crook. Well, I'm not a crook.' But Nixon's problem was simple. His audience did not believe him. And yet, the incident that triggered the implosion of his presidency – the break-in at the Democrat party Headquarters in the Watergate building in Washington DC in June 1972 – was, from a different perspective, not so much a crime as part of the customs and practices of American politics.

In his book *The Ends of Power* (1978), Bob Haldeman, the 'advance man' who organized Richard Nixon's political campaigns, reproduces a picture of himself with Dick Tuck, a Democrat widely credited with re-creating the practice of 'dirty tricks' in its modern form. Assessing Haldeman's role in the Watergate scandal, Theodore White suggests that '[d]irty tricks are as old as American campaigning, as old, indeed, as electoral politics, dating back to republican Rome. But they had been elevated to a minor dark art by . . . the celebrated Democratic prankster Dick Tuck, a political wit who had specialized . . . in plaguing and pin-pricking Richard Nixon's campaigns.'[12] It was Tuck who, in 1960, had managed to ensure that the fortune cookies on the menu at a lunch honouring Nixon had all contained the message 'Kennedy will win'. In Haldeman's political world, however, such humour was notably absent. Instead, 'dirty tricks' became a way of trying to sabotage opposition campaigns in which breaking and entering for political purposes could be condoned.

Once the Watergate burglars were arrested, and found to have links to members of the Nixon White House, the media had their story. It was pursued with remarkable tenacity by *The Washington Post*, and made heroes out of its investigative journalists, Bob Woodward and Carl Bernstein. Paul Johnson argues, in fact, that Watergate effectively became a media-inspired 'putsch against the executive'. He suggests that '[t]he media in the 1970s . . . felt that they were in some deep but intuitive sense the repository of the honor and conscience of the nation and had a quasi-constitutional duty to assert it in times of crisis, whatever the means or the consequences.'[13] Though the case is over-stated, it does draw attention to the central role of the media in being able to mould the terms of contemporary political debate, as had been the case too with the Vietnam war. This time, however, it was newspapers rather than television that led the charge. Watergate was not as compelling visually as the war, yet, as Ben Bradlee, then editor of The *Washington Post*, observed twenty years after the event, '[n]o news story has ever grabbed and held Washington by the throat the way Watergate did. No news story in my experience ever dominated conversation, newspapers, radio and television broadcasts the way Watergate did.' Moreover, television did make a critical contribution. In October 1972, Walter Cronkite made Watergate the central item in two consecutive news programmes on CBS. Once again, then, it proved instrumental in altering the climate of political opinion. According to Bradlee, after Cronkite's show of support, other editors starting taking the story seriously, although it was another year before 'the rest of the American press not only joined the hunt for the truth but contributed solid, original reporting of their own.'[14] For Katherine Graham, the newspaper's publisher, 'Cronkite gave us great credit, and the still photos of the *Post* and its headlines in the background helped enormously. . . . CBS had taken the *Post* national.' But it would not have been the story it became unless there had been some substance to the investigation. Watergate thus came to symbolize the potential for the executive to abuse the constitutional powers of the office in pursuit of the preservation of political self-interest. In the end, that is why the power of the story is both compelling and enduring.

The way in which the Watergate cover-up finally unravelled confirmed the capacity of the media to influence political events. When Nixon was succeeded by Gerald Ford, Katherine Graham recalled that 'tee shirts were printed with his picture on them, together with the caption "I got my job through The Washington Post", a slogan also used by our classified-ad department.'[15] Like Lyndon Johnson before him, Nixon blamed the media for his downfall. But at the same time both would agree to television interviews after they had left office to attempt to justify their presidential actions: LBJ with Walter Cronkite, and Nixon with David Frost. When his turn came, moreover, Nixon was careful to put on record his belief that

[t]he greatest concentration of power in the United States today is not in the White House; it isn't in the Congress and it isn't in the Supreme Court. It's in the media. And it's too much. . . . It's too much power and it's power that the Founding Fathers would have been very concerned about. Because the Founding Fathers balanced the power. . . . And when you have balanced power, you have checks, each on the other. There is no check on the networks. There is no check on the newspapers.[16]

And yet as the interviews themselves demonstrate, politicians – even ex-presidents – have to embrace the media if they are to have any say in how their actions are interpreted. It is a symbiotic relationship, a marriage of convenience, which, when it sours, can only lead to acrimonious recriminations over who was at fault in the divorce.


## Spinning through Hollywood


It is like writing history with lightning. And my only regret is that it is all so terribly true.
*Woodrow Wilson on seeing D.W. Griffith's*
Birth of a Nation (*1915*)


The media compose the mood music of American politics. As William Randolph Hearst demonstrated, the headlines that grab most attention have to do either with personal tragedy, war or scandal. So the 1960s and 1970s provided television, radio and newspapers with some outstanding stories. Following what William Manchester called the 'one brief shining moment'[17] that was Kennedy's presidency came the twin disasters of Vietnam and Watergate. These were news stories that transcended their times and the retelling of them has been mediated through popular culture. JFK's assassination spawned an industry of interpretations: investigative analysis, memoir, fictional representations. So too did Vietnam and Watergate. How, though, could these powerful stories be fitted into the continuing narrative of American history? One way was to present the assassination as a pivotal moment, representing a tragic 'loss of innocence'. Thereafter the war in Southeast Asia and the domestic scandal that forced a president to resign reflect the contours of an American political system in which things had gone badly awry. In this scenario, had Kennedy lived, it would all have been different: no war, no Watergate. Even if the reality of Lyndon

Johnson in power is accepted, another variation can be played on the
counter-factual theme. So if Robert Kennedy had lived instead of
being assassinated in 1968, then Nixon would not have been elected,
and history would have found its way back to the right path: RFK
would have ended the war, and, of course, would have had no part in
a 'third-rate burglary attempt'. Kennedys did things properly. In these
terms, then, the Watergate scandal has all the elements of political
tragedy. Even if it was not a story that could be adapted easily for
TV news (although it did become the basis for a television mini-series,
*Washington – Behind Closed Doors*), it was fashioned by Hollywood
screenwriters into a movie that became a major box-office success and
reinforced in the popular imagination the idea that the media can and
should hold politicians to account for their actions.

*All the President's Men*, the title of Bob Woodward and Carl
Bernstein's account of their part in the revelations of Watergate, published in 1974, is reminiscent of Robert Penn Warren's novel *All the
Kings Men* (1946): a portrait of Huey Long, the governor of Louisiana
in the 1930s. A populist demagogue – nicknamed the Kingfisher –
who flourished in the corrupt politics of the contemporary south, he
was assassinated on the steps of the state legislature in Baton Rouge.
As Brian Neve observes, T. Harry Williams, Long's biographer,
argued that the novelist's premise had been that 'the politician who
wishes to do good may have to do some evil to achieve his goal': an
apt allegory for Nixon. The film of the same name, released in 1949,
won three Oscars, including that for Best Picture, and, according
to Neve, critics saw in it 'the potential for democratic authority, as
well as the need for constraints on that legitimate power, once
established.'[18] In this context, too, it indeed recalls *Citizen Kane*: the
rise and fall of the media tycoon is mirrored in the biography of the
Louisiana governor whose political ambition was the presidency. A
further connection between the worlds of media, popular culture and
politics is suggested by the subsequent career of the film's director,
Robert Rossen. He lost his studio contract after he had been named
as a communist by witnesses testifying to the House Committee on
UnAmerican Activities (HUAC) – where Richard Nixon had first
established his political reputation – in 1951.

Woodward and Bernstein wrote with Hollywood in mind. The film
of the same title appeared in 1976, two years after the book had been
published. Its opening pages helpfully list the cast of characters who
will appear in it, and the fact that the authors knew that it would
become a movie – the screen rights were being sold while it was being
written – makes it read almost like a Hollywood script. The book
ends with a defiant president delivering his 1974 State of the Union

address in which he declared that he had 'no intention whatever of ever walking away from the job that the American people elected me to do'. By the time the film appeared, audiences knew the eventual outcome of the story: Nixon resigned six months later. To entertain, though, the film has to dramatize the story and make heroes of its principal characters. Casting helped. Robert Redford and Dustin Hoffman, who play Woodward and Bernstein, were immediately associated with certain screen images. Redford brought to his part the persona developed in earlier films as a clean-cut resourceful hero with a sense of integrity. Hoffman was the character actor, with successful screen credentials in such films as *The Graduate* (1967), *Midnight Cowboy* (1969) and *Little Big Man* (1970). Together their names sold the film: their endorsement of the movie – which Redford helped to produce – became an endorsement of its message.

The dramatic tension in the plot was provided by the shadowy, elusive and enigmatic character of 'Deep Throat'. He was, according to the book, Woodward's 'source in the Executive Branch who had access to information at CRP (the Committee to Re-elect the President) as well as at the White House. His identity was unknown to anyone else. He could be contacted only on very important occasions. . . . Their discussions would be only to confirm information that had been obtained elsewhere and to add some perspective.' 'Deep Throat' – the title of a celebrated contemporary pornographic movie – would arrange meetings with Woodward by drawing a clock-face with the nominated time on it on a page of the journalist's copy of the *New York Times*. 'Woodward did not know how Deep Throat got to his paper.' It sounds implausible enough to be part of a Hollywood movie script, which, of course, it became. But this kind of detail again authenticates the source as someone used to clandestine behaviour: the scenario, after all, would not be out of place in a spy story.

In the movie, 'Deep Throat' clearly has all the answers to the Watergate conspiracy. The frustrating thing for Woodward, but not perhaps for the audience, who appreciate the growing suspense, but who also know the eventual outcome of the story, is that he refuses to reveal them. Instead he gives clues as to the ways in which the investigation should proceed: he is the guide, giving Woodward the road-map through the complexities of the conspiracy. Throughout the narrative he also acts as a commentator on the political process. He berates Woodward for writing an inaccurate story that implicated Bob Haldeman in the management of illegal funds, allowing the White House to deny the report vociferously. According to Deep Throat, it was 'the worst possible setback. You've got people feeling sorry for Haldeman. I didn't think that was possible.' Then, in the book, 'Deep

Throat' lays out an analysis of how the investigation should proceed. 'A conspiracy like this . . . a conspiracy investigation . . . the rope has to tighten slowly around everyone's neck. You build convincingly from the outer edges in. . . . If you shoot too high and miss, then everybody feels more secure. Lawyers work this way. I'm sure smart reporters must, too.'[19]

In *All the President's Men* authenticity is easy to establish insofar as the audience can relate the investigation to an actual event that did indeed lead to a cover-up being exposed and a president resigning. In looking at the way in which the movie approaches its task, however, it is nevertheless interesting to observe the way in which TV images are used to help establish the context of the story. It is as if television itself – a 'neutral' medium that preserves scenes from the past – in turn makes the images conveyed in the film authoritative by associating them with contemporary media accounts. So television is a constant back-drop to the action. On the eve of the Watergate arrests, there are images of Nixon on television addressing a joint session of Congress on his return from a summit meeting in Russia, which took place a couple of weeks before the break-in. The scene sets up the idea of the president at his most powerful: the focus of national attention, the holder of the most important political office in the land, who is about to fall from grace. Throughout the film, glimpses of Nixon's re-election campaign are seen and press conferences denouncing Woodward and Bernstein are mediated through television. Finally, as Nixon's 1972 electoral triumph is being relayed on a TV in The *Washington Post* newsroom, the two journalists are shown furiously typing the stories that will bring him down. It was Nixon whose activities in the White House appeared to confirm the paranoid style in American politics and whose impact upon popular culture was to inspire the conspiracy movies that appeared in the aftermath of his resignation.

Television forces politics to become part of America's visual culture. It is ironic for the media, in this sense, that their cameras were absent from a defining event of the television age: the assassination of John F. Kennedy. The most famous film of the tragedy, Abraham Zapruder's home movie, became familiar to audiences only twenty-eight years after the event, through its incorporation in Oliver Stone's film *JFK* (1991). Stone's film narrative, however, can only mediate an interpretation of a critical moment in contemporary American history by using generic formulas familiar enough to those who had enjoyed the dramatization of Nixon's downfall.

The casting of Kevin Costner, who had made the award-winning *Dances With Wolves* (1990), as Jim Garrison, the lawyer turned investigator from Louisiana, who sets out to expose the cover-up behind the assassination, was another example of an established star taking on the role of ordinary hero. The 'Deep Throat' character is the equally shadowy, elusive and enigmatic Colonel 'X', an invented source, but once more the 'insider' who can reveal aspects of the conspiracy to those, like Garrison, who are trying to uncover it in the public's interest. *JFK* also makes prolific use of TV coverage. From the opening montage of news stories, which significantly includes President Eisenhower's farewell address, warning the country of the dangers of excessive power concentrated into the 'military-industrial' complex, television exists as a backdrop to the action, recording again contemporary events: the assassination itself and its aftermath, and later the further assassinations of Martin Luther King and Bobby Kennedy. Stone, however, goes beyond the simple use of TV as a device to locate the narrative in an authentic historical context. His repeated use of flash-backs, in black and white, gives a documentary feel to the material, connecting his interpretations of events with the accepted authenticity of the television record of Kennedy's presidency.

Movies thus act as cultural reference points that help to define the contours of contemporary American politics. Ian Scott indeed argues that 'politics has always played, and Hollywood came along to enhance, a game of spectacle and idealization. Hollywood reflects and indeed encourages the kind of mythmaking that American politics itself has constantly engaged in, and for this reason alone its politics have an acute sensibility to the cinematic medium that is worth investigating.'[20] So films that deal explicitly with important events in American political history – *All the President's Men* and *JFK* – and that achieve box-office success effectively mould a mass audience's perception of the past. To know Watergate only via Hollywood is to accept that the heroes of Watergate were two investigative journalists, no matter that congressional committees, grand juries, special prosecutors and lawyers were also involved in trying to find out what had occurred. In the end, Woodward and Bernstein did not force Nixon to resign. It was the collapse of his political support in a Democrat-dominated Congress that left him no alternative. Indeed, as journalists on *The Washington Post* themselves recalled twenty years after the film's release,

[t]he most gratuitous visual inaccuracy in 'All the President's Men' is the repeated depiction of Woodward and Bernstein laboring alone in an empty newsroom. The truth is that almost everyone in the newsroom . . . became swept up in the Watergate coverage. . . . We were

part of the paper and we knew what was happening and nobody believed us. It was like being in combat together.[21]

Yet that reality would have been harder for Hollywood to depict.

In similar fashion, but with even more ambition, *JFK* seeks to persuade its audience of the existence of a conspiracy to assassinate the president through the construction of a visually compelling and entertaining narrative. Its version of the event, if believed, suggests that a labyrinthine plot was devised and triggered because Kennedy, having failed to bring down Castro in Cuba, was reluctant to commit America further to the war in Vietnam. So Cubans, organized crime (the Mafia had lost control of lucrative casinos in Havana), high-ranking members of the 'military-industrial complex' who wanted a war in Southeast Asia, and even Lyndon Johnson himself are implicated in the conspiracy. The controversy provoked by Stone's film, however, revolved not simply around his interpretation of the historical moment. It also addressed the issue of the film-maker's power to persuade: *JFK* becomes the accepted popular view of what may have occurred in Dallas in November 1963. Stone, like D.W. Griffith before him, is able to use the medium to 'write history with lightning'. But just as on closer scrutiny *Birth of a Nation* is a flawed interpretation of the nation's past, so *JFK* should be regarded as a stunning example of the director's craft: no more, no less.

War not only sells newspapers. It is also a subject with box-office appeal. Following the Second World War and the war in Korea, a generation of Americans came of age without direct experience of being involved in conflict. Instead a vicarious knowledge of war was supplied by Hollywood, and in particular by stars associated with the genre, notably John Wayne. Despite Wayne's attempt to 'sell' the Vietnam war in *The Green Berets* (1968), however, it became apparent to participants that the war in Southeast Asia was not a narrative scripted by Hollywood. Indeed, during and after the event the movie industry had difficulties coming to terms with such a controversial conflict. And yet, over a quarter of a century after the last American military helicopters clattered away from the US Embassy in Saigon, as North Vietnamese forces finally unified their country, it is Hollywood that mediates popular images of the first television war. Films such as *The Deer Hunter* (1978), *Apocalypse Now* (1979), *Platoon* (1986) and *Full Metal Jacket* (1987) have brought different perspectives to bear upon the complexities of the war in Vietnam. More simply, in *Rambo: First Blood Part II* (1985), Sylvester Stallone famously posed the question: 'Do we get to win this time?' before refighting it on celluloid. War is entertainment, as, in a media-dominated world, news is 'infotainment' and political ideas are expressed as 'soundbites'.

# Conclusion: The Politics of Communication

Anchormen have . . . become mythical characters, larger by far than the scouts of folklore who led the covered wagons across the trackless plains.

*Theodore White*, America in Search of Itself (*1982*)

Throughout the twentieth century, the challenge for American politicians, in common with those elsewhere, was to adapt to technological developments that made the politics of communication at once easier and more challenging. Election campaigns still may be shaped by traditional political activities – direct contact with potential voters, town-meetings, speeches, debates between candidates – but as the media's influence has grown, first through the widespread circulation of newspapers, then through radio and finally through television, the electorate no longer need personally to witness political performances. In the nineteenth century, politicians such as Abraham Lincoln and Stephen Douglas could draw large audiences to debates staged as part of an election campaign for the Senate in Illinois, who might make up their minds on the basis of their oratory. In 1960, the essential drama of the Kennedy–Nixon debates revolved around who looked better on television. Contemporary politicians – notably presidents – may thus acquire the kind of celebrity hitherto reserved for Hollywood film stars. It was thus entirely appropriate when a former Hollywood star became president. Ronald Reagan was the best actor to occupy the White House since Franklin Delano Roosevelt.

Ronald Reagan's understanding of media was profound. In 1933, just after Franklin Roosevelt became president, Reagan, then twenty-two, was hired as a radio announcer by a local station in Iowa. Four years later he was under contract with Warner Brothers studio as an aspiring Hollywood actor. After the war, as his movie career declined, he went into television, hosting a drama series sponsored by General Electric. His work for the corporation also involved public appearances and speeches to audiences across America. In a survey conducted in 1958, he emerged as one of the most recognized men in the country, which gave him a huge amount of political capital. Eight years later he spent some of it in running successfully for the governorship of California, which became a springboard for his eventual election to the White House in 1980.

His presidency was one of the most visually compelling performances in contemporary American political history. Nicknamed 'the great communicator', it was Reagan's experience in front of a camera that enabled him to establish an effective relationship with his audience.

Colin Powell recalls how he witnessed the closing scenes of Reagan's presidency. The television cameras were part of the event. For Powell,

> [t]his was the conclusion of a big dramatic production. Here we were, his senior staffers, all of us who directed him and scripted him and made him up and gave him his cues. And here were the cameramen, the sound guys, the light holders and the grips. And there, all alone against the backdrop of the Oval Office, was Ronald Reagan shooting his last take.[22]

Here, then, the historical memory of a president is being constructed exclusively for television, and the production values are those of a Hollywood movie.

At the core of the contemporary relationship between American politicians and the media, therefore, there is a battle for control over images. The presidency in particular has become part of the 'infotainment' industry. In a culture of celebrity, the president is the unchallenged star of the political firmament. What he decides or does is news. How he projects himself in the role of leader, however, is also an important index of his political stature. The media help to establish popular images of the president, commentating on both style and performance. Those who are able to seize the initiative in that process – Roosevelt, Kennedy, Reagan – are able to influence perceptions. But they have to understand how the media work, be prepared to co-operate with them, and ultimately feel at ease with them. Those who cannot maintain control of their image in the media – Johnson, Nixon – in the end may only cast themselves as its victims.

At the same time, whatever issues determine the president's political agenda, the priorities that drive the commercialized and competitive world inhabited by the media may be different. The essence of news is that it is transitory. The spotlight falls upon an incident, an event, a story. It stays until the subject is exhausted, and then it moves on. Very often, there is little opportunity to contextualize; instead the drama of the moment is what counts. In such an atmosphere it is very difficult for politicians to appear in control of events; very often their role is to react to them. Nevertheless, the president remains a key actor, for the significance of a story is greatly enhanced if he is involved. In his novel *American Hero* (1995), Larry Beinhart observes that there is always 'some new goddam problem . . . being picked out by the media to be the new crisis that the president, and only the president, must supply leadership for.'[23]

Yet problems of leadership can occur when political and media agendas diverge. Again, the careers of Johnson and Nixon are illustrative of that reality. LBJ's Great Society was, in its intent, the most radical transformation of American society attempted in the twentieth century. Yet the most compelling images for the media during his administration were not to be found in the war on poverty, but rather in the war in Vietnam. Similarly, Nixon's super-power diplomacy was in some ways the most creative attempt by a Cold War president to influence the ways in which America perceived the wider world. But it was the domestic scandal of Watergate that would always overshadow his international achievements. So the most complex problem that faces a contemporary president is to establish and maintain control of his image and his agenda in the context of what the media define as the most newsworthy events of the time.

The media in America historically have been privately owned and subject to little regulation: the first amendment's guarantee of freedom of speech is jealously preserved. Yet as sources of information have proliferated, from newspapers to radio to television, to the personal computer and the internet, so those issues of control have become more difficult still. Formerly the network 'anchormen' became – like Walter Cronkite – mythical characters in their own right because they not simply were trusted to read the news but also were believed on those dramatic occasions when they commented upon it. Now new pioneers can exploit fresh forms of media by, say, starting a rumour on the internet and seeing it eventually become real. Bill Clinton's affair with an intern was first revealed not by mainstream media but on the Matt Drudge website.

Yet if the president must compete for media attention in a culture of celebrity, then it is important to provide scenarios in which he can take a leading role. Beinhart's novel takes this premise to a logical conclusion. He imagines George Bush, in office, unpopular and out-of-touch with the mood of the country, acting upon a memo: the legacy of his former chief political strategist, Lee Atwater. In it, Atwater recalls that Margaret Thatcher's political career was transformed by her success in winning the Falklands war. The same outcome could occur in America if it is accepted that in modern times war has become a media spectacle: the logic of the argument is that wars should be fought that look good on television. In the novel, then, the Gulf War is scripted, financed and produced by Hollywood professionals to boost the president's political fortunes. The novel was itself filmed as *Wag the Dog* (1997), with the story reinvented to suit the times in which it was made: now a president whose career was threatened by the revelations of a sex-scandal is the one who is saved by a made-for-television war. In August 1998, four days after he had owned up on nationwide television to his affair with Monica Lewinsky, Bill

Clinton authorized military action against terrorist bases overseas. The media saw the connection immediately and the president's press secretary had to stonewall questions about the 'Wag the Dog' theory: whether political life was imitating Hollywood's art.

News media may provide the first rough drafts of history, but there is no doubt that Hollywood's retelling of stories from the nation's past helps to mould contemporary attitudes as well. More than this, movie images and inventions can provide idealized portraits of political leadership. So audiences may like the idea of a President Bill Pullman saving the world from alien invasion in *Independence Day* (1996). They may prefer Michael Douglas in *The American President* (1995) or Harrison Ford in *Air Force One* (1997) to real-life occupants of the White House. On television, Martin Sheen seems to be a more effective president in *The West Wing* than some of those who have been elected to the position. On the other hand, movies can suggest too that American politicians are by nature corrupt, by instinct manipulative and by inclination conspirators against the public good: scenarios that retell, mirror or exaggerate the various and varied scandals that stain the nation's political life.

The media's power has always been that of persuasion, but with the technology of television it is no longer sufficient to use simply the spoken or written word to make political statements. Now, the techniques of persuasion must incorporate the visual: power is invested in images as well as arguments. In November 1951, the installation of a coaxial cable joining the east and west coasts of America was completed, allowing the technology of television to begin effectively to mould national political opinions. Since then, what Theodore Roosevelt called the 'bully pulpit' of the presidency has preached to the nation through television. Yet, in the decades that followed, with an accelerating pace, the executive struggled to control the news agenda. While presidential press conferences could make news headlines, so could images of civil rights protestors confronting police in the south, or American soldiers at war in Vietnam. The 'credibility gap' was the penalty politicians paid for using the new media. People heard one message from their leaders and saw another when watching their television. And the images seem more convincing than the words. Moreover, new technologies have allowed a proliferation of the channels of television communication, such that presidential vulnerability is compounded. Indeed, while fewer people now rely on network news for information, cable television viewing has increased, particularly in the last decade, and dedicated news channels such as CNN have grown in influence. So managing the media is still the key skill for a successful political career. But it may prove an impossible task.

In 1998, Kenneth Starr, the independent counsel investigating President Clinton's affair with Monica Lewinsky – and whose media image became that of a puritanical witch-hunter – issued his report. It was made available first on the internet. The printed version was published later. Like television in the 1950s, the internet represents a new tool of communication, the political impact of which is still in its infancy. At the turn of the twenty-first century there were more than forty-five million Americans subscribing to the internet. It offers new possibilities of interactive communication. On the one hand that makes it an ideal democratic medium: all who have access to it can add their voice to contemporary political debates. On the other, complete freedom of communication may be abused by those who seek converts to the privatized world of their own particular prejudices.

At the same time, the internet has become yet another outlet for the major corporations that dominate not simply the American communications industry, but increasingly also the global media market as well. The proliferation of the technologies of mass communication – newspapers, book and magazine publishing, radio, television, satellite and cable broadcasting, film, video and the internet itself – has been mirrored by the consolidation of a small number of media empires. In the United States, by the end of the 1990s, Time-Warner, Disney and News Corporation had become the three major players domestically and internationally, with interests ranging from print media to broadcasting, to the music industry, to theme parks and the ownership of professional sports teams. In January 2001 the merger between the internet company America Online and Time-Warner – the biggest such deal in the history of American business – created the largest media company in the world, with a potential influence reminiscent of that enjoyed by J.P. Morgan when he dominated the US steel industry a century earlier. In this sense, therefore, the opportunities for increased democratic participation afforded by the internet have to be measured alongside the attempts to monopolize this new medium of communication. In the brave new world of the internet, at the beginning of the twenty-first century, almost half of all page visits were to the most popular hundred websites, and those who used the net spent nearly a fifth of their time viewing only the top ten sites. Very few internet waves seemed worth surfing.

Technology, however, still drives the politics of communication. In turn, the media map the contours of American politics. They are the source of information about the political process, and they are the means by which politicians may speak to the nation. From the days of Pulitzer and Hearst they have provided the commentary upon the political game and those who play it. Crucially, they have operated in a commercial environment: America is more or less unique amongst modern industrial nations in not having elements of its media which are government-controlled. In defining their proper role within a democratic republic, they have nevertheless to choose between becoming the unelected watchdog, holding to account those who have achieved the legitimacy of a democratic mandate, or behaving as the politician's poodle: supporting the aims and objectives of those in positions of power. When that choice is framed in the context of the competitive demands of a market-driven economy, it may, from time to time, be a hard one to make. When the media are adversarial, politicians call foul and cast themselves as victims of an illegitimate, unelected and thus unaccountable power that they cannot control. In the 'big stories' of the 1960s and 1970s that pitted them against the political establishment – the Vietnam war and the Watergate scandal – the media were, to a large extent, on the right side of the moral and the political argument. That may not always be the case. But like politicians themselves, the media ultimately must be held to account in the court of public opinion. In the end, therefore, the influence of the media upon the nation's politics is neither as extensive as those who cast themselves as its victims might suggest, nor as powerful as investigative reporters might hope. The battle between politicians and the media for the hearts and minds of their audience is one that is fought day by day, issue by issue and story by story. However, while the essence of news is its immediacy, the fundamental antagonisms that divide the nation are the result of historic faultlines that run deep within its society and its culture. Power, whether the prerogative of politicians or of the media, is thus never an end in itself. If power is political capital, to have meaning, it must not only be accumulated, it must also be spent. Those who have power can be players in the political game; those who do not remain the dispossessed, relying upon the altruistic concern of others to give them a chance to become recognized as equal shareholders in the enterprise that is America, unless and until they themselves can achieve reform. It follows, then, that there will always be political faultlines on the borders where those who want to alter the shape of American society confront the beneficiaries of the status quo. If the acquisition of power allows voices to be heard, then the purpose of power is to determine what is done – and what is left undone – in the realm of public policy. And this in turn will continue to mould the character of the nation's political life.

# Faultlines

E Pluribus Unum
*Motto on the Great Seal of the United States*
*of America (1776)*

When John Adams, Thomas Jefferson and Ben Franklin suggested the Latin phrase – translated as 'one from many' – as the inscription on the Great Seal of the United States in 1776, what they had in mind was the forging of a nation from its disparate states. Yet that idea could be extended into the ideal of integrating people from diverse backgrounds, cultural and ethnic identities, into one community. As a nation made up of immigrants, the image of America as a 'melting-pot' is a seductive one. Crèvecoeur had asked the famous question, 'What then is the American, this new man?', and his optimistic reply, describing how the land moulds those who come from elsewhere into a new race, with a national character that suggests both its difference and its potential, is, for the historian Arthur Schlesinger, Jr, 'still a good answer – still the best hope'.[1] On the other hand, the history of America is defined by the struggles of many for both inclusion and acceptance in the community. The contours of contemporary American politics are shaped by the consequences of that past. Race remains the deepest and most prominent faultline within the American polity. But there are others. Many issues, among them those of class, gender and sexuality, divisions between generations, industrial and agricultural perspectives, urban and rural priorities, and commercial and environmental concerns, also cause political collisions and arguments. The portrait painted of an America that is able to accommodate such diversity is one on which the paint may be cracked and sometimes peeling away; and the fundamental challenge it faces is a problem of colour.

# Race

'As I remember, you used to *laugh* at all this Afro-centric business. I remember one night – when was it? – '87 – '88 – you made so much fun of Jesse Jackson and his "African-American" pro-nouncement at that press conference – you remember? – wher-ever it was – Chicago, I think – that press conference where he started everybody using "African-American" instead of "black"?'
. . .
'Well', said the Mayor . . .'times change. Times change, times change, and the polls change.'

> *Tom Wolfe*, A Man in Full (*1998*)

Wolfe's novel is set in Atlanta, the city at the heart of the old Con-federacy, and now the symbol of the 'New South'. The conversation is between a lawyer and the mayor: both successful professionals, both black. They are meeting to discuss the problem that threatens to tear apart the political and social fabric of the city: a star Georgia Tech football player, Fareek Fanon, has been accused of date-rape – his alleged victim, the daughter of one of the wealthiest members of Atlanta's white business community. It may be a coincidence that the footballer shares his name with Frantz Fanon, the author of *The Wretched of the Earth* (1967), a book that was influential in the radical-ization of the civil rights movement in the 1960s. But as the mayor says, 'times change'. Yet the political challenges associated with the racial divide in America remain.

In 1944, Gunnar Myrdal fulfilled his $300,000 commission from the Carnegie Foundation by publishing a book, entitled, in the language of the times, *An American Dilemma: The Negro Problem and Modern Democracy*. Judging by the book's length (over a thousand pages), the problem was a formidable one. Myrdal, from Sweden, admitted that 'America is truly a shock to the stranger.' As an outsider, how-ever, he also recognized the strength of the shared values of the nation, its commitment to democratic republicanism. This represented a 'social *ethos*, a political creed' and was 'the cement in the struc-ture of this great and disparate nation'. Given that common idealism, Myrdal argued that the contemporary status of blacks in the commun-ity 'represents nothing less than a century-long lag of public morals' as they were denied still 'the elemental civil and political rights of formal democracy'. Having discussed the dimensions of race and the prejudices it produces, the growth of the African-American population, and its migration from the rural south to the urban north, the economic and the political context in which blacks lived, as well as issues of justice, social inequality and stratification, leadership and community, he ended the book with an analysis of America's dilemma: *'America is free to choose whether the Negro shall remain her liability or become her opportunity.'* If, after the Second World War, the nation was to assume a position of world leadership, then it would be impossible to claim the moral high-ground for republican democracy, with its animating principles of equality and liberty, while still denying rights to a significant minority on the basis of their colour. This, together with existing social trends within the nation, would mean that change would come, but it should be 'engineered'. Myrdal's conclusion was that racial attitudes could be altered through deliberate effort: 'In a sense, the social engineering of the coming epoch will be nothing but the drawing of practical conclusions that "human nature" is changeable and that human deficiencies and unhappiness are, in large degree, preventable.'[2] But where and how was such social engineering to take place?

Myrdal's book was extremely influential among leading American intellectuals, among them Thurgood Marshall, then head of the National Association for the Advancement of Colored People (NAACP) Legal Defense and Education Fund, who would become the first African-American appointed to the Supreme Court, following his nomination by Lyndon Johnson. Marshall's strategists in the campaign for civil rights were 'legal realists', arguing that whatever the Founders had intended, the law should reflect contemporary political and sociological realities. They found a sympathetic audience among liberal justices on the Supreme Court, who were also impressed by Myrdal's work. The result was the seminal decision taken in the case of *Brown* v. *Board of Education of Topeka* (1954), which effectively undermined the doctrine of 'separate but equal' on which the system of racial segregation in America's southern states had been built.

The *Brown* decision was a critical step forward in the campaign for equality of treatment for African-Americans. But it did not result in immediate change. Rather, it became – like Myrdal's book – part of the foundations on which the mass campaign for civil rights was constructed during the late 1950s and 1960s. Orchestrated by such leaders as Martin Luther King, Jr, and taking its doctrine of non-violent civil disobedience from the pre-Civil War writings of Henry David Thoreau, actions such as the Montgomery Bus Boycott, the sit-ins to end segregation in public places, the Freedom Rides, which did the same for interstate transportation, and the famous March on Washington forced the issue of civil rights to the top of the domestic political agenda. Another example of the politics of spectacle – television images of the white police in southern states using violence against peaceful black demonstrators had a galvanizing impact upon public opinion – the campaign for civil rights defined the times in which it took place.

For all its success in forcing the pace of change, however, the civil rights movement could not dismantle entirely the legacy of racism that it confronted. But it did help to clarify two approaches to the problem of the racial divide within America. On the one hand, in the tradition of the Myrdal book, the *Brown* decision and Martin Luther King's leadership is the belief that through changing attitudes it is possible to achieve peaceful racial integration within American society. On the other, black nationalists argue that separatism should replace segregation: that African-Americans should celebrate their historical, cultural and racial difference, and should co-exist with but not accommodate themselves to the dominant white society around them. In the 1960s, under the leadership of Malcolm X, black nationalists also argued that the only effective response against racist violence from whites was confrontation.

Again, religion helped to define these two perspectives. The non-violent civil rights movement had strong roots in the black churches of the south – where Martin Luther King was a baptist minister. Black nationalism found its religion in the Nation of Islam, and the teachings of Elijah Mohammad. As Michael Dyson suggests, while in prison for offences ranging from drug-dealing to illegal gambling and burglary, Malcolm X was 'drawn to the Nation of Islam because of the character of its black-nationalist practices and beliefs: its peculiar gift for rehabilitating black male prisoners; its strong emphasis on black pride, history, culture and unity; and its unblinking assertion that white men were devils, a belief that led Muhammad and his followers to advocate black separation from white society'. In their public statements in the mid-1960s, then, Martin Luther King and Malcolm X appeared to endorse two diametrically opposed viewpoints. Michael Dyson again observes that

> [w]here King advocated redemptive suffering for blacks through their own bloodshed, Malcolm promulgated 'reciprocal bleeding' for blacks and whites. As King preached the virtues of Christian love, Malcolm articulated black anger with unmitigated passion. While King urged nonviolent civil disobedience, Malcolm promoted the liberation of blacks

by whatever means were necessary, including (though not exclusively, as some have argued) the possibility of armed self-defence. While King dreamed, Malcolm saw nightmares.[3]

These conflicting outlooks were nowhere better dramatized than in the boxing ring. In 1962, Floyd Patterson was about to defend his world heavyweight title against Sonny Liston. The NAACP and civil rights leaders were on his side: Patterson seemed superior as a role model and representative for the black community than was the challenger, whose media image was that of a street-fighter with a conviction for armed robbery. According to David Levi-Strauss, 'President Kennedy invited Patterson to the White House to tell him he had to beat Liston because the future of civil rights hung in the balance.' Patterson lost. Then, in 1964, after Cassius Clay beat Liston, he announced he had joined the Nation of Islam, renouncing his former name – his grandfather had been a slave – and becoming Muhammad Ali. As Malcolm X had told him before the contest, 'This fight is the truth. It's the Cross and the Crescent fighting in a prize ring – for the first time. It's a modern Crusades – a Christian and a Muslim facing each other with television to beam it off Telstar for the whole world to see what happens.' When Patterson fought for the title again the following year, he announced that Ali had 'taken the championship . . . and given it to the Black Muslims, who don't want to be a part of our world'. For Patterson to beat him 'would be my contribution to civil rights'.[4] Ali won.

And yet, if each side framed their opposition to the heritage of racial prejudice in a different language, there was still a measure of common ground upon which both were prepared to stand. Malcolm X left the Nation of Islam, and, following a trip to Mecca in 1964, started to moderate his opinions and the stridency of his language. Meanwhile, according to James Cone, by the late 1960s King 'began to move toward an acceptance of Black Power and even advocated "temporary segregation" as the only way to achieve genuine integration. . . . He became so militant that a *New York Times* reporter told him he sounded like a nonviolent Malcolm X.'[5] Moreover, it was opposition to the Vietnam war that united the different sections of the African-American community. When Muhammad Ali refused to be drafted for the war – 'Man, I ain't got no quarrel with them Vietcong' – he became an iconic symbol for the anti-war movement. Having been stripped of his title in 1967 because of his stand against the war, his eventual success in regaining it after knocking out George Foreman in Zaïre in 1974 is as much a political statement as it is a sporting achievement. By 1967 too Martin Luther King was openly voicing his

opinion that America was engaged in 'one of history's most cruel
and senseless wars'. Even before this, however, he had become aware
that his outlook on the more immediate issues confronting African-
Americans was now becoming not that dissimilar from Malcolm X's
perspective. The two men had arranged a meeting in 1965, but Malcolm
had been assassinated two days before it was to take place. Three years
later, the now openly more radical King was also shot dead.

If the goal of the civil rights movements was to claim for blacks
many of the political and social rights denied them in the segregated
south, there is no doubt that it was, by and large, achieved. But having
the right to eat in a restaurant in Atlanta alongside white people does
not mean that everyone can afford to do so. The economic status of
many African-Americans has remained an unresolved issue. Affirmat-
ive action programmes to bring about greater equality of opportunity
for blacks have been resisted by those who think themselves corres-
pondingly disadvantaged. In 1978, Allan Bakke, a white man who
had been unsuccessful in his application for admission to the University of California at Davis Medical School, won a Supreme Court
case in which it was argued that his rights had been violated because
quotas for the admission of minorities set by the university discrimin-
ated against him. Evidently, there was – and remains – resistance to
attempts at Myrdal's 'social engineering' to achieve better racial integration. Yet as Justice Blackmun put it in his opinion on the *Bakke*
case, '[i]n order to get beyond racism, we must take account of race.
There is no other way. And in order to treat some persons equally, we
must treat them differently.'

The issue of race in American society thus remains an intensely
politicized area of public debate. Language itself is an example. In *The
New Republic* in March 1981, in an interview with Thomas Le Clair, the
novelist Toni Morrison drew attention to the fact that as an African-
American '[t]here are certain things I cannot say without recourse
to my language.' She was referring to the vernacular English spoken
by many black people. Moreover, Morrison argued, '[i]t's terrible
to think that a child . . . comes to school to be faced with books that
are less than his own language. And then to be told things about his
language, which is him, that are sometimes permanently damaging. . . .
This is a really cruel fallout of racism.'[6] Should language be a source
of separation or integration?

Karen De Witt, writing in the *New York Times* in December 1996,
took the view that vernacular English enriched the vocabulary of
Standard English, pointing out that '[t]he language of black America
bubbles up from the streets, percolates through its music, infiltrates
the entertainment industry and spills out into the language of all

Americans.' She was reacting to a decision made that month by the board of supervisors for the Oakland Unified School District that highlighted Toni Morrison's concern. It had endorsed the argument that many African-American children were being taught in Oakland schools in a language – Standard English – that was not their primary means of communication. Their lack of proficiency contributed to their poor academic performance. So the board recognized that the children were speaking a distinctive and different language, and that the academic curriculum should reflect that reality.

It ignited an intense debate over whether Ebonics – the name is a fusion of 'ebony' and 'phonics', otherwise called 'African-American Vernacular English' or 'Vernacular Black English' – indeed should be regarded as a language. In January 1997, the Linguistic Society of America, meeting in Chicago, passed a resolution in support of the board's decision. It argued that '[c]haracterizations of Ebonics as "slang", "mutant", "lazy", "defective", "ungrammatical", or "broken English" are incorrect and demeaning.' Moreover, '[t]he distinction between "languages" and "dialects" is usually made more on social and political grounds than on purely linguistic ones.' The resolution concluded that

> [t]here is evidence from Sweden, the US, and other countries that speakers of other varieties can be aided in their learning of the standard variety by pedagogical approaches which recognize the legitimacy of the other varieties of a language. From this perspective, the Oakland School Board's decision to recognize the vernacular of African American students in teaching them Standard English is linguistically and pedagogically sound.

The statement is not only interesting in itself. The fact that the society felt obliged to issue it demonstrates the extent of the controversy the decision had caused.

In the 1950s, it was the Supreme Court that took the initiative in trying to engineer changes in social attitudes through its interpretation of the Constitution and the laws. During that time it was Chief Justice Earl Warren who had mobilized the Court in the cause of reform. But as he recognized in his memoirs (published posthumously in 1977), 'the tragedy of the situation is that because of the resistance die-hard segregationists have made, advances have come about only after torrid litigation or after federal legislation which has emphasized the unfairness of the white supremacy theory to the point that deep bitterness against whites is felt by all minority groups – blacks, Chicanos, Puerto Ricans, Asians, and American Indians'.[7] Moreover, it is the criminal justice system itself that has often exposed the realities of the contemporary climate of race relations in the United States.

The beating administered to Rodney King by Los Angeles police in 1991, well publicized because it was recorded on video and became a media event, thus – like the trial and acquittal of O.J. Simpson – was an example of the politics of racial spectacle. According to the American Civil Liberties Union, 'police abuse against people of color is a legacy of African American enslavement, repression and legal inequality.' Moreover, a less liberal Supreme Court has strengthened police powers, which may invite such abuse. As a result of its decision in *Whren* v. *U.S.* (1996), the police effectively have the power to stop and search any vehicle that has committed a traffic offence. As the ACLU point out, 'because state traffic codes identify so many infractions', if the police want to stop a driver, 'all they have to do to come up with a pretext for a stop is to follow the car until a driver makes an inconsequential error or until a technical violation is observed.' This power, when associated with the practice of racial profiling, results in a new offence: 'driving while black or brown'.

Racial profiling grew out of the 'war on drugs' as a product of the activities of the Task Force on Crime in South Florida, instigated by President Ronald Reagan, and under the direction of his vice-president, George Bush. The Task Force was to combat drug smuggling in the area. The Florida Highway Patrol contributed to the effort by issuing guidelines for the police on 'The Common Characteristics of Drug Couriers'. Officers were advised to look out for drivers wearing 'lots of gold', or who did not 'fit the vehicle', and also to be suspicious of 'ethnic groups associated with the drug trade'. This encouragement of the practice of discriminatory stops and searches of minority groups spread across the country. The impact of such racial profiling was plain. In the early 1990s, a judge in New York city admitted having 'no recollection of any defendant in a Port Authority Police Department drug interdiction case who was not either black or Hispanic'.

Increasing media attention to the issue amplified its political importance. In February 2001, President George W. Bush raised the problem of racial profiling in a speech to Congress, saying that '[a]s government promotes compassion, it also must promote justice. Too many of our citizens have cause to doubt our nation's justice when the law points a finger of suspicion at groups instead of individuals. All our citizens are created equal and must be treated equally. It [racial profiling] is wrong and we will end it in America.' He immediately instructed his attorney-general, John Ashcroft – whose own commitment to civil rights had been questioned during his confirmation hearings – to 'review the use by federal law enforcement authorities of race as a factor in conducting stops, searches and other investigative procedures'.

Yet if the federal government takes the lead, it still relies on individual states to follow and the habits of mind in police forces across the nation to change. In March 2001, after civil rights activists brought a legal action to a federal court accusing the city of Cincinnati, Ohio, of a 'thirty-year pattern of racial profiling', the city council banned the practice and ordered police officers to record the race of people they stopped. But a couple of weeks later, riots broke out in the city following the death of an unarmed African-American, shot by a police officer while being apprehended. He was the sixteenth such victim – all of them black – shot by Cincinnatti police since 1995. The battle between civil rights and racial prejudice is an enduring one: the product of the nation's history that remains its perennial political problem, overshadowing all others. At the same time, however, other faultlines also define the contours of contemporary American politics.

## Class

You don't understand! I could've had class. I could've been a contender. I could've been somebody, instead of a bum, which is what I am.

*Marlon Brando in* On the Waterfront (*1954*)

Capitalism – the American economic creed – is about competition. Under its rules there are winners and losers: it results in social stratification in terms of the distribution of wealth. As such, it creates classes, defined not necessarily through birth or inheritance, as elsewhere, but certainly in terms of occupation, income and social status. And yet, just as the problem of race is ever-present in discussions of contemporary American politics, so the issue of class is often strangely absent from debates. Indeed, as a divisive force in American society, it should have been a contender. But it is not. So how does class fit into an analysis of antagonisms within the American polity?

The psychology of escape that influenced the minds of those who emigrated to America from those European societies in which the vestiges of feudalism remained allowed them too to participate in an adventure in the new world of the American Dream. In other words, immigrants left behind ideas of deference and class rigidity and entered a world in which wealth was the principal indication of social standing. Social and economic mobility could be achieved simultaneously through application and individual effort. America was a 'land of opportunity' in which the language of progress might be shared. 'From rags to riches' becomes the economic equivalent of the political journey 'from log-cabin to White House'. In such an atmosphere, class divisions may still exist, but class conflicts are diminished. Why advocate the overthrow of a system in which individuals still aspire to succeed and are convinced that they will be able to achieve a better life and standard of living?

It follows that the ideology of class conflict – Marxism – found few converts in the United States. Indeed, belonging to the American Communist Party should have had the social cachet of being a member of a rather exclusive club instead of being regarded as a threat to the stability of the nation itself. As Robert Gorman observes,

> [e]ven in the 1930s, when the CP was fairly stable and unified, Federal government repression was minimal, the Soviet Union was perceived as a potential anti-fascist ally, and working class America was in the throes of economic and social upheaval, Marxism was politically impotent everywhere but in scattered immigrant communities and native-born sectors that had special needs, resources, and characteristics.[8]

At the same time, however, class-based antagonisms fuelled the development of labour unions, and have been most visible in the violent history of industrial disputes.

One of the earliest recorded labour disputes in America occurred in 1636 when some fishermen from Maine rebelled against their employer after he witheld their wages. Two hundred and fifty years later, in 1886, a policeman was killed by a bomb thrown during a workers' demonstration in Haymarket Square, Chicago. The forces of law and order opened fire immediately: one demonstrator was shot dead, many were wounded. Subsequently eight anarchist leaders were arrested, and although none of them were identified as the bomb-thrower, four of them were executed. That reality of confrontation that connects colonial New England fishermen and Chicago workers of America's industrial revolution seems to symbolize the ongoing battle between capital and labour during the time in which both have organized: one in pursuit of greater efficiencies in production for profit, the other to fight for better wages, employment rights and conditions within the workplace.

Such conflict indeed became the hallmark of America's industrializing economy. As the development of railroads symbolized the expansionist spirit of the post-Civil War era, so, in 1877, a series of strikes that disrupted the nationwide movements of trains seemed at one stage to threaten greater consequences. The spectre of revolution appeared to grow out of the unrest. Rioting strikers confronted the federal militia and police in states and cities across the country before the strikes were over.

In the twentieth century, the automobile would replace the train as the icon of American industrial achievement. Henry Ford achieved his ambition to 'build a motor car for the great multitude', and for a time his 'Model T' not only became the mass object of desire in the fulfilment of the American Dream, but also made him one of the richest men in America. The American automobile industry established itself in Detroit, Michigan: a city that had acquired a reputation as a place where business – organized in the Employers' Association of Detroit – was strongly anti-union. Indeed, it was not until 1936 that the United Automobile Workers union was formed, and became the representative organization for workers at General Motors and at Chrysler. By 1937, only Ford still resisted the union. In May that year, a group of union organizers, including the future president of the UAW, Walter Reuther, were handing out leaflets at the Ford plant. They were attacked and beaten on the orders of Harry Bennett, the man Ford had appointed to oversee the company's labour relations. The incident, captured by a press photographer, encapsulates the violence that continued to characterize employer–worker relations during the twentieth century. It would be another four years before the Ford motor company allowed the UAW to organize in its factories.

As Robert Lacey observes in his history of Ford, Harry Bennett, in addition to his unlawful attempts to prevent unionization in the company, was also allowed 'to develop the relationships that led to one of the more extraordinary chapters in modern industrial history: the establishing of day-to-day working links between Ford Motor Company and organised crime'. So 'by the middle of the 1930s', Bennett – and by extension the company itself – had established 'a network of underworld connections with hoodlums of largely Italian origin, and the unholy alliance came into its own in the battle which Ford fought against the unions with increasing ferocity as the decade went by'.[9] Yet the automobile industry was not unique in its criminal connections: by the 1930s, critics of American capitalism argued that big business and crime were effectively synonymous: notably during the era of Prohibition. At the same time, however, the union movement was also prone to corruption.

For many, therefore, the stereotypical image of the labour 'boss' became the character of Johnny Friendly, the New York longshoreman played by Lee J. Cobb in *On the Waterfront* (1954). It seemed confirmed in the career of Jimmy Hoffa. As Harold Evans puts it, 'Hoffa, mobsters like to say, is now a hubcap. The longtime leader of the International Brotherhood of Teamsters was abducted and murdered on July 30 1975, his body most likely disposed of in a car compactor.'[10] During the 1960s he had been the most significant target of attorney-general Robert Kennedy's investigation into the links between organized crime and unions: a connection that once again became the background for fiction in works such as James Ellroy's novel *American Tabloid* (1995). The issues and concerns of organized labour in the United States have sometimes appeared overshadowed by the more dramatic narratives of corruption and crime that resonate in American popular culture. Such stories indeed suggest that in the absence of a truly radical agenda, underpinned by a distinctive ideology, unions have been more prone to infiltration by those seeking criminal gain than by those intent on undermining the business of America.

Mari Jo Buhle, Paul Buhle and Harvey J. Kaye, in their edited collection called simply *The American Radical* (1994), thus argue that '[t]he Industrial Revolution and a rapid increase in population . . . focused attention on the working class.'[11] But among the forty-six biographical vignettes of those they consider as influential radicals in American history, they can find room for only one union leader: Eugene Debs, who, from 1900 onwards, became perhaps better known as the five-time presidential candidate for the American Socialist Party. Before and after the merger of the American Federation of Labor and the Congress of Industrial Organizations in 1955, the dominant mood in American unionism was not to pursue a radical agenda. George Meany, for many years president of the AFL–CIO, was no political firebrand. True, some union activists, such as Walter Reuther in the automobile industry and Cesar Chavez, who organized migrant fruit-pickers in California into the United Farm Workers, agitated for, and achieved, reforms. But the combined power of corporate capitalism and federal government support for it has proven, historically, difficult for unions to overcome.

In 1947, for example, Senator Robert Taft steered the Taft–Hartley Act through Congress. Overtly anti-labour, it made the closed shop illegal, held unions liable in breach of contract cases and also prevented them from contributing to election funds. It also introduced loyalty oaths for union leaders, who had to proclaim themselves non-communist. While it was being discussed in Congress, two members of the House of Representatives travelled to Pennsylvania to debate its merits. One, a Republican, was for the legislation, while the other, a Democrat, was against it. Thirteen years later, Richard Nixon and John F. Kennedy were to participate in further political debates. The Taft–Hartley Act, moreover, effectively solidified links between trade unions and the Democrats that were only weakened in the 1980s when Ronald Reagan succeeded in gaining the support of many so-called 'blue-collar' workers.

Yet in 1981, the president himself demonstrated his attitude towards unionism. Ronald Reagan dismissed over twelve thousand air-traffic controllers who had defied the law by striking. Edmund Morris suggests that the then leaders of the Soviet Union might have taken note of a photograph 'of the leader of the air-traffic controllers' union being taken to prison in chains'. Furthermore, 'as Sovietologist Richard Pipes remarked, [it] was the kind of image totalitarians understood. It showed that the president was no mere cowboy, but a sheriff capable of hard action.'[12] The values of frontier individualism might always be preferred to those of union collectivism: even by a president who could boast of leading the first strike ever of the Screen Actors Guild.

So class antagonisms have, in the main, been expressed in terms of the ongoing battles between capital and labour in America. Class struggle occurs within the ideological confines that are the outcome of continuing faith in the 'American Dream'. In turn this renders alternative visions of society either threatening or irrelevant. But class represents still a formidable faultline in the American polity. For contained within the idea of class is a core understanding that American society is stratified, and that to understand this reality a radical vision is required. It follows that the radicalism that has promoted social change within the United States, whether in terms of civil rights or workers' rights, flows from a common discontent with the existing social contract. And this much is also evident in tracing the contours of other faultlines as well.

## Gender

If particular care and attention is not paid to the ladies, we are determined to foment a rebellion, and will not hold ourselves bound by any laws in which we have no voice or representation.
*Abigail Adams, letter to John Adams (1776)*

It was Abigail Adams who also admonished her husband, as he took part in the political discussions that led to the formation of the American republic, to 'remember the Ladies, and be more generous and favorable to them than your ancestors.' John Adams and his fellow Founding Fathers did not take much notice of her. As Gunnar Myrdal pointed out, in *An American Dilemma*, the issues surrounding the status of women – and indeed children – in American society were obviously similar to those that bore directly upon the 'Negro problem'. Moreover, in the battle for civil and political rights,

> women suffragists received their political education from the Abolitionist movement. Women like Angelina Grimke, Sarah Grimke, and Abbey Kelly began their public careers by speaking for Negro emancipation and only gradually came to fight for women's rights. . . . [T]he leading male advocates of woman suffrage before the Civil War were such Abolitionists as William Lloyd Garrison, Henry Ward Beecher, Wendell Phillips, Horace Greeley and Frederick Douglass.[13]

If the rhetoric of liberty and equality were to mean anything, not only did the Constitution have to be colour-blind, but it also should not privilege roughly half of humanity at the expense of the other half.

The Women's Rights Convention, held in the Wesleyan Chapel in Seneca Falls in 1848, thus approved the 'Declaration of Sentiments' drafted by Elizabeth Cady Stanton. Having outlined the extent of contemporary discrimination against women, it included an obvious demand: '[B]ecause women do feel themselves aggrieved, oppressed, and fraudulently deprived of their most sacred rights, we insist that they have immediate admission to all the rights and privileges which belong to them as citizens of these United States.' It took another seventy-two years for women to gain the right to vote.

The history of the women's movement in the United States was defined initially in terms of this political struggle. And yet at the same time it was clear that to achieve the right to vote was to gain only partial acceptance of the equality of women in what remained, throughout the nineteenth century and beyond, a patriarchal society. In 1855, Lucy Stone became the first recorded example of a woman who kept her own name after marriage; others who followed her practice were known as 'Lucy Stoners'. Only in 1872 did Congress pass legislation requiring women employed by the federal government to be paid equally for equal work. In the following year, however, the federal legislature acted in response to a moralist crusade instigated by the founder of the New York Society for the Suppression of Vice, Anthony Comstock. The so-called 'Comstock Act' revised the law governing the federal postal service and, in addition to prohibiting the sending of obscene literature through the mail, included in its definition of obscenity any information that promoted contraception or abortion. Comstock, who personally policed his act, continued to promote his puritan agenda. It was not until 1936 that the Supreme Court ruled that information on birth control did not constitute obscene material.

In 1921, the year after the nineteenth amendment to the Constitution had been ratified, giving women the right to vote, Margaret Sanger established the American Birth Control League; in 1942 it would become the Federation of Planned Parenthood. In 1923, a constitutional amendment was proposed in Congress, which failed to pass, but which was subsequently routinely reintroduced until in 1943 its wording was revised and it became known as the Equal Rights Amendment. The coincidence in the timing of these initiatives reflects the twin concerns of the women's movement after suffrage had been achieved. As Gunnar Myrdal pointed out in the 1940s, the problems of a 'paternalistic order of society', although diminishing, still determined the status of women in America, but '[i]n the final analysis, women are still hindered in their competition by the function of procreation.'[14] If there were those who saw the battle between labour and capital as a dispute over the ownership of the means of production, for women, then, the pursuit of equality might also revolve around control over the right of reproduction.

Just as the women's movement had been part of the fight against slavery in the nineteenth century, so its contemporary impetus emerged from the struggle for civil rights in the 1950s and beyond. With the issue of the vote long settled, its energies could be focused on other areas of discrimination. The 1964 Civil Rights Act prohibited discrimination in the workplace not only on grounds of race, religion and national origin, but also on the basis of gender. The Equal Employment Opportunity Commission was set up to review cases of discrimination, but what was perceived as its lacklustre performance in pursuing the 50,000 sex discrimination complaints brought to it during the first five years of its existence led to demands for more activism. By 1966, the National Organization of Women (NOW) had been formed. One of its founders was Betty Friedan, whose book *The Feminine Mystique* (1963) had deconstructed the traditional view of a woman's role in American society, and was a source of inspiration for the emerging women's liberation movement.

In 1970, Gloria Steinem, a leading activist in the movement – and the architect of *Ms* magazine – argued in a commencement address at Vassar College that the 'movement that some call "feminist" but should more accurately be called humanist [was] a movement that is an integral part of rescuing this country from its old, expensive patterns of elitism, racism and violence'. The following year, Friedan and Steinem were among the founders of the National Women's Political Caucus, which supports women running for political office. It was not until 1984 that Emily's List (Early Money Is Like Yeast: It Makes the Dough Rise) was established to help fund feminist candidates, but the political impact of the women's movement, and the way in which it has altered perceptions of gender issues in the United States, should not be under-rated. On the other hand, however, a ten-year effort to ratify the Equal Rights Amendment, which was finally passed by Congress in 1972, failed: when the Constitutional time limit was reached, only thirty-five of the thirty-eight states needed to agree its incorporation in the document had voted in favour of it.

In 1973 the Supreme Court's decision in the case of *Roe* v. *Wade* meant that anti-abortion laws in forty-six states were now unconstitutional. The political repercussions – and shockwaves – of the case are resonating still in American society and culture: the arguments over abortion remain at the centre of contemporary political debate. For individuals, the issue is expressed in the language of rights: the 'right to choose' confronts the 'right to life'. But advocates of each actively campaign for the support of the state: seeking either legal protection – as given in *Roe* v. *Wade* – or legal prohibition in a situation where individuals still face a complex and difficult decision. As Norman Mailer – not necessarily regarded as a supporter of feminism – put it, writing in 1972, 'if at its most tragic abortion is the decision to kill the memory of an extraordinary night, and so can be cruel and unendurable, close on occasion to creating insanity in the woman, still abortion is the objective correlative of sanity.' It is an admission that '[m]y nature is divided between the maximum of my romantic moments and the minimum of my daily self-calculation, too divided to permit this child to live.' Mailer suggests that 'abortion is therefore an act of self-recognition (which is a step to sanity).' And yet, at the same time, he admits that 'the decision not to have an abortion is another kind of sanity, which states, "I am committed to the best moments I have known and take my truth from that".'[15] The intellectual may see both sides of the divide, but religious groups – notably fundamentalists – who try to set a strict moral agenda for individuals and the nation remain as committed in their advocacy of the 'right to life' as liberals – and feminists – are to the 'right to choose'. Pro-life campaigners have picketed abortion clinics. Some have gone further. A number of doctors and nurses have been killed in attacks, and the more radical pro-life groups see nothing incongruous in espousing violence that might result in death as a means to their ends. In this war, there is little room for compromise. In 1989, as a result of its decision in *Webster* v. *Reproductive Services*, the Supreme Court sanctioned the right of individual states to prevent public money being spent on abortion services, and to ban public hospitals from carrying them out. The battle continues: in the courts, in the media and on the streets.

Feminism has helped to revolutionize the status of women in contemporary American society. In many spheres of working, cultural, sporting and social life, glass ceilings have been either shattered or splintered. And yet, barriers can take a long time to come down. Sally Ride is widely regarded as the first American female astronaut. In fact, she was the first to go into space: twelve women were part of the original astronaut programme, and became contemporaries of John Glenn, the first American to orbit the Earth. None of them were selected to participate in the Mercury, Gemini or Apollo missions. John Kennedy's famous pledge had been, after all, to put a *man* on the moon and return him safely to earth before the 1960s came to a close.

The campaign for women's rights in American society – like the achievement of civil rights in general – thus remains a struggle. Moreover for contemporary activists, the goal of equality is still elusive, not least because of divisions within the women's movement itself. So Christina Hoff Sommers, for example, suggested in *Who Stole Feminism?* (1995) that there is now a distinction between 'equity feminism' – the campaign for equal rights – and 'gender feminism', which has become a dominant force in academic circles, in women's studies programmes in universities. In an interview in the *Dartmouth Review* in 1998, Sommers argued that it seems now that '[o]nly women from the cultural left have the right to interpret the lives of women. Conservative women, politically moderate women, libertarian women, traditionally religious women, have all been thoroughly marginalized.' So while 'equity feminism' still exists, 'the reasonable feminism on the campus has been hijacked by a group of rather eccentric women who view American society as oppressive and patriarchal.'[16] For non-violent direct action and black power, read 'equity' and 'gender' feminism.

At the beginning of the 1990s, Susan Faludi published *Backlash: The Undeclared War Against American Women*, which explored the idea that the successes of the women's movement had sparked a reaction against it, founded in the fear that women were indeed on the verge of gaining equality. Indeed, it is possible to see such a phenomenon in the establishment of such organizations as the Promise Keepers, led by Bill McCartney, a former football coach at the University of Colorado. Right-wing, fundamentalist-inclined and well financed, the Promise Keepers have little time for either equity or gender feminists. Another prominent member of the organization, Tony Evans, urges men to 'reclaim' the role of leadership within the family, arguing that '[o]ver the last thirty years, this role reversal has given rise to a feminist movement specifically designed to assert the role of women. Now a lot of women don't like to hear me say this, but I believe that feminists of the more aggressive persuasion are frustrated women unable to find the proper male leadership.'[17] That view might lead to an interesting debate with, say, Betty Friedan or Gloria Steinem. Effectively, the Promise Keepers stand against the women's movement again focuses attention on the politics of gender. Bill McCartney has been a supporter of Operation Rescue, a militant anti-abortion group, and the agenda that he and his followers support indeed represents a formidable backlash against the progress towards greater equality and civil rights made during the last half of the twentieth century.

The Promise Keepers speak to those who feel threatened. After the political and social upheavals of the 1960s, and coincident with the nation's failure to win the war in Vietnam, the traditional dominant figure in American society – the white, Anglo-Saxon, Protestant male – seemed a haunted and threatened species. A perceived 'crisis of masculinity' gave rise to a number of responses, of which the Promise Keepers appears as one of the more extreme. Another analysis of the condition of contemporary American males came from a former activist against the Vietnam war, Robert Bly, whose 'book about men', *Iron John* (1990), combined a mixture of pop psychology and anthropological advocacy and had widespread populist appeal. Bly argued that men's psychological growth has been stunted as a result of inadequate fathering and the lack of the mentoring that is essential to their development from child to adulthood. As Bly wrote in a contribution to another book, *Wingspan* (1992), '[i]n no traditional society was the training of young boys left in the hands of the father alone. The entire male community participated in this important work. Our father didn't have these connections either – he was as lost as we are.' Corporate capitalism is once more to blame for reinforcing male role models that provide economic rather than emotional security. Bly's view of the average American man in the 1950s 'lonely crowd' is a familiar stereotype, examples of which could still be seen in the 1980s. This man 'got to work early, laboured responsibly, supported his wife and children and admired discipline. Reagan is a sort of mummified version of this dogged type.' Such men had 'many qualities' that 'were strong and positive' and yet 'underneath the charm and the bluff there was, and there remains, much isolation, deprivation and passivity.'[18] Bly's solution to the problem of the dysfunctional American male comes via group therapy sessions, which may involve poetry readings and can take the form of spiritual retreats. This, then, becomes a contemporary model for men's liberation: for its advocates, it complements rather than attacks the women's movement. What it reflects is a realization that social and cultural change can be embraced by both men and women, and this may yet bring about political repercussions, as stereotypical gender roles are broken down, discussed and reformulated.

# Sexuality

That summer – it was 1978 – estimates of the gay population of San Francisco ranged from 75,000 to 150,000. If the oft-cited figure of 100,000 were correct, this meant that in this city of less than 700,000 people, approximately one out of every five adults and one out of every three or four voters was gay. A great proportion of these people – half of them or more – had moved into the city within the past eight years. . . . At that time most San Franciscans still contrived to ignore the growing gay population in their midst.

Frances FitzGerald, Cities on a Hill (1986)

As with gender, so sexuality has emerged as a political faultline in contemporary American society. In *Cities on a Hill* Frances FitzGerald described the Castro, 'the first gay neighborhood in the country', which by the end of the 1970s was a significant influence in the municipal politics of San Francisco. More than that,

> Castro activists thought of it as the cutting edge. Gay liberation was a civil rights struggle, but it was much more than that. Now that the feminist movement had passed its radical phase, gay activists saw themselves as the avant-garde of the sexual revolution and the revolutionary change in sex and gender roles. Specifically, their goal was to overturn one of the oldest and strongest taboos in the culture, but beyond that it was to challenge all the conventions surrounding the 'traditional' nuclear family.

Gay liberation, however, like all movements for civil rights in America, has encountered strong political opposition, and has had its share of martyrs.

It first attracted attention in New York. In 1969, a raid by the police on the Stonewall Inn in Greenwich village, 'a bar', wrote FitzGerald, 'that catered to effeminate young street people and drag queens among others, provoked a riot, out of which came the Gay Liberation Movement'. It became part of the contemporary counterculture, and many activists migrated to the west coast – despite the fact that Ronald Reagan was governor of California from 1967 to 1974, and had promised at the start of his administration not to pass any gay rights legislation. Nevertheless, by the mid-1970s, the political power of gay activists in San Francisco was beginning to bring about a change in the cultural climate. In 1977, Harvey Milk successfully campaigned as a gay candidate for election to the city Board of Supervisors. The following year, he was actively involved in defeating the initiative put forward by John Briggs, a state senator, who, with the support of fundamentalists, had proposed that any schoolteacher who appeared to promote homosexuality should be sacked. As FitzGerald notes, for Briggs, the 'moral decay in this country', of which gay liberation was a part, had become 'a greater danger than Communism'.[19] But even former governor Reagan opposed the Briggs initiative as a threat to civil liberties. It was voted down in the 1978 elections in California. Three weeks later, Harvey Milk was assassinated.

If Susan Faludi identified a backlash against the women's movement, so too was gay liberation attacked during the 1980s and 1990s, not least because of the high-profile issue of AIDS. The AIDS virus, first identified in the United States in 1981, became identified in the popular mind with two groups whose lifestyles ran counter to those of the moral mainstream: intravenous drug users and homosexuals. For fundamentalists, the scourge of AIDs could be presented as divine retribution upon the gay community. But the disease also provided a context for the Supreme Court decision in *Bowers* v. *Hardwick* (1986), which permits states to pass anti-sodomy laws, criminalizing homosexual sex on the grounds that it runs counter to inherited social, moral and religious traditions. A similar argument could be used to justify other forms of discrimination against gays, such that political gains made by the gay liberation movement were effectively reversed.

The political impact of anti-gay sentiment was felt by the then newly elected President Clinton in 1992, attempting to honour a campaign pledge to remove discrimination against homosexuals who joined the military. Opposition, not least from within the military establishment, forced him into retreat. Eventually a policy was decided: 'don't ask, don't tell'. The government would not investigate the sexual orientation of those serving in the armed forces, but the military could still prevent those who were openly gay from enlisting. It was an unsatisfactory compromise. For the president, however, the issue was clear. In a speech in Boston on 25 April 1993, he commented on the controversy: 'You are free to discriminate in your judgments about any of us – how we look, how we behave, what we are. Make your judgments. But if we are willing to live together according to certain rules of conduct, we should be able to do so. That is the issue for America.'

It was also the issue for individual states to judge. In Colorado – where the Promise Keepers had found their leader – an amendment to the state constitution effectively reversed any state laws protecting gay rights. In the resulting court case, *Romer* v. *Evans*, the Colorado State Court declared the amendment unconstitutional: the state could not discriminate on the grounds of sexual orientation, and that to do so was contrary to the fourteenth amendment: the equal-protection clause of the Constitution. The case was appealed to the Supreme Court, which in May 1996 upheld the Colorado Court's decision, but on different grounds. In Justice Kennedy's opinion, agreed by the majority of the Court, '[w]e cannot accept the view that . . . prohibition on specific legal protections does no more than deprive homosexuals of special rights. To the contrary, the amendment imposes a special disability upon those persons alone. Homosexuals are forbidden the safeguards that others enjoy or may seek without constraint.' Kennedy thus argued that '[a] State cannot so deem a class of persons a stranger to its laws.' President Clinton approved the decision, commenting that the Colorado amendment had been 'bad policy . . . inconsistent with our common values'. Yet given its stance in *Bowers* v. *Hardwick* it seemed that the Supreme Court was showing signs of inconsistency.

Indeed, Justice Scalia, in his dissenting opinion in the *Romer* case – supported by Chief Justice Rehnquist and Justice Clarence Thomas – argued that '[i]f it is rational to criminalize the conduct, surely it is rational to deny special favor and protection to those with a self-avowed tendency or desire to engage in the conduct.' The amendment was 'Colorado's reasonable effort to preserve traditional American moral values'. The majority opinion meant that the Court had been forced to 'take sides in this culture war'. Scalia thus pointed out that, for example, a law firm is able to refuse to give employment to an individual 'because the applicant is a Republican; because he is an adulterer; because he went to the wrong prep school or belongs to the wrong country club; because he eats snails; because he is a womanizer; because she wears real-animal fur; or even because he hates the Chicago Cubs.' But if the basis of the rejection is disapproval because the applicant is gay, then this contradicts the decision of the Association of American Law Schools that its members be willing to hire homosexuals. Scalia believes that gays should not enjoy such 'special protection' simply because of their sexual orientation.

The Colorado state legislature remained equally unsympathetic to gays. In 2000 it approved a 'no homosexual marriage' law, which also denied the legality of same-sex marriages carried out in other states. For Donald Cavanaugh, editor of a Colorado-based internet site called Second Class Action, the arguments presented in support of this 'are all religious and moralistic'. However, he argues, '[h]omosexuality has no moral relevance in the world of civil law. Morality is an issue for religion not state governments. The morality of homosexuality is a religious debate, not a secular one.' And yet, this misses the point. Historically, religion and morality have been fundamental to the shaping of American culture and society, and continue to influence profoundly the nation's laws.

# Conclusion: The Culture of Prohibition

I saw the best minds of my generation destroyed by madness,
starving hysterical naked,
dragging themselves through the negro streets at dawn looking
for an angry fix.

*Allen Ginsberg, 'Howl' (1956)*

Ginsberg was right to call his poem 'Howl'. Whether the issue is race, class, gender or sexuality, the tradition of protest in American society cannot be separated from the history of resistance to change, which has been a fundamental characteristic of the nation's political culture. At the core of both protest and resistance, moreover, there lies the influence of religion. If the civil rights and black power movements gained their impetus from the support of black churches and the militancy of the Nation of Islam, so the symbol of white racism is the burning cross of the Ku Klux Klan, and contemporary white separatist groups have links to religious fundamentalism. In the nineteenth century, the Gospel of Wealth, which justified capitalist accumulation, was preached with the same fervour as the Social Gospel, demanding greater economic and social justice. Religious groups such as the Promise Keepers establish and maintain a strict moral agenda that sets them against feminists and activists for gay rights alike.

So religion provides a way of mapping the two sides of many of the political divisions within American society. Radical and reactionary, religion provides a moral compass that is a useful guide to political outlooks. Abolitionism was founded upon religious sentiment. So too was Prohibition. Yet contemporary attitudes towards alcohol – and drugs – in America, while shaped by faith, are also the product of history. In this sense, it is no accident that the success of abolitionism in many ways provided an impetus towards prohibition, particularly in the south. As the political momentum that would result in the eighteenth amendment grew during the early years of the twentieth century, a traveller in the south could observe that in that region '[t]he presence of the negro . . . is a tower of strength to the prohibitionist.' Fear of the impact of alcohol upon the now freed slaves was used as one more political device to reinforce networks of power and control in a society that had moved from oppression to repression. When Gunnar Myrdal was researching *An American Dilemma*, the fact that the consumption of alcohol in the south was segregated struck him forcefully: 'In Mississippi, which is an absolutely dry state, the author saw more hard drinking than he has ever before witnessed.

Will Rogers is said to have remarked that "Mississippi will hold faithful and steadfast to prohibition as long as the voters can stagger to the polls." '[20]

Prohibition, though, appealed to a wider cross-section of the nation than those who saw it as a way of reinforcing political controls over a racial minority. In the midwest, Henry Ford, 'a temperance crusader', was among those who endorsed the decision taken in a popular referendum that led to Michigan becoming a 'dry' state even before the eighteenth amendment took effect. Yet as his biographer points out, '[t]he Prohibition experiment transferred some $2 billion a year from brewers, distillers, and their shareholders into the hands of murderers and crooks, making possible the extraordinarily embedded role that organised crime plays in modern American life.' For those who supported the attempt to force temperance on an evidently unwilling nation, however, faith defied logic. So Ford himself 'threatened, in the event that Prohibition were repealed, to shut down his production line'.[21] Mike Gray recounts the conversion to common sense of another pioneer of America's automobile industry. Henry Joy, a founder of the Packard Motor Car Company, eventually took a more sanguine view of the issue. He was in favour of Prohibition until forced to accept that it would not work, and admitted that: 'I made a mistake. I was stupidly wrong. America must open its eyes and recognize that human nature cannot be changed by legal enactment.'[22] But even after the eighteenth amendment was repealed, this would not stop further crusades, inspired once more by racist fear and religious fervour.

Until 1903, those who were deprived of alcohol could drink Coca Cola instead; it contained cocaine. But for most of the twentieth century – and beyond – America's battle against drugs has both stigmatized and criminalized the use and abuse of certain substances, and has had a number of social repercussions. Drugs were a threat, not least because of their supposed connection with racial minorities. As David Musto argues, '[t]he Chinese and their custom of opium smoking were closely watched after their entry into the United States about 1870,' while in the south there was the fear that 'Negro cocaine users might become oblivious of their prescribed bounds and attack white society.' The result was that by 1875 San Francisco had passed a local law that illegalized the smoking of opium in 'opium dens', and southern representatives in Congress saw the political capital that could be made from supporting the anti-narcotic legislation introduced in the House of Representatives in 1913 by Francis Harrison, a Democrat from New York and a member of Tammany Hall. The measure was passed the following year. By then, according to Musto,

[p]rominent newspapers, physicians, pharmacists, and congressmen believed opiates and cocaine predisposed habitués towards insanity and crime. They were widely seen as substances associated with foreigners or alien subgroups. Cocaine raised the spectre of the wild Negro, opium the devious Chinese, morphine the tramps in the slums; it was feared that use of all these drugs was spreading into the 'higher classes'.[23]

Coinciding with the campaign to enforce temperance through Prohibition, and gaining support too from those whose religion sponsored such moral crusades, the control of narcotics might be achieved by simple congressional legislation rather than by the sledgehammer of constitutional amendment.

The Harrison Act required anyone selling opiates and cocaine to be licensed. Doctors could still prescribe them. But shortly after it became law, its full impact was felt when those enforcing it argued that drug addiction was not a disease, and that therefore addicts could not be said to be under the care of doctors, who could then legitimately prescribe them their drugs as part of a treatment. As Steven Duke and Albert Gross observe, '[t]he courts at first seemed to reject this bizarre interpretation', but by 1919, and again against the background of Prohibition, the Supreme Court, in *Webb* v. *United States*, 'upheld the constitutionality of the Act and the criminal prosecution of a physician who prescribed for addict maintenance and the pharmacist who filled the prescription'. The repercussions of this decision were felt during and after the Prohibition era: the profits from the illegal trade in alcohol provided organized crime with the capital to diversify into the drugs trade when the eighteenth amendment was repealed. 'The underworld took over where the Court had forbidden medical doctors to tread, in the maintenance of addicts.'[24] At the same time, as the provisions of the Harrison Act were strictly enforced, so the prison population grew. By 1928, among the federal prison population, those convicted as a result of the Act far outnumbered those who had broken the law on alcohol prohibition.

In 1930, the Federal Bureau of Narcotics was established, and Harry Anslinger was appointed as its head. Mike Gray quotes Anslinger's biographer, John McWilliams, describing his subject as 'a cross between William Jennings Bryan and Reverend Jerry Falwell': a fundamentalist crusader against drugs. Like J. Edgar Hoover, Anslinger's influence ultimately lay in his longevity: he controlled the FBN until the 1960s. In the 1930s, he was instrumental in creating the climate of opinion that led to passage of the Marijuana Tax Act of 1937, which effectively outlawed the drug. Until the mid-1930s, according to Gray, '[o]utside of the temperance organizations and a handful of lawmen, most Americans had never heard of marijuana, but along the Mexican border it was a different story.' The economic depression influenced attitudes towards Mexican workers: they became stigmatized as the Chinese had before them, and their drug use magnified their threat to American society. The bandwagon started to roll. 'Once again the specter of superhuman, sex-crazed savages sent a ripple of fear through the South, and once again it proved irresistible to politicians and the press. The Hearst news media – including radio stations – were particularly active in spreading accounts of this new scourge.' Yet by the time Congress decided to act, there were still some who appeared unenlightened. Sam Rayburn, when asked in the House of Representatives about the bill that would ban the drug, replied that he thought '[i]t has something to do with something that is called marihuana. I believe it is a narcotic of some kind.'[25] When marijuana too was made illegal, the main framework of America's contemporary policy on drugs had been constructed.

Since then, the nation's 'war on drugs' has continued, boosted on occasions – notably during the Reagan presidency – for political purposes, but ultimately, as its critics suggest, self-defeating and unwinnable. And yet those involved in it, from politicians, to enforcement agencies, to drug-traffickers themselves, all have a vested interest in maintaining the status quo. Decriminalizing banned substances would have a severe impact on all aspects of the drug economy, and, as some critics have argued, would also threaten fundamental aspects of the nation's existing power structure. Thus, the war on drugs becomes another example of the influence of the 'military-industrial complex' in national politics. It helps to shape foreign policy by identifying those nations that – and individuals who – threaten the United States through producing and trafficking in drugs. Domestically, anti-drugs laws result in the imprisonment of predominantly impoverished and non-white members of the community, who otherwise might represent a threat to existing social, economic and political structures. In this context, it is revealing that a study published in June 2000 by the Human Rights Watch found that up to 90 per cent of those imprisoned in state prisons for drug offences are black: another form of racial profiling.

Contemporary attitudes towards illicit drugs in the United States are thus rooted in history, and demonstrate that the combination of religious moralism, racist scare-mongering and desire to maintain the political and economic status quo that can be seen again and again in patterns of resistance to demands for radical social change. From this perspective, the nation that sees its origins in the liberal values of the Declaration of Independence and its history as a struggle to extend them to wider sections of its community also attempts to maintain a cultural agenda that is often framed by a desire to conserve the traditional social order. It is the fundamental tension between these two essentially incompatible goals that creates the dynamic that defines the faultlines in its political culture. Religion provides a context within which the development of these opposing views can be understood. And so missionaries and crusaders will continue to debate the future of the nation according to their distinctive interpretations of its traditions, its heritage and its past.

# In Country

My dear Rick, when will you realize that in the world today, isolationism is no longer a practical policy.
*Sydney Greenstreet to Humphrey Bogart in* Casablanca (*1942*)

In his farewell address to the nation on 11 January 1989, Ronald Reagan – who, as a Hollywood actor, according to industry mythology, had been considered for the part eventually played by Humphrey Bogart in *Casablanca* – reminisced. He confessed he had been thinking of the 'shining city upon a hill'. The president explained his preoccupation to his audience:

The phrase comes from John Winthrop, who wrote it to describe the America he imagined. What he imagined was important because he was an early Pilgrim, an early freedom man. He journeyed here on what today we'd call a little wooden boat; and like the other Pilgrims, he was looking for a home that would be free. I've spoken of the shining city all my political life, but I don't know if I ever quite communicated what I saw when I said it. But in my mind it was a tall, proud city built on rocks stronger than oceans, windswept, God-blessed, and teeming with people of all kinds living in harmony and peace; a city with free ports that hummed with commerce and creativity. And if there had to be city walls, the walls had doors and the doors were open to anyone with the will and the heart to get here. That's how I saw it, and see it still.

Reagan then asked the rhetorical question:

And how stands the city on this winter night? More prosperous, more secure, and happier than it was eight years ago. But more than that:

after two hundred years, two centuries, she still stands strong and true on the granite ridge, and her glow has held steady no matter what storm. And she's still a beacon, still a magnet for all who must have freedom, for all the pilgrims from all the lost places who are hurtling through the darkness, toward home.

It was a typical and classic statement of American patriotism.

Winthrop's image of the puritans' colonial settlement resonates in American political culture. But the idea of the 'city on a hill' may be interpreted in differing ways. Does it mean that America is a fortress, strategically situated to avoid invasion from the world outside? Or, as Reagan suggested, is it to act as a beacon, a place of pilgrimage for others who wish to emulate its example and a stockade from which further 'errands into the widerness' may be launched? American attitudes towards the wider world often have been framed in terms of these competing visions. The nation's foreign policy has thus been seen in terms of phases of withdrawal and engagement – isolationism and internationalism – within the sphere of international relations.

Other perspectives may be more illuminating. For a vital impulse that can be traced throughout the nation's history is that of the expansion of political control across the continent, and the extension of political influence across the world. Articulated in the language of 'manifest destiny', this was a secular version of the 'providential mission' that had inspired Winthrop and his followers. At the same time, however, American foreign policy – like that of any other nation – is framed by contemporary perceptions of its self-interest. In these terms, as the United States has grown from relative obscurity to undeniable ubiquity as the world's most powerful country, politically, economically, militarily and culturally, there have been those who have aggressively cold-shouldered the wider world, and those who have sought to achieve their ambitions through international networks of diplomacy and alliances.

As the most influential voice in foreign affairs, moreover, the president has been able to emphasize either a unilateral or a multilateral approach to this pursuit of the national self-interest. But even chief executives may be constrained by political events, by others with political influence, and ultimately by public opinion. Some presidents, then, have been able to define the contours of American foreign policy, not least through establishing doctrines that have acted like marker buoys, guiding the nation on its voyages through international waters. But others have found themselves overwhelmed by the shoals and eddies stirred up as a result of their encounters with the wider world, their political ambitions shipwrecked. To venture out of the 'city on a hill' and go 'in country' is to take a political risk: for dealing with the world outside may prove to be a more complex task than first it might appear.

## Talking the Talk

The woods are lovely, dark and deep
But I have promises to keep
And miles to go before I sleep
And miles to go before I sleep.
  *Robert Frost, 'Stopping by Woods on a Snowy Evening' (1923)*

Frost's poem was a favourite of John F. Kennedy's, who invited the poet to read another of his works at the presidential inaugural ceremony in 1961. That occasion, though, was made memorable by Kennedy's own words and his promise that 'we shall pay any price, bear any burden, meet any hardship, support any friend, oppose any foe to assure the survival and the success of liberty.' Throughout the history of the republic, presidential rhetoric provides a key to understanding the contemporary culture and dominant political perspectives that together form the crucible within which American foreign policy has been formed.

Consider George Washington. In 1796, his farewell address established the tradition that others have since followed – including Ronald Reagan almost two centuries later – of using the pulpit of the presidency to offer some reflections upon the past and future of the republic. In terms of the nation's foreign policy, moreover, Washington's advice has often been interpreted as an argument in favour of American isolationism. But it is not necessarily so. The president who had won the battle for colonial self-determination thus saw clearly that, having become an independent nation, the United States had to chart its foreign policy so as to move away from involvement in the contemporary world of European power politics. In his view,

Europe has a set of primary interests which to us have none or a very remote relation. Hence she must be engaged in frequent controversies, the causes of which are essentially foreign to our concerns. Hence, therefore, it must be unwise in us to implicate ourselves by artificial ties in the ordinary vicissitudes of her politics or the ordinary combinations and collisions of her friendships or enmities.

Here, the president is advocating not disengagement from the world –
isolationism – but rather that the United States should not become
embroiled in the imperial adventures of another country. Indeed,
'[w]hy, by interweaving our destiny with that of any part of Europe,
entangle our peace and prosperity in the toils of European ambition, rivalship, interest, humor or caprice?' It was a common-sense
approach to defining America's self-interest. And it led Washington
to conclude that '[i]t is our true policy to steer clear of permanent
alliances with any portion of the foreign world' (a sentiment reiterated
by Thomas Jefferson in his first inaugural address in 1801 when he
defined one of 'the essential principles of our Government' as 'entangling alliances with none'). In other words, America's future should
not be hostage to the political fortunes of other nations, although
Washington also recognized that 'we may safely trust to temporary
alliances for extraordinary emergencies', if the United States itself
was threatened.

Washington's farewell address in 1796 became a symbol for those
who later advocated isolationism, while overlooking the fact that his
advice was written for his contemporaries rather than for posterity.
Once again the politics of nostalgia becomes a formidable force in
helping to frame political attitudes and ideas. The president's words
become articles of faith. In terms of providing a guide to the nation's
foreign policy, moreover, Washington's farewell address was only a
start. A little over a quarter of a century later, America's declaration
of its international independence was given yet more force in the
first of the doctrines that have periodically attempted to define the
nation's perspective on the wider world.

As the products of the interplay between cultural and ideological
forces in American political life, foreign policy doctrines thus have
been articulated as much for a domestic as for an international audience. National resolve has been stiffened by an appeal to these
generalized principles defining America's conduct abroad. Doctrines
have acted as talismans to guide the nation through the intricacies of
foreign affairs. They also have incorporated the cultural and ideological assumptions of America's liberal democratic tradition, reflecting
the nation's sense of its unique place in the world, the power of its
example, its concept of mission and its preference for unilateral action
in foreign affairs.

In 1823, therefore, the last president from the so-called 'Virginia
dynasty' – following Washington, Jefferson and Madison – included
in his Annual Message to Congress the statements that became the
enduring principles of the Monroe Doctrine. It was prompted by
the concern that European imperialists were planning to recapture the

former Spanish colonies in Latin America, which, during the previous eight years, had joined the United States and Haiti as independent republics. America's self-interest was again defined in opposition to that of Europe: it had more in common with its New World neighbours to the south than the Old World it had left behind. For Monroe, '[w]ith the movements in this hemisphere we are of necessity more immediately connected, and by causes which must be obvious to all enlightened and impartial observers.' If the issue was the preservation of independence and republicanism in the face of attempts to reimpose imperialism, the United States had clear principles at stake. Monroe challenged all those European nations who threatened the Americas.

> We owe it, therefore, to candor and to the amicable relations existing between the United States and those powers to declare that we should consider any attempt on their part to extend their system to any portion of this hemisphere as dangerous to our peace and safety. . . . [w]ith the Governments who have declared their independence and maintained it, and whose independence we have acknowledged, we could not view any interposition for the purpose of oppressing them, or controlling in any manner their destiny, by any European power in any other light than as the manifestation of an unfriendly disposition toward the United States.

So Europe should leave the Americas alone, although the circumlocutions that Monroe employed demonstrate that the hope was that the language of diplomacy would be sufficient to achieve that objective. In practice, the United States was not yet powerful enough to resist European incursions into what it came, in time, to regard as its backyard, if not its own dominion. Again, though, what Monroe expressed was not an isolationist sentiment. Rather, it acknowledged that the nation's self-interest remained distinct and separate from the political ambitions of Europe.

Cecil Crabb indeed argues that '[i]solationist mythology to the contrary, state papers like President Washington's Farewell Address, the Monroe doctrine, and other sources did not commit the United States absolutely and without qualification to a general position of noninvolvement or 'nonentanglement' in the affairs of the world, or even to a blanket policy of nonparticipation in the affairs of continental Europe.'[1] And as Albert Weinberg pointed out, Americans should reflect upon the idea that '[t]he true objective of their historic caution was not isolation . . . but an ideal interpreted to the nation by Washington as 'the command of its own fortunes".'[2] What America desired was freedom of manoeuvre in both domestic and foreign affairs, unhindered by the power politics of European empires. Monroe's message came, after all, only eleven years after the war of 1812, during which the British had set fire to the White House.

Nevertheless Washington's farewell address and Monroe's Doctrine have been associated with an attitude of isolationism that seems to run counter to the ideology of the Truman Doctrine: the basis of America's international interventionism following the Second World War. On the other hand, the cultural and ideological forces underpinning American perspectives on the wider world imply an essential continuity in the nation's outlook, and the major doctrines of the nineteenth and twentieth centuries complement rather than contradict each other.

During the early years of the republic, therefore, America's mission involved the gradual domestic creation of Madison's 'extended sphere': the continental consolidation of the republican democratic ideal. That purpose was introspective, and as such it was sustained by a doctrine that was a warning to the world not to interfere with America's hemispherical concerns. It was a unilateralist rather than an isolationist statement of foreign policy principle. After the Second World War, however, the mission became global in an American world of cultural certainties and ideological absolutes that its dominant religious and democratic traditions reinforced.

Indeed, as America's power increased during the nineteenth century, through territorial acquisitions justified as part of its 'Manifest Destiny', and through industrial and economic development, it appeared that the United States itself was as much a threatening presence to its immediate neighbours as Europe had been in Monroe's time. If the nation was to chart its own course in international affairs, then the Monroe Doctrine could be reinterpreted by a later generation to justify the very interventionism in Latin America that Europe had been warned against. Theodore Roosevelt's 'corollary' to the Monroe Doctrine came just four years into the 'American Century' after the United States had gained an entry into the world of European imperialism through its success in the Spanish–American war of 1898. Then it had acquired the Philippines as a colony, and Cuba as a protectorate. Now, Roosevelt argued, America's power justified further interventionism south of the border: not just Panama, but also the Dominican Republic, Haiti and Nicaragua soon would feel the force of Yankee political, economic and military ambition, setting the pattern and style of future American conduct in Latin America.

Roosevelt thus proclaimed that

[c]hronic wrongdoing, or an impotence which results in a general loosening of the ties of civilized society, may, in America, as elsewhere,

ultimately require intervention by some civilized nation, and in the Western Hemisphere the adherence of the United States to the Monroe Doctrine may force the United States, however reluctantly, in flagrant cases of such wrongdoing or impotence, to the exercise of an inter- national police power.

As the United States began to realize its potential as an actor on the world stage, it began to assume the role of defending what it defined as 'civilized' values and principles, justifying interventionism not sim- ply in Latin America but also elsewhere.

The Truman Doctrine of 1947, which mapped the contours of Cold War American foreign policy, was in some senses merely an extension of the rhetoric that had gone before, although its implications for the conduct of American foreign policy were more profound. It globalized the Monroe Doctrine and reinforced Roosevelt's 'collorary'. Whereas, in the nineteenth century, Monroe had warned European imperialists to stay out of America's hemisphere, now President Truman told the forces of international communism that America would resist them anywhere and everywhere. So communism – which Truman defined as totalitarianism – became the global enemy of democracy, and, like Theodore Roosevelt before him, the president argued that America should be a policing power. For William Appleman Williams, the argu- ment, resting as it did on the analysis of foreign policy experts like George Kennan, was flawed. So Kennan's 'famous "Long Telegram" of 22 February 1946, and the shortened version that appeared as the "X" article in the July 1947 issue of *Foreign Affairs*, provided a simplistic and self-contradictory analysis of Soviet behaviour that divided the world into two camps – The Civilised West and the Evil Eastern Empire': a characterization that would echo down the years.[3]

For Truman, in the words of his doctrine, 'totalitarian regimes imposed upon free peoples, by direct or indirect aggression, undermine the foundations of international peace and hence the security of the United States.' The president then made the commitment: 'I believe it must be the policy of the United States to support free peoples who are resisting attempted subjugation by armed minorities or by outside pressures.' The stage was set for the battles to come: including – but not limited to – those in Korea, Cuba and also Vietnam.

In this context consider too the prophetic analysis of the Truman Doctrine by Henry Wallace in a speech at Madison Square Gardens, New York, on 31 March 1947. 'Sooner or later,' he suggested,

Truman's program of unconditional aid to anti-Soviet governments will unite the world against America and divide America against herself. . . . The Truman program must turn the world against America. At our command freedom . . . will become a catchword for reaction. Once we grant unconditional loans to the undemocratic Governments of Greece and Turkey, then, in the name of freedom, every Fascist dictator will know that he has credit in our bank. Today it is the Governments of Greece and Turkey. Tomorrow it may be Peron and Chiang Kai-shek. Our banks will give dollars; our arsenals will give weapons. When that is not enough our people will be asked to give their sons.

Wallace's prediction foreshadows the record of American's Cold War military interventionism, not only in Korea, but also at the Bay of Pigs in Cuba, and then emphatically in Vietnam. However, the subsequent attempts to assimilate such experiences in America's cultural and political life have shown that the core values that influence perspectives on the wider world are deeply rooted, and it is difficult for them to be disinterred and redefined. In retrospect Americans might have preferred it had they listened to Henry rather than to Harry in 1947. To do so, however, ultimately would have been to deny the consequences of the nation's sense of its mission to promote the cause of democracy worldwide.

   Indeed, although it never acquired the dignity of a doctrine, Woodrow Wilson's rhetoric also became very influential in moulding such American perspectives on the wider world – not least because it expressed an idealist vision for the 'American Century'. In April 1917, speaking to both Houses of Congress, the president argued the case for American entry into the First World War. The significance of the moment is illustrated in Gore Vidal's fictional re-creation of it in his novel *Hollywood* (1990):

> Everything seemed unreal, the dusky ill-lit chamber, the April rain on glass, the straining faces not to mention ears, many of them cupped as half-deaf statesmen tried to amplify for themselves the voice of the nation that had broken its long silence – last heard, when? Gettysburg? 'Last best hope of earth'? Government of, by and for the people. All these ultimate, perfect, unique concepts to describe mere politics. Nations were wordless embodiments, hence, the extraordinary opportunity for the eloquent man on the right rainy April evening to articulate the collective yet inchoate ambition of the tribe.[4]

Wilson took his chance.

   On 2 April 1917, in his message declaring war on Germany, he said 'the world must be made safe for democracy. Its peace must be planted upon the tested foundations of political liberty. We have no selfish ends to serve. We desire no conquest, no dominion. We seek no indemnities for ourselves, no material compensation for the sacrifices we shall freely make.' Wilson committed the country to its democratic mission, with repercussions upon its foreign policy that have reverberated ever since.

After persuading the United States to join in the First World War, Wilson's major foreign policy achievement was to have been the peace treaty that ended it and that created the League of Nations as a forum for collective security, for which he could claim credit as a principal architect. But the Treaty of Versailles and the Covenant – that puritan word again – that established the League failed to gain the necessary support of two-thirds of the Senate, and Wilson's vision collapsed. This could be taken as evidence that America was in the grip of isolationism: rejecting engagement with the world, and turning inward on itself. Advocates of such a view, indeed, might then find justification for such a withdrawal from the world stage by selective quotations from Washington and Monroe among others to justify such sentiment. Yet even if isolationism was a contemporary characterization of American foreign policy between the wars, and became, as William Appleman Williams referred to it, 'the folklore of American foreign relations', he and other historians have argued effectively that it was a myth. The desire to avoid 'entangling alliances' may have led to an intense debate about the extent to which the nation should become involved in international institutions, but the United States has, throughout its history, remained engaged at some level with the rest of the world. Indeed, as Williams pointed out in 1954, '[i]t is both more accurate and more helpful to consider the twenties as contiguous with the present instead of viewing those years as a quixotic interlude of low-down jazz and lower grade gin, fluttering flappers and Faulkner's fiction, and bootlegging millionaires and millionaire bootleggers.'[5] Nevertheless, there was – and is – a genuine division of opinion within the country as to the extent to which America should commit itself militarily to overseas interventionism in support of the rhetorical principles espoused by presidents such as Woodrow Wilson, and, given the experience of the post-Second World War period, Harry Truman as well.

## Ordering the World

We won't lose, 'cause we're Americans.
                                    Go Tell the Spartans (*1978*)

George Washington had preferred temporary to permanent alliances with other nations. During the Cold War, however, the United States built up a number of multilateral defence pacts with the sole purpose of attempting to contain the threat of international communism yet which continue to endure. The North Atlantic Treaty Organization was set up in 1949, followed by the ANZUS Pact in 1951, the Southeast Asia Treaty Organization in 1955 and the Central Treaty Organization in 1959. Bilateral agreements with other nations – notably Israel and Saudi Arabia – reinforced these international networks. Institutions such as the United Nations, the International Monetary Fund and the World Bank buttressed the contemporary framework of collective security that the United States has had a major role in constructing, and in which it remains the actor who cannot be ignored.

If the international order has structure, it also needs purpose. During the Cold War, America's objective seemed plain: expressed in the language of 'containment' of communist expansion, principally in the developing areas of the world, and in the context of Eisenhower's 'domino theory', which suggested that if one country came under communist influence, a chain reaction would take place, with neighbouring nations becoming vulnerable to ideological contagion. Containment justified American interventionism overseas on an unparalleled scale, and the domino theory assumed that unless such action was successful, the United States itself might become increasingly encircled by hostile forces. In a world that also lived under the threat of nuclear conflict – the Cuban Missile Crisis demonstrated just how easy it might be for threat to escalate to war – presidents, whether Democrats or Republicans, remained committed to a common rhetoric, the credibility of which was finally exposed by the failure of interventionism in Vietnam.

During the Cold War, therefore, the United States was concerned not so much about the idea of imperialism as with the imperialism of an idea. Itself the product of a colonial struggle for self-determination, America's claim that its democratic values were the way of the future stemmed from its successful rejection of British imperialism. Its republic was a model to be admired and imitated by all societies that sought a similar freedom.

America's distinct sense of its mission – as articulated by presidents such as Woodrow Wilson – thus affected the way in which it approached its task. If the European method of colonial expansion was condemned – although in the 1890s the United States, encouraged by the Hearst newspapers, flirted with that form of overt imperialism – America's interventions overseas could be defined as a series of 'errands into the wilderness', reminiscent in style to their puritan original, and ones in which religious evangelism could still play a part.

For the puritans, then, Catholicism, established as a faith in the new world through Spain's colonial domination of South America, could be contained through Protestant settlement and evangelism in North America. This missionary impulse was preordained. Christianity had spread westwards from the Middle East to Europe, and Protestantism would now claim the New World across the Atlantic. Missionary work was accepted as part of the puritan – and Christian – commission in colonial America. It took time. By the mid-1640s, however, puritans – notably John Eliot – had learned the language of the natives they encountered, and could claim some converts. From that point on, there was an increase in such activity. In 1649, the New England Company was formed in Britain with the express purpose of converting the Indians. By 1658, the Society for Propagating the Gospel in New England had printed Eliot's Indian Bible.

It was significant, however, that, as Henry Bowden observes, '[t]he Spanish Franciscans and French Jesuits, often among the first Europeans to come into contact with native peoples, lived with or near the tribes they wanted to convert. Puritan ministers never lived among their native charges during the seventeenth century,' even when missions to the Indians assumed a more prominent role in their ambitions.[6] Instead, they seemed to prefer the construction of strategic hamlets where Christian natives would live. As R. Pierce Beaver put it,

> [t]o Eliot the best means to the desired end appeared to be the establishment of towns of 'Praying Indians'. There under the eyes of ministers, teachers, and native evangelists the converts could be isolated from contamination by evil pagan influences and the bad example of many settlers, and there be nurtured in Christian knowledge and trained in the ways of English civilization.[7]

Living apart from natives, who were clustered into purpose-built settlements, was a distinctive method of puritan missions during the seventeenth century.

A century after Eliot had begun his work among the Indians, Jonathan Edwards inspired the religious revivalism of the Great Awakening and further evangelical activity. Out of the Great Awakening came a theological doctrine, moreover, that subsequently influenced the character of American overseas missions. Samuel Hopkins, a contemporary theologian whose thinking was deeply affected by Edwards' ideas, argued the case for 'disinterested benevolence' as a Christian creed.

Hopkins suggested that the essence of Christianity lay in the individual's capacity to disengage from thoughts about future prospects of redemption or indeed damnation. Instead, an effort should be made to live according to a rigorous code of altruistic conduct, not as a means to salvation, but in order to attain that state of grace whereby salvation might at least be a possibility. In Oliver Elsbree's words, '[o]nly by attaining a complete mental indifference toward one's own future reward or punishment could a man attain to a true Christian life. In its crudest form this state of mind implied a willingness to be damned for the glory of God.'[8] Christians should not live in anticipation that by their piety or through their conduct salvation was assured.

Christians were invited to ask not what God could do for them, but what they might do for God. Disinterested benevolence implied the submergence of individual concerns to the greater demands of God and the Christian community. Hopkins, in turn influenced later religious reformers, and especially those who came together in the nineteenth century on the American Board of Commissioners for Foreign Missions. Of these, the most influential was Rufus Anderson. Although not himself a keen missionary – 'I had no passion for foreign travel' – Anderson did visit Hawaii to inspect the work of Christian conversion there, and in a book about that experience, and elsewhere, he considered in detail the proper role of the evangelist abroad. Anderson viewed the missionary enterprise as a series of 'errands' to the un-Christian and uncivilized of the world. The aim was to search and convert. Native pastors could consolidate the gains made as a result of the American missionaries passage. 'The experience on the Hawaiian Islands', wrote Anderson, 'shows that missions should be prosecuted with the expectation, and upon the plan, of gradually giving place to a native ministry.' Furthermore,

> [i]t is not incumbent on us to prosecute missions anywhere, with American laborers, until the entire people is converted, nor until idolatry and superstition have been banished from every part of the community. The native churches will themselves *need* missionary ground to be left for them to operate upon, in order for the preservation and growth of their own religious life. The grand object of missions is *to plant the gospel institutions effectively*. The missionary's vocation, as a soldier of the cross, is to make conquests, and to go on, in the name of his divine Master, 'conquering and to conquer'; committing the maintenance and consolidation of his conquests to another class of men, created expressly for the purpose. The idea of *continued conquest* is vital to the spiritual efficiency of missions.

Conquerors for Christ rather than colonists for Christ, American missionary activity in this light mirrors the secular impulse for continued expansion – extending the 'sphere' – domestically in the nineteenth century and subsequently overseas. Anderson's missionary became 'the pioneer of Christian institutions', an evangelical counterpart of those whose mission was to keep the world safe for democracy.[9]

The American missionary as pioneer should be constantly on the move, spending life on the frontier between those who had accepted the faith and those who had yet to do so. There should be no pause to cultivate converts. William Hutchinson quotes Anderson's view that '[t]he missionary, first of all, is a planter only. What will appear in the harvest, indeed whether or not there will be a harvest, is up to God.' The American approach potentially involved endlessly shifting the scene of missionary action. So as Hutchinson observes, '[e]ven more than earlier embodiments of the errand ideal, the foreign mission effort placed a premium on activism and motion, doing and going. To set an example, to send forth beams from the American hilltop, was seen as essential but not sufficient. Americans as Christ's special messengers were a people sent as well as chosen.' Yet the essence of such activity was that it took place largely on its own terms. America's missionaries had no need of dynamic interaction with the wider world. They could arrive hermetically sustained in the self-confidence of their message, proselytize and move on. For Hutchinson,

[t]he Andersonians proposed a stance resembling (not by accident) the mediating ideal later proclaimed when the United States acquired overseas colonies. One goes in, imposing values and making available (though Anderson would say not imposing) a model for the society. But one then gets out, for practical reasons but also because the model itself, influenced heavily by democratic and congregational ideologies, dictates that churches and peoples must be self-governing.[10]

Americans might thus journey abroad to spread their spiritual and also their secular gospel while paradoxically caring little for the world they visited, except insofar as it represented a filter for their own ambitions. Needing to learn little from cultural encounters overseas, they might arrive and depart with their ignorance intact.

The puritans had avoided living among the natives they sought to convert, and had established defensive stockades for those who accepted their faith. Samuel Hopkins had provided through the doctrine of disinterested benevolence the motivation for renewed missionary activity in the era after the Great Awakening. And the evangelists of the nineteenth century, among them Rufus Anderson, saw their work as a constant process of proselytizing, moving on and finding fresh challenges. The implications of America's methods of mission that are revealed in their spiritual dimension also resonate in their secular context. Deliberate isolation from other cultures may lead to an incapacity to engage in cultural dialogue. Disinterested benevolence may be part of that political altruism that many Americans would claim to characterize their interventions abroad. And the constant desire to seek out new territories in which to test the 'idea of America' abroad may lead to international engagement at a global level. The cultural roots of those assumptions, buried deep in American history, were, however, to be challenged decisively in Vietnam.

The missionary's role in spreading the unique American gospel was thus vital. The crusading spirit of religion was allied with an unquestioning acceptance of the democratic faith. Missionaries, because of their faith, took for granted that their way of life was the right one: their culture, their values, their societies were better than those of the nations they sought to convert. Christianity and democracy became the hallmarks of the developed world. That effortless belief in the superiority of their civilization – their culture – meant that those who proselytized abroad could largely ignore the cultural values of the societies that they wished to enlighten.

Take China. American missionaries approached it in the nineteenth century under the self-confident banner that they could win 'China for Christ'. Some attempts to accomplish this impressive task might have given them pause. One Baptist evangelist, the Reverend I.J. Roberts, whose enthusiasm was such that when he sang 'Onward Christian Soldiers' in the right climatic conditions it could be listened to three miles away, so influenced one convert, Hung Hsui-ch'üan, that this self-appointed younger brother of Christ was inspired to conquer southern China during the Taiping Rebellion (1851–64). Nearly twenty million people died in the process.

Nevertheless, the missionary effort continued. In 1900, a poll in the *Boston Herald* found that the clergy were one of the most convinced expansionist groups in the country. China in particular appeared to be a place for missionary activity. Despite the frustrations that accompanied the missionaries there, the importance of the self-assigned undertaking was such that it was not to be modified in the light of any cultural differences that were encountered abroad. Instead, the assumption of superiority meant that setbacks were regarded often as problems to be overcome by the crusaders rather than manifestations of a desire on the part of the natives to ignore or subvert the message of these religious and social engineers.

Politicians subscribed to a similar orthodoxy. By the end of the nineteenth century, expansionists were looking to fulfil the nation's 'manifest destiny' beyond its own frontier. Yet in their perspective on the wider world it was assumed that the United States had nothing to gain from an understanding of innately inferior cultures. Indeed it remained the nation's task to reform the heathen. Christianity, in association with capitalism and, if necessary, with the help of the military, would achieve the objective. As Theodore Roosevelt said in a speech at the Minnesota State Fair on 2 September 1901,

> [b]arbarism has, and can have, no place in a civilized world. It is our duty toward the people living in barbarism to see that they are freed from their chains, and we can free them only by destroying barbarism itself. The missionary, the merchant, and the soldier may each have a part to play in this destruction, and in the consequent uplifting of the people.

At the dawn of 'the American Century', then, the nation's sense of self-confidence in the superiority of its spiritual and secular values remained undiminished.

As Louis Hartz suggested, the nation's political culture was shaped fundamentally by its lack of a feudal past. In turn this also influenced the characterization of its overseas mission. European imperialists, in a way that was reminiscent of their feudal inheritance, and the class system it engendered, appreciated the value of a network of reciprocal obligations tying them to their colonies. The British concept of the 'dual mandate' encapsulated this idea. As David Healy points out, it 'resembled a contractual obligation: the backward peoples owed to civilized society whatever natural bounties civilization required for its use, while the civilized world had an obligation to spread the blessings of progress among the barbarians.'[11]

In the same way, the French colonial policy of assimilating native cultures recognized the need to engage in a process of dialogue that would necessarily take time. Whereas the American approach potentially involved endlessly shifting the scene of the missionary action, these British and French ideas justified the need to colonize and to dig in for a long haul. And in turn this had implications for the cultural relationships that might develop between nations. The imperial connection implied some degree of cultural contact and exchange.

America's mission, rooted in the religious fervour that had inspired the puritans, and amalgamated with the nation's faith in the values of Jefferson's Declaration of Independence, was a distinctive outcome of the nation's sense of itself as different – a place apart. Where Europeans considered a dialogue with foreign cultures in the process of imperial control and assimilation, America's unique sense of purpose and anti-imperialist rhetoric made its native culture largely impervious to such external influences. Secure in their beliefs, many Americans would journey overseas to spread their spiritual and secular gospel while paradoxically caring little for the world they visited. They imported to the United States few, if any, of its concerns.

The result could even be the paradox of an expansionist nation periodically appearing to turn away from the world at large, for the ethnocentrism and cultural introspection that this methodology of mission compounded can explode from time to time in the isolationist impulse, which, taken to an extreme, might even deny the prospect of foreign mission itself. That was the outcome of the internal contradictions resulting from a cultural drive that tried to teach the world without being prepared to learn from it in return: the result of which contributed to America's defeat in the Vietnam war. In the post-Vietnam period, moreover, an initial reluctance to engage militarily overseas – the so-called 'Vietnam Syndrome' – meant that the nation appeared to oscillate between separation and mission, militarily choosing between isolationism and interventionism, while nevertheless still seeing itself as a globally committed super-power.

During the Cold War there were few who, like Louis Hartz, saw 'the American consensus as the result of a pretension to uniqueness, a pretension that an ironic and comparative historical consciousness can hope to dissolve'. That sense of irony was submerged in a world of ideological absolutes. Hartz himself queried 'whether a nation can compensate for the uniformity of its domestic life by contact with alien cultures outside it'. After Vietnam, the verdict should remain open.

If cultural ethnocentrism implied ignorance of strange societies, so ideological absolutism was marked by suspicion of foreign ideas. To enter the maze of American liberal thought was, to Europeans, to look into an ideological hall of mirrors. As Hartz observed, 'Burke equaled Locke in America.' Through their act of emigration, dissenters from feudal values became the political and philosophical establishment in the New World. Once there they brooked no ideological argument. This liberal absolutism meant that polemics were stifled by a domestic consensus that considered philosophical debate largely irrelevant. Ideological conversations abroad with those who argued that there might be philosophical alternatives to American liberalism became that much more difficult to sustain.

Given this overwhelming agreement, the issue Hartz raised was 'whether American liberalism can acquire through external experience that sense of relativity, that spark of philosophy which European liberalism acquired through an internal experience of social diversity and social conflict'.[12] The strength of ideological 'Americanism' suggests, however, that there was little need to participate in discussions with the world outside, for there was nothing to be gained by genuine debate, and the force of dialogue was dissipated into competing monologues.

If Americans could only engage in reluctant philosophical argument among themselves, and alien ideas were seen as suspicious, how could they export a creed that ignored other nations, cultures and societies, and indeed considered them often as threats to the American way of life?

Nevertheless, this unique phenomenon – the United States – has tried to inspire the re-creation of its spiritual and democratic republican values abroad. In cultural and ideological terms, however, it could be argued that at times it has lacked the subtle conceptual understanding necessary to the task. This analysis becomes all the more relevant in a world that has moved beyond the ideological certainties of the Cold War, for what if, after all, that mission has been accomplished? American politicians can argue that it is democracy rather than communism that has finally been given global endorsement. What is happening in the former Soviet Union, Eastern Europe and elsewhere is evidence. What happened in Tiananmen Square is forgotten.

In President Bush's 1990 State of the Union address, for example, the rhetoric was naturally self-congratulatory and endorsed the triumphalist perspective. Reviewing the previous year, he suggested that the history of that time had fulfilled 'the long-held hopes of the American people'. Events indeed could be taken to 'validate the long-standing goals of American policy – a policy based on a single, shining principle: the cause of freedom'. Later in the speech the president recalled playing catch with children in Poland: 'little leaguers' who were 'ready to go from Warsaw to the World Series'. A symbol of America's democratic culture beckons the youth of Eastern Europe. The world appeared poised to be made over in the American image.

Yet it could not be forgotten that an earlier crusade undertaken in the name of that 'single, shining principle' of freedom turned into the 'bright shining lie' that was Vietnam. America's mission, sustained by its sense of exceptionalism, characterized by its insensitivity towards foreign cultures and ideological absolutism at home – the 'other' is seen as 'alien' or 'unAmerican' – disintegrated in Southeast Asia. Then, there was a lack of an appreciation of cultural relativism and a failure to understand the possibility of ideological diversity. Now, despite the political transformations that have taken place in the world since the collapse of communism and the break-up of the Soviet Union, it may be equally mistaken to assume that this is an indication of a universal impulse to imitate American cultural life or to aspire to American ideological values.

The concept of mission that, free from the encumbrances of a feudal past, helped to make America's political culture perversely impervious to foreign influences has led also to a lack of interest in the world except as a laboratory for experiments in 'Americanism'. As products of this culture of ignorance, some of America's leaders, and even those who might be expected to know better, have exhibited a certain lack of geopolitical sophistication. George Bush's vice-president, Dan Quayle, was an outstanding example of the apparent *ingénue* with respect to the wider world. But it was Lyndon Johnson who lamented, 'I keep confusing Nigeria with Algeria because both end in "geria".' Or, there was Henry Kissinger's equally understandable question: 'What's Chad?'[13] George W. Bush could probably have answered him after his electoral experiences in Florida, but during the election campaign, his inability to name the contemporary leaders of several other nations raised doubts about his grasp of foreign policy issues.

The perception of the world as a bi-polar divide, geographically in the nineteenth century and ideologically in the twentieth, has nevertheless consistently conditioned American attitudes towards the world beyond its frontiers. The nation's enemies have been defined historically in both racial and ideological terms as aliens, who threaten the norms of its – predominantly Anglo-Saxon and Protestant – republican democratic tradition. The nation's apparent incapacity to appreciate cultural and ideological relativism – the persistent refusal to see the need for Hartz's ironic and comparative historical consciousness – effectively reinforces such a perspective on the wider world. So international communists, Latin American drug-dealers, Middle Eastern dictators and terrorists worldwide variously have become preoccupations of the nation that at home and abroad has traditionally defined its adversaries as public enemies whose existence represents a threat to the democratic health of the nation and the world.

## After Vietnam

> May the Force be with you.
> *Alec Guinness as Obi Wan-Kenobi in* Star Wars *(1977)*

The impact of America's war in Vietnam upon the nation's politics, culture and society has been profound. John Hellman, in *American Myth and the Legacy of Vietnam* (1986), argued that

> Americans entered Vietnam with certain expectations that a story, a distinctly American story, would unfold. When the story of America in Vietnam turned into something unexpected, the true nature of the larger

story of America itself became the subject of intense cultural dispute. On the deepest level, the legacy of Vietnam is the disruption of our story, of our explanation of the past and vision of the future.[14]

The major foreign policy débâcle of 'the American Century' altered the nation's sense of itself and the way it saw the world. After Richard Nixon had declared the war over, having achieved a so-called 'peace with honour', his four immediate successors in the White House – Ford, Carter, Reagan and Bush – had to confront the legacy of the 'Vietnam Syndrome' – a national reluctance to intervene militarily overseas. Even Ronald Reagan, who unashamedly redefined America's mission in Southeast Asia as 'a noble cause', could only fight wars in Latin America by proxy. The Iran–Contra scandal was the outcome of his administration's attempt to fund an overseas mission from the profits of illegal arms dealing: a course of action taken in the knowledge that American public opinion would not countenance the possibility of 'another Vietnam'.

In his inaugural address in 1989, George Bush argued that a twenty-five year 'statute of limitations' should be invoked to permit the nation to move beyond its experience of war in Southeast Asia. 'This is a fact,' Bush continued, 'the final lesson of Vietnam is that no great nation can long afford to be sundered by a memory.' Two years later, after the Gulf War, he was exultant before the American Legislative Exchange Council: 'By God, we've kicked the Vietnam syndrome once and for all.' But when Bush proved reluctant to prolong the mission in the Gulf in an effort to topple Saddam Hussein's autocratic regime in Iraq – fearing that Vietnam's quagmire might become a desert quicksand – his boast seemed empty. Saddam still controlled Iraq when Bush's son came to the White House in 2001. In between time, Bill Clinton, whose own relationship with the Vietnam war was a characteristically controversial element of his political career – he managed to avoid the draft through drawing a high lottery number, rather than dodging it altogether – became, towards the end of his second term, the first president to visit Vietnam since the war ended. The repercussions rumble on: in 2001, Senator John Kerry's role in the conflict became a matter of public debate. In the same year, Christopher Hitchens in *The Trial of Henry Kissinger* alleged that the former secretary of state conspired with supporters of Richard Nixon during the 1968 election campaign to sabotage peace talks aimed at ending the Vietnam War by promising the South Vietnamese that if Nixon became president they might gain better terms in a settlement with Hanoi. The statute of limitations on the legacy of the war has apparently not run out.

In an article published in 1982 in the prestigious journal *Foreign Affairs* (where George Kennan had argued the case for containment in 1947), William McNeill suggested that '[i]n the absence of believable myths, coherent public action becomes very difficult to improvise or sustain.'[15] If Vietnam represented, as John Hellmann observed, a 'disruption of our story', after the conflict ended it was left to popular culture – and to Hollywood – both to mediate the experience of the war, and to re-create the mythologies that America's defeat had shattered.

Hellmann thus argues that George Lucas's film *Star Wars* (1977) satisfied 'the need of a national consciousness deep in the collective amnesia of the post-Vietnam era for escape into a fantasy world that could substitute for the lost landscape of American myth'. He also observes that, '[s]ignificantly, writers in religious publications were among the most receptive', notably to the two sequels released in the 1980s (*The Empire Strikes Back* and *The Return of the Jedi*), because they realized that in those films 'spiritual allegory could probe contemporary concerns deep below specific political positions.' The initial escapism of *Star Wars*, a fantasy in which the forces of good, acting according to the principles of the Truman Doctrine, stand up to and overcome the forces of evil, was in keeping with the mood of the moment. Yet the immediate sequels did suggest that, in the aftermath of Vietnam, more complex cultural issues needed to be addressed.

The climax of *The Empire Strikes Back* (1980) is thus the confrontation between the hero, Luke Skywalker, and the villain (revealed as his real father), Darth Vader. Evil wins. For Hellmann, Luke fails because he has pursued his mission 'without first calculating the odds against his success and acquiring a fuller self-knowledge'. In this way, 'he duplicates the essence of the American error in Vietnam of making a momentous decision on the basis simply of right intention and past luck.' When Luke 'leaps into an abyss' it becomes 'a metaphorical equivalent to the chaos into which the post-Vietnam American psyche leapt as it fled the spectre of impossible failure and self-revelation'. The hero survives, but has at some level to acknowledge that he has suffered a traumatic defeat.

In *The Return of the Jedi* (1983), the final part of the initial trilogy of films, having discovered that Darth Vader is his natural father, and, as Hellmann observes, during their final confrontation, after 'renouncing at last the use of his light sword', Luke 'pulls back from the will to power he has inherited from his corrupted parent, in effect pulling back from the tendency of self-righteous pursuit of mission'. The phrase 'will to power' comes from the German philosopher

Friedrich Nietzsche, who saw it as a character trait separating the leader from the led: those who have the 'will to power' – the 'force' – are able to transcend the narrative action, to exercise control over their destinies rather than leave their fate up to the chance outcomes of historical circumstance. It is significant in this context that John F. Kennedy, who was president at the time when Vietnam was becoming a pressing political and military foreign policy problem for the United States, was seen by his contemporaries as just such an existential hero, who might use his 'will to power' in an effort to win the Cold War confrontation with international communism.

For Hellmann, then, '[t]he fantasy Lucas has presented Americans in *Star Wars* is a redreaming of American memory that includes the Vietnam experience as a traumatic passage to a higher plane of under-standing.'[16] Whether this was a self-conscious intent is debatable. Lucas's biographer, John Baxter, describes how, after 'Skywalker Ranch' had been constructed from the profits of the first movie, Joseph Campbell, the noted scholar of anthropology and cultural mythmaking was invited to speak there. John Williams, who composed the music for the film, recalled that, '[u]ntil [Campbell] told us what *Star Wars* meant – started talking about collective memory and cross-cultural shared history – the things that rattle around our brains and predate language, the real resonance of how the whole thing can be explained – we regarded it as a Saturday-morning space movie.' Indeed, even as the sequels to the original film were produced, for some critics the significance of the moment had passed. A review of *The Return of the Jedi* in *The Washington Post* points out that the *Star Wars* 'phenomenon has gone too far to avoid being self-conscious about its impact and reputation. The original may have answered a unique cultural craving in 1977, but the sequels are bound to be more and more dependent on whatever's happened in the chapters that preceded them.' Thus it proved when Lucas returned to his mythic landscape in *The Phantom Menace* (1999).

Nevertheless, the fact that *Star Wars* was influential in shaping the cultural climate of the time meant that it could be appropriated as a political symbol. Ronald Reagan, whose rhetoric made frequent use of the idioms of popular culture, thus popularized his Strategic Defense Initiative – a missile defence system that would use laser technology to protect America against a nuclear attack – as 'star wars'. As Baxter observes, however, 'Lucas sued' when Reagan appropriated his 'trade-mark'. So if '[r]eal mythology, by its very nature, is communal, and open to interpretation by all', Lucas 'hadn't given us a mythology; we could only rent it.'[17]

# Conclusion: Back to the Future

America does not go abroad in search of monsters to destroy.
She is the well-wisher to freedom and independence of all. She is
the champion and vindicator only of her own.
*John Quincy Adams in a speech made on 4 July 1821*

If the experience of defeat in Vietnam has had continuing repercussions
upon American politics, society and culture, so the unravelling of the
Soviet Union, and the collapse of communism as its ideology of choice,
has had a similar dramatic impact upon American perceptions of the
wider world. The 'Vietnam Syndrome' counselled against military
interventionism abroad, but the post-Cold War international system
appeared to give the last remaining superpower the opportunity to
fashion a 'New World Order', with the United States as its leader. Yet
the basic thrust of American foreign policy is still the same. As Brian
Hocking points out, '[o]ne of the key preoccupations of successive
generations of US policymakers – from George Washington's Farewell Address to Congress in 1796 to Ronald Reagan's attachment to
the Strategic Defense Initiative – has been the conquest of potential
vulnerability through maximum self-reliance and minimum dependence
on others.'[18] Agreement on the need to preserve national self-interest
does not, however, mean that there is still a consensus on the means
to that end.

In President Clinton's first inaugural address in 1993, therefore,
there was a clear recognition of the interdependence of domestic and
foreign policy. 'To renew America we must meet challenges abroad
as well as at home. There is no clear division today between what is
foreign and what is domestic – the world economy, the world environment, the world Aids crisis, the world arms race affect us all.' But
as the president who was elected with a declared interest in the importance of domestic issues found – like others before him – that it was
in the sphere of foreign policy that his political reputation might be
forged, the mood of the country became more difficult to judge.
Clinton's peace initiatives in the Middle East and his support for the
peace process in Northern Ireland could draw widespread domestic
support as they did not involve the deployment of American forces
overseas. The prospect of military interventionism in support of
humanitarian causes – in the Balkans, or in Somalia – drew a more
ambivalent response from the American public. Indeed, the suspicion
that the foreign and domestic agendas of the American government
were too closely entwined is a contemporary concern among those for

whom the phrase 'New World Order' has implications of a conspiracy that once more reflects upon the paranoid style of American politics.

At its most extreme, such a worldview may erupt in the form of domestic terrorism shown in the Oklahoma City bombing in 1995. Initially feared to be an act perpetrated by international enemies of the United States – Islamic extremists were among those immediately under suspicion – the fact that it was Timothy McVeigh, an American who had fought in the Gulf War, who was eventually convicted and executed for the crime focuses attention upon the extremist political attitudes that may prompt such actions. So the federal government becomes not simply an enemy but part of an international plot to amalgamate its power with that of a world government, which will attack the fundamental liberties of America's citizens. Such actions as the destruction of the Branch Davidians' compound at Waco in Texas by federal authorities seem to confirm the plan: for right-wing militia groups and fundamentalists, multilateralists such as Bill Clinton were proving their credentials as potential candidates for the 'presidency' of the United Nations. The only way to maintain freedom in such a threatening world is thus to be prepared to fight another American War of Independence against such New World Order imperialist ambition. John Quincy Adams' monsters exist at home – there is indeed no need to travel abroad in search of them.

Timothy McVeigh's was the first federal execution to take place in the United States since 1963, when John F. Kennedy refused clemency for Victor Feguer, a kidnapper and murderer, judged guilty of a federal crime since his victim was transported across state borders. In 1953, Julius and Ethel Rosenberg had, like McVeigh, transgressed more directly against the government through their alleged acts of nuclear espionage and they were sent to the electric chair. The continued use of the death penalty in America, which, along with countries such as China and Iraq, insists on this ultimate sanction, is at odds with contemporary policy in other democracies, and serves to highlight American exceptionalism in a different way. If McVeigh's execution aroused protest against the death penalty abroad, however, it could be safely ignored at home. In the same way, George W. Bush, whose home state of Texas was among those most enthusiastic in its use of capital punishment, came to the White House with a far more unilateralist perspective on the wider world than his predecessor.

Thus, in the first months of his administration, the first president to be inaugurated in the twenty-first century seemed intent on preserving American self-interest irrespective of the international repercussions of his foreign policy. In March 2001, he rejected the Kyoto agreement on global climate change, inviting opposition worldwide from environmentalists who saw America's disproportionate consumption of energy as a major factor contributing to the problem. His supporters may argue that the president planned a more realistic overall approach to environmental issues, despite his links to the oil industry, and concern to maintain American economic growth. It appears, however, that national priorities will continue to determine responses to international initiatives on the environment.

The same seemed true of Bush's efforts to revive Star Wars – the missile defence system promoted during Ronald Reagan's presidency – as a cornerstone of America's strategic security in the post Cold War era. Despite the administration's view that nuclear threats from so-called 'rogue states' and international terrorism – the new enemies to replace the forces of international communism – justified the renewed initiative, other nations saw it as a potentially destabilizing policy that was unlikely to achieve its aim of protecting the United States from foreign threats, both imagined and real. While it is true that the Strategic Defense Initiative could not have prevented the terrorist attacks of 11 September 2001, in their aftermath the search for domestic security became an even more important political priority in which, for the Bush administration, Star Wars has a significant role to play.

Bush was simply inheriting the tradition of independence argued for in foreign policy by George Washington, James Monroe and Theodore Roosevelt. In a world moving beyond the rigidities of the Truman Doctrine, the voices of presidents past still echo in the minds of those who have succeeded them, with the emphasis on the tactics of foreign relations rather than its strategy. So as William Pfaff argued in *Foreign Affairs* in 2001, '[a]n implicit alliance has emerged in Washington since the Cold War's end: internationalist liberals, anxious to extend American influence and to federate the world's democracies, and unilateralist neoconservatives, who believe in aggressive American leadership for the world's own good, have joined forces in what some call the New Wilsonianism.' Woodrow Wilson's influence remains central to both Democrat and Republican visions of a New World Order.

Pfaff quotes the arguments of William Kristol and Robert Kagan, published in *The National Interest* the previous year: 'Today's international system is built not around a balance of power but around American hegemony. . . . American hegemony, then, must be actively maintained, just as it was actively obtained. . . . [I]t is precisely because the United States infuses its foreign policy with an unusually high degree of morality that other nations feel they have less to fear from its otherwise daunting power.' The assumption is that definitions of American morality may be universally accepted as absolute principles rather than relative concepts. As Pfaff observes, '[i]t is hard to explain why Wilson's fundamentally sentimental, megalomaniacal, and unhistorical vision of world democracy organized on the American example should continue today to set the general course of American foreign policy under both Democrats and Republicans.' Nevertheless, '[t]he country is still in the intellectual thrall of this self-righteous clergyman-president who gave to the American nation the blasphemous conviction that it, like he himself, had been created by God "to show the way to the nations of the world how they shall walk in the paths of liberty".'

The attitudes of America's leaders remain intact – even after the traumatic failure of interventionism in Vietnam. They have been shaped by the weight of history, culture and traditions of rhetoric. So, Pfaff concludes, '[t]he United States . . . has pursued its mission to reform the world, a pious and unrealistic hope turned into a foreign policy.' Moreover,

> America's optimism about such world transformation has yet to be broken. It underpins the case for hegemony and prevails on virtually every side of the orthodox policy debate. The idea that history is tragedy is not to the American taste. This is why the United States is a dangerous nation while remaining a 'righteous' one. The puritanism of its cultural origins was intolerant of sinners and impatient with God's roundabout and unhurried ways. The United States is still impatient for progress. Its vision of reform expresses its conviction of singular virtue and national exception, which by happy coincidence reinforce national economic interest and the extension of national power. The risk to the United States is a classical one: self-destructive hubris, leading to barren tears.[19]

It is a prospect that might give pause to presidents who seek to define American – and their own – leadership by venturing out of the City on a Hill and going 'in country'. Nevertheless, it may be a temptation that proves simply too hard to resist and a challenge that remains too great to ignore.

The events of 11 September 2001 dramatically demonstrated that the City on a Hill is not invulnerable. The response to it – the declaration of a lasting war on international terrorism – is, however, another example of moral absolutism defining the nation's foreign policy. Pfaff's warning remains relevant, for the search for lasting security may remain elusive. The United States cannot assume that others will share its hope and its vision for a 'New World Order'. Remaking the world in its image is indeed a utopian dream. Enemies remain.

# Back on the Raft

A monarchy is a merchantman, which sails well, but will sometimes strike on a rock, and go to the bottom; whilst a republic is
a raft, which would never sink, but then your feet are always in
the water.
*Fisher Ames, Speech to the House of Representatives (1795)*

For Fisher Ames, who helped to draft the first amendment to the
Constitution, the raft was the great metaphor that, although sometimes leaky, guaranteed the survival of America's democratic republic. Over the last forty years, however, it has become more waterlogged.
For there has been a fragmentation in America's political culture. On
the one hand, there are those who see the future in the creation of a
truly multi-cultural society. In this new world, the faultlines of race,
class, sex and gender may be recognized, but also can be accommod-
ated on the raft, as different histories are retrieved and valued as
competing narratives in the story of America. On the other hand,
those who oppose such a vision defend the politics of nostalgia. They
retain a simple faith in the traditional narrative of America's celebratory history, in which the Declaration and the Constitution symbolize
enduring political values and principles, and the heritage of religious
faith moulds attitudes to the nation and the wider world. The battle
between these two opposing viewpoints – postmodernist and modern-
ist, liberal and conservative, humanist and fundamentalist – can be
seen, moreover, in the twin dramas of Watergate and the attempt
to impeach Bill Clinton, which, as two examples of the media-driven
politics of spectacle, helped to define American politics during the
closing decades of the twentieth century.

America is an old country: geologically, geographically and anthropologically. But in cultural, psychological and political terms it sees itself as new. It is the fact of its 'discovery' by Europeans that produces such a foreshortened view of its history. America – 'the first new nation' – only celebrated the bicentennial anniversary of achieving independence from European colonial control less than thirty years ago. As a place of refuge – escape – or as a 'land of opportunity', America initially defined itself as the antithesis of the 'Old World': Europe. Its experiment with new forms of government, a written constitution and the institutions of republican democracy was framed also in that context. The United States was a place apart from Europe and indeed the rest of the world.

'Was the discovery of America a blessing or a curse to mankind? If it was a blessing, by what means are we to conserve and enhance its benefits? If it was a curse, by what means are we to repair the damage?' One European response to finding America, typified by the Abbé Raynal's question, posed in 1777 and for which he offered a cash prize for the best answer, was to observe the American experience initially in less than flattering terms. In France, contemporary intellectuals discussed whether all things American were 'degenerate' or not: a debate that continues to this day. Alexander Hamilton, in *Federalist 11*, took the argument seriously enough to use it as a justification for America's rejection of European political dominance. 'Our situation invites and our interests prompts us to aim at an ascendant in the system of American affairs.' Europe had for too long thought of 'the rest of mankind as created for her benefit'. It had led to 'men admired as profound philosophers' thinking that Europeans enjoyed 'a physical superiority' and 'that all animals, and with them the human species, degenerate in America – that even dogs cease to bark after having breathed awhile in our atmosphere.' Hamilton sees the opportunity to expose the fallacy of these assertions.

> Facts have too long supported these arrogant pretensions of the Europeans. It belongs to us to vindicate the honour of the human race, and to teach that assuming brother, moderation. Union will enable us to do it. . . . Let Americans disdain to be the instruments of European greatness! Let the thirteen States, bound together in a strict and indissoluble Union, concur in erecting one great American system, superior to the control of all transatlantic force or influence, and able to dictate the terms of the connection between the old and the new world!

It was an ambition that took two centuries to achieve, and in this sense there is a certain irony that the contemporary debate over the future of European integration and the adoption of a single currency is reminiscent of that which took place in Philadelphia in 1787, and then in America throughout the nineteenth century.

American politics thus can be approached with an appreciation of America's history of discovery and settlement by Europeans and of the manner by which it achieved its independence. The ideas suggested by Thomas Jefferson in the Declaration of Independence – of natural equality and God-given rights to life, liberty and the pursuit of happiness – emerged from the crucible of a revolution. They would define the work undertaken by James Madison as the principal architect of both the Constitution and the Bill of Rights, which in turn would become the documents that define the framework and the structure of America's raft of republican democracy.

There is thus a sense of continuity that still connects contemporary American political thought to its origins and the subsequent history of the republic. It is self-evident in political rhetoric and the impact of religion upon the cultural life of the nation. It is also symbolized in the nation's capital. The Washington Monument, the Jefferson Memorial and the Lincoln Memorial are reminders not only of America's founding period, but also of the fact that the Union could be preserved ultimately only through the trauma of civil war. The different locations of the institutions of the federal government – the executive, the legislature and the judiciary – emphasize the separation of powers: the White House, the Capitol and the nearby Supreme Court building. The National Archives house the original documents: the Declaration of Independence and the Constitution. The nation's inventions, explorations and technological achievements are kept and recalled in the museums of the Smithsonian Institution. And the Vietnam war memorial remains a stark reminder of the failure of a mission.

Architecture and artefacts, memorials and museums, however, cannot map entirely the contours of American politics. The importance of religion remains another feature of the political landscape. From the puritan settlement of colonial Massachusetts, through the revivalism – the Great Awakening – of the 1740s, and on to the revolution itself, religion underpins political ideas. During the nineteenth century, the philosophy of transcendentalism, which emphasized the primacy of individual conscience, became a force, once again in Massachusetts. Ralph Waldo Emerson and Henry David Thoreau placed religion at the centre of their ideas, and it was the conflict between a religious-based morality and the law that prompted Thoreau's essay on 'civil disobedience'. Religious fervour inspired abolitionists and prohibitionists alike. During the twentieth century and beyond, fundamentalism has incorporated a distinctive political agenda, while it looks for converts in the age of televangelism. Money is power in religion as well as in politics; indeed it is the organization of religion as a corporate business that nowadays makes it influential in the nation's political life: an American phenomenon.

Despite Hamilton's wish, though, the United States has not escaped entirely from the influence of Europe. Indeed, innovative interpretations of the natural and physical world by European scientists have helped to shape American political ideas and attitudes. In the nineteenth century, it was Charles Darwin's theory of evolution that was taken to endorse the competitive spirit of American capitalism. The 'survival of the fittest' as part of the process of 'natural selection' appeared to correspond to the political and social realities of the New World. But the concept of evolution also challenged fundamentals of America's religious faith – and contributed to a continuing battle of beliefs. Then, in the twentieth century, it was Albert Einstein who changed the world.

In 1905, Einstein's publication of the first outline of the theory of special relativity took issue with the mechanistic certainties of Newtonian physics and suggested an altogether more complex, if no less understandable, universe. Einstein's deconstruction of established concepts of space and time, and his suggestion that instead of being regarded as absolutes they should be seen as relative values, was an imaginative leap that would have a profound impact on the twentieth-century mind, for the idea of relativity permeated not simply physics, but also other spheres of cultural life. If Darwin's *On the Origin of Species* had fundamentally changed the religious and philosophical environment of the nineteenth century, through applications of its argument outside the field of natural science, so too did Einstein's theory of relativity now begin to revolutionize thought beyond the frontiers of physical science. The concept of relativity, translated to the world of culture and morality, meant that existing political and religious faiths might be questioned once again by the challenges of postmodernism. But in terms of twentieth-century history, the idea of relativity still found its most important experimental outcome in the field of atomic research.

In August 1939, Einstein, who had escaped the persecutions of fascist Germany to find refuge in the United States, sent a letter to Franklin Roosevelt, in which he outlined the theoretical construction of 'extremely powerful bombs of a new type' that were the product of a nuclear chain reaction. This kick-started government support for the American research that culminated in the Manhattan project. It was Einstein's fear that Germany might be already engaged in a similar enterprise that prompted his concern. In fact, he worried unnecessarily: it became evident in the closing stages of the war in Europe that the race to produce the atom bomb had had only one entrant. Some of the scientists who had produced the bomb in America now argued against its use. The death of Roosevelt on 12 April 1945, just prior to the first successful testing of the device, effectively truncated any extended discussion of the issue. As president, and initially ignorant of the bomb's existence, Truman nevertheless made a swift decision. Less than a month after the test, on 6 August 1945, Hiroshima was bombed, and the Manhattan project culminated in the age of nuclear weaponry.

Relativity, with its denial of the objective reality of space and time, had led to the creation of a weapon that threatened to obliterate space and time themselves. The sense of anxiety that characterized Cold War American society – particularly in the 1950s – was thus the product of Einstein's revolutionary idea. In a century during which the nation had experienced economic depression, two world wars and the holocaust, life in the age of nuclear weapons and super-power confrontation was yet another challenge to be faced. The history of the times was indeed the history of crisis.

At the core of American political culture, moreover, there is a tendency to respond to fears through attempting to control, restrict, prohibit or contain them. Although, for example, Jefferson argued for the individual's right to liberty, it was controlled both by an emphasis on the morality of religion, and by the social pressures towards conformity. Similarly, in the Constitution, the sphere of federal authority was restricted through the balancing of layers of government, the separation of powers and the system of checks and balances. The Bill of Rights became a defensive stockade to protect individuals from being threatened by the interference of the state. This impetus towards containment is illustrated too in the treatment of those who initially were excluded from the raft of American democracy.

In the nineteenth century, Native Americans were contained upon reservations; in the twentieth, blacks have been contained in ghettoes (and, during the Second World War, Japanese-Americans in camps). Class conflict has been contained by widespread faith in the potential of the American Dream. The common reaction towards those who stood on the banks while the river of America's celebratory history flowed past also extended to the treatment of women and to gays: their rights were contained until their protests became impossible to ignore and they were invited to try to swim to the raft. Prohibition of alcohol and drugs represents an attempt not simply to legislate public morality, but also to incorporate a political agenda of discrimination against those judged still to be outside the mainstream of American society. The ultimate form of containment for criminals – the death penalty – is an expression of the fear of those who by their actions and conduct refuse to accept the rule of law. Fear of the contamination of national ideals by unAmerican ideologies also helped to mould attitudes towards the wider world, such that the policy of containment overseas became a way of defending 'the American way' at home, and indeed may be seen as a predictable response to the anxieties of the age.

In 1950s America, therefore, the decay of the absolute in the face of relativity was resisted by an effort to preserve the 'vital center' in cultural and political life. This involved a celebration of the idea of exceptionalism, which moulded the ideological and political rhetoric of the time. The threat of nuclear conflict also emphasized the need for leadership, legitimizing the development of 'the imperial presidency'. At the same time, the policy of containment supported expansionist ideals – 'errands into the wilderness' – and the commitment of national resources to fight ideological enemies abroad. Nowhere did this have more damaging consequences than in Vietnam.

The failure of the nation's mission in Southeast Asia resulted in cultural shocks and aftershocks that undermined the consensus politics of the time, already disturbed by the domestic campaign for civil rights. In the drama of this cultural and political change, the role of John F. Kennedy is pivotal. In his life, and especially in his death, JFK precipitated and then symbolized the transformations in America's political culture – the 'loss of innocence' – that also resulted from the overwhelming confrontation in Vietnam. This would ultimately call into question the intellectual rationale of the Cold War and the political calculus of military interventionism. It was the war in Southeast Asia that forced many Americans into a public and populist questioning of the assumptions of the 'idea of America' itself. Defeat in Vietnam achieved something unique. It made many Americans see the futility of war; its legacy has been its 'syndrome'.

The war itself might seem a postmodern metaphor – with its fluid lines of battle, its apparent lack of clear-cut objectives, and the conflicting and confusing justifications for its prosecution – images aptly captured in Francis Ford Coppola's cinematic representation of it, *Apocalypse Now* (1979). But Vietnam is not a postmodern conflict – ahistorical and detached from any political and cultural context. Rather it remains a symbol of the erosion of the credibility of Cold War America's dominant self-image, which celebrated the nation's sense of its providential destiny and mission. In other words, failure in Vietnam is a defining moment in contemporary American political culture. It dramatizes the realities of living in a world of relative values, where outcomes cannot be predicted, where chance encounters shake cultural

certainties. After Vietnam, the sense of political and cultural disloca-
tion was complete. And American politicians have had to grapple
ever since with the consequences. As Norman Mailer put it: 'Vietnam,
hot damn.'

One of the consequences of the political divisions caused by the
Vietnam war was the increasing mistrust of the power of national
government, personified in the presidency, and then symbolized in
Richard Nixon's actions during Watergate. It was his political opponents in Congress – the majority of them Democrats – who would
eventually have the power to remove him from office: a fate he escaped
through resignation. To what extent, then, was the move to impeach
Bill Clinton an act of political revenge by fundamentalist Republicans
upon an opponent they saw as morally corrupt – not least because
of his apparent refusal to fight in Vietnam? What is evident is that in
the contemporary polarized world of American politics, few hostages
are taken.

On both sides of the cultural divide, however, political attitudes
are also conditioned by traditional fears. Nixon's conduct in office
confirmed the historical American fear of political power. Clinton's
apparent lack of moral integrity demonstrated a disregard for the
codes of voluntary behaviour that temper individual freedom with
self-restraint. The fear was that the self-indulgence of the first representative of the 'baby-boomers' to reach the White House represented
an abuse of liberty. The behaviour of first Nixon and then Clinton thus
recalls the observation of the Reverend Henry Cumings in a sermon
preached on 28 May 1783 during the seedtime of the republic, that
'power abused ceases to be lawful authority and degenerates into
tyranny. Liberty abused or carried to excess is licentiousness.' In these
terms, both presidents dived off the raft of American democracy, and
acted beyond the borders of constitutional and individual propriety.

On 11 September 2001 the early morning news on American television was dominated by speculation that Michael Jordan, the former
basketball star, was planning to return to the professional game. The
importance given to such an event illustrated not only the centrality
of sports and celebrity in contemporary American culture, but also
the prevailing lack of curiosity about what might be headline news
in the rest of the world. And then everything changed. The terrorist
attack on the World Trade Center in New York, and the Pentagon,
across the Potomac river from Washington, DC, together with the
crash of another hi-jacked jet in Pennsylvania, which might otherwise
have targeted the Capitol or the White House itself, dramatically
affected cultural sensibilities and the political agenda. The architec-
tural symbols of the military-industrial complex – its economic base in

New York city, its military headquarters and the focus of its political power in Washington, DC – were destroyed, damaged and threatened. It was a defining moment for the first presidential administration of the twenty-first century.

Yet both the attack and the response to it also illustrate some of the themes discussed in this book. Terrorists find recruits among those to whom American foreign policy, particularly in the Middle East, appears economically vindictive, militarily ruinous, politically inept and religiously insensitive: an aggressive crusading spirit that threatens their fundamentalist Islamic faith. For many Americans, whose belief in the transcendent appeal of the political rights and civil liberties that they enjoy is equally strong, and who are convinced that the 'city on a hill' is still both an example and a refuge, the shock of finding that others detest their political aspirations and their cultural values is made the more profound because of their prior ignorance that such different sensibilities could exist in the wider world.

The attack manipulated the politics of spectacle. The media images of a jet crashing into one of the towers of the World Trade Center – the other having been hit already by another plane – were seared into the national consciousness through constant repetition: Hollywood could hardly have provided a more dramatic scenario or plot. The cameras witnessed the buildings' collapse. The rescue and recovery efforts that followed, at the scene where most casualties occurred, dominated the twenty-four-hour news coverage: the attack on the Pentagon and the crash in Pennslyvania became almost sub-plots in the story in part because the images they provided were neither so visually chilling nor so compelling.

The response focused attention once more upon the potential for presidential leadership. George W. Bush faced critical political deci- sions and challenges in an atmosphere where his every reaction and action, statement and assertion, was the subject of immediate and obsessive scrutiny. Was his initial absence from Washington an act of prudence or vacillation? Until the White House managed to influ- ence the media commentary – releasing information that the president himself had been a potential target of the terrorists – the verdict seemed open. Could he actually declare 'war on terrorism'? Not without Congress's support – which was given almost without qualification. Was he diplomatic in calling the new national mission a 'crusade'? It offended some Islamic members of the coalition of nations necessary to support his political aims. Should the initial search for Osama bin Laden in Afghanistan – the Soviet Union's Vietnam – be articulated in the language of the western gunfighter – he was a renegade who was wanted 'dead or alive' – or did this too betray a cultural insensitivity.

Bush, though, like other presidents before him, would be judged in terms of his ability to meet the challenge of the contemporary crisis and define the nation's course in the effort to overcome it.

Following 11 September, in an atmosphere in which tension was heightened as a result of the discovery of mail deliberately contaminated with anthrax spores, the question arises as to how far civil rights might be eroded in the drive for increased domestic security. John Ashcroft, the attorney-general whom earlier in the year the president had charged with putting an end to 'racial profiling', appeared to condone the arrest of Arab Americans as terrorist suspects. The FBI was given permission to eavesdrop on privileged attorney-client conversations. Also, those accused of terrorism would stand trial in military rather than civil courts. Just as in the 1950s, when anti-communist fervour meant that individuals were sometimes denied the very freedoms upon which American democracy was founded, so now too there is a danger that anti-terrorist measures might threaten civil liberties. In the end a 'war on terrorism' might be as open-ended and politically self-defeating as the 'war on drugs', which, in some ways, it closely resembles. The enemy is shadowy, elusive and the measure of triumph in such a conflict is difficult to assess. Can this war be won militarily, diplomatically, economically or politically? Any victory claimed may only be temporary: until the next outrage occurs. Success may only be relative, and the resources required to contain the threat may turn out to be limitless. But, following the vicissitudes and triumphs of the 'American Century', the rhetoric of the nation's leaders made clear the assumption that it now faced a fresh 'rendezvous with destiny'. And if courage is, as Ernest Hemingway believed, 'grace under pressure', in the immediate aftermath of 11 September 2001, there could be no doubting America's resolve.

For Mark Twain, the raft was the craft that took Huckleberry Finn and the fugitive slave Jim on their great adventure down the Mississippi. It could provide them with a sanctuary as they negotiated their individual futures at a time when the issue of slavery still challenged the 'idea of America' itself. War came. The Union and 'the idea of America' survived into the twentieth century – the 'American Century'. At the beginning of the new millennium, therefore, the United States still lights out for the territory that will define the future contours of its political life and culture. The raft floats on.

# Notes

## Chapter 1   Lighting Out for the Territory

1   L. Hartz, *The Liberal Tradition in America*, New York: Harcourt Brace Jovanovich, 1955, pp. 3 and 65.
2   A. Smith, *The Wealth of Nations*, London: George Routledge and Sons, 1893, p. 457.
3   Hartz, *The Liberal Tradition*, p. 65.
4   L. Hartz, 'The Nature of the Revolution', *Senate Committee on Foreign Relations, 90th Congress 2nd Session*, Washington, DC: US Government Printing Office, 1968.
5   A. de Tocqueville, *Democracy in America*, vol. 1, New York: Vintage Books edition, 1945, p. 31.
6   T.B. Macaulay, *The History of England*, vol. 1, London: Dent, pp. 102 and 69.
7   Tocqueville, *Democracy in America*, vol. 1, p. 301.
8   N. Campbell and A. Kean, *American Cultural Studies*, London: Routledge, 1997, pp. 9 and 22.
9   F.J. Turner, *The Frontier in American History*, New York: Henry Holt, 1920, p. 4.
10   W.E. Du Bois, *The Souls of Black Folk*, New York: W.W. Norton and Co., 1999, p. 11.
11   S. DuBois Cook, 'Democracy and Tyranny in America', in W. Havard and J. Bernd, eds, *200 Years of the Republic in Retrospect*, Charlottesville: University of Virginia Press, 1976, pp. 276 and 294.
12   H. Lofgren and A. Shima, *After Consensus*, Gothenburg: Acta Universitatis Gothoburgensis, 1998, p. 1.
13   A.L. Smith, 'Is There an American Culture?', in R. Maidment and J. Mitchell, eds, *The United States in the Twentieth Century: Culture*, London: Hodder and Stoughton, 1994, p. 308.
14   M. Barone, 'Our Country: The Shaping of America from Roosevelt to Clinton', in B. Shafer, ed., *Present Discontents*, Chatham, NJ: Chatham House Publishers, Inc., 1997, p. 43.

15 J. Kingdon, *America the Unusual*, New York: Worth Publishers, 1999, p. 2.

16 W. Whitman, 'The Eighteenth Presidency', in *The Collected Writings of Walt Whitman*, vol. vi, edited by E. Grier, New York: New York University Press, 1984, p. 2122.

17 N. Mailer, 'Huckleberry Finn – Alive at 100', in *The Time of Our Time*, Boston: Little, Brown and Co., 1998, pp. 1054 and 1058.

## Chapter 2   The Politics of Nostalgia

1 D. Boorstin, *The Genius of American Politics*, Chicago: University of Chicago Press, 1953, p. 10.

2 N. Hawthorne, *The Scarlet Letter*, Harmondsworth: Penguin, 1983, p. 246.

3 G. Wills, *Under God: Religion and American Politics*, New York: Simon and Schuster, 1990, pp. 63 and 68.

4 A. de Tocqueville, *Democracy in America*, vol. 1, New York: Vintage Books edition, 1945, p. 46.

5 N. Campbell and A. Kean, *American Cultural Studies*, London: Routledge, 1997, p. 100.

6 Tocqueville, *Democracy in America*, vol. 1, p. 45.

7 H. Evans, *The American Century*, London: Jonathan Cape, 1998, p. xvi.

8 C. Milner, 'National Initiatives', in C. Milner, C. O'Connor and M. Sandweiss, eds, *The Oxford History of the Amercian West*, New York: Oxford University Press, 1994, pp. 157 and 161–2.

9 S. Lynd, *The Intellectual Origins of American Radicalism*, London: Wildwood House Ltd, 1973, pp. 7–9 *passim.*

10 L. Hartz, *The Liberal Tradition in America*, New York: Harcourt Brace Jovanovich, 1955, pp. 72–3.

11 George Bancroft quoted in A. Craven, *Civil War in the Making*, Baton Rouge: Louisiana State University Press, 1959, p. 22.

12 H.B. Stowe, *Uncle Tom's Cabin*, New York: W.W. Norton and Co., 1994, p. 383.

13 Wills, *Under God*, pp. 15–16 and 19. Wills also comments (p. 20) that Billy Graham 'has been, over the years, the most admired man in America'.

14 J. Walsh, 'American Soul-Searching: Talk Shows and the Culture of Confession', *Borderlines: Studies in American Culture*, 5:3 (1998), p. 235.

15 Wills, *Under God*, pp. 17–18.

16 Walsh, 'American Soul-Searching', p. 237.

17 R. Morris, 'The Revolution and the Third World', in G. Bilias, ed., *The American Revolution*, New York: Holt, Rinehart and Winston, 1980, pp. 180–1.

18 Boorstin, *Genius*, pp. 156 and 159.

19 B. Appleyard, 'The Prophet Motive', *Sunday Times*, Culture Section, 30 July 2000, pp. 6–7.

## Chapter 3  The Challenge of the Constitution

1  R. Neustadt, *Presidential Power*, New York: John Wiley and Sons Inc., 1976, p. 323.
2  D. Caute, *The Great Fear*, New York: Simon and Schuster, 1978, p. 150.
3  T. White, *America in Search of Itself*, New York: Warner Books, 1983, p. 45.
4  R. Nixon, *RN: The Memoirs of Richard Nixon*, New York: Grossat & Dunlap, 1978, p. 223.

## Chapter 4  The Framework of Government

1  Fillmore was immortalized by H.L. Mencken's hoax story, published in the *New York Evening Mail* in 1917, which claimed that he had introduced the first bathtub to the White House.
2  A. Schlesinger, Jr, *The Imperial Presidency*, Boston: Houghton Mifflin Co., 1989.
3  R. Neustadt, *Presidential Power*, New York: John Wiley and Sons Inc., 1976, p. 74.
4  R. Stein and K. Bickers, *Perpetuating the Pork Barrel*, Cambridge: Cambridge University Press, 1997, p. 4.
5  G. Stephanopoulos, *All Too Human: A Political Education*, London: Hutchinson, 1999, p. 23.
6  P. Schroeder, 'Congressional Bull****', in B. Murphy, ed., *Portraits of American Politics*, Boston: Houghton Mifflin Co., 2000, p. 121.
7  M. Lerner, 'John Marshall's Long Shadow', in F. Friedel and N. Pollack, eds, *Builders of American Institutions*, Chicago: Rand McNally and Co., 1963, p. 122.
8  Ibid., p. 123.
9  A. de Grazia, 'The Myth of the President', in A. Wildavsky, ed., *The Presidency*, Boston: Little, Brown and Co., 1969, p. 65.

## Chapter 5 Playing the Political Game

1  Cited in H. Evans, *The American Century*, London: Jonathan Cape, 1998, p. 79.
2  R. Chernow, *The House of Morgan*, New York: Simon and Schuster, 1990, p. xii.
3  C.W. Mills, *The Power Elite*, New York: Oxford University Press, 1956, p. 4.
4  P. Lyon, *Eisenhower: Portrait of the Hero*, Boston: Little, Brown and Co., 1974, p. 408.
5  R. Kehler and M. Jezer, 'Campaign Cash: Dollars versus Democracy', in B. Miroff, R. Seidelman and T. Swanstrom, eds, *Debating Democracy*, Boston: Houghton Mifflin Co., 1999, p. 236.
6  Mills, *The Power Elite*, p. 166.

7   Kehler and Jezer, 'Campaign Cash', p. 239.
8   H. Rockoff, 'The "Wizard of Oz" as a Monetary Allegory', *Journal of Political Economy*, 98 (1990), p. 750.
9   B. Hammond, *Banks and Politics in America*, Princeton: Princeton University Press, 1957.
10  A. de Tocqueville, *Democracy in America*, vol. 1, New York: Vintage Books edition, 1945, p. 427.
11  P. Trescott, *Financing American Enterprise*, New York: Harper & Row, 1963, p. 21.
12  Hammond, *Banks and Politics in America*, pp. 723–4.
13  E. Morris, *Dutch: A Memoir of Ronald Reagan*, London: HarperCollins, 1999, pp. 113 and 447.
14  R. Hofstadter, 'The Paranoid Style in American Politics', in *The Paranoid Style in American Politics and Other Essays*, Cambridge, Mass.: Harvard University Press, 1996, pp. 5 and 37–8.
15  P. Robertson, *The New World Order*, Dallas: World Publishing, 1991, pp. 118–25 *passim.*
16  K. Armstrong, *The Battle for God*, London: HarperCollins, 2000, p. 175.
17  Ibid., p. 177.

## Chapter 6   Making Headlines

1   A. de Tocqueville, *Democracy in America*, vol. 1, New York: Vintage Books edition, 1945, p. 195.
2   J. Dos Passos, *USA*, Harmondsworth: Penguin, 1966, p. 1113.
3   D. Halberstam, *The Powers That Be*, New York: Alfred A. Knopf, 1979, p. 9.
4   R. Nixon, *Six Crises*, New York: Pyramid Books, 1968, pp. 109–34 *passim.*
5   R. Nixon, *RN: The Memoirs of Richard Nixon*, New York: Grossat & Dunlap, 1978, p. 219.
6   A. Sperber, *Murrow: His Life and Times*, London: Michael Joseph Ltd, pp. 439 and 572.
7   Nixon, *RN*, p. 329.
8   Halberstam, *The Powers That Be*, p. 514.
9   D. Halberstam, *The Best and the Brightest*, London: Pan Books, 1973, p. 797.
10  Nixon, *RN*, p. 330.
11  T. White, *Breach of Faith*, New York: Atheneum Publishers, 1975, p. 322.
12  Ibid., p. 155.
13  P. Johnson, *A History of the American People*, New York: HarperCollins, 1997, p. 896.
14  B. Bradlee, 'Watergate: The Biggest Story', *Washington Post* special on Watergate, 14 June 1992.
15  K. Graham, *Personal History*, London: Weidenfeld and Nicolson, 1997, pp. 470 and 497.

16  D. Frost, '*I Gave Them a Sword*', London: Macmillan, 1978, p. 191.
17  W. Manchester, *One Brief Shining Moment: Remembering Kennedy*, Boston: Little Brown and Co., 1988.
18  B. Neve, *Film and Politics in America*, London: Routledge, 1992, pp. 142 and 143.
19  B. Woodward and C. Bernstein, *All the President's Men*, New York: Simon and Schuster, 1974, pp. 71–2 and 196.
20  I. Scott, *American Politics in Hollywood Film*, Edinburgh: Edinburgh University Press, 2000, p. 6.
21  K. Ringle, 'Journalism's Finest 2 Hours and 16 Minutes', *Washington Post* special on Watergate.
22  Cited in E. Morris, *Dutch: A Memoir of Ronald Reagan*, London: HarperCollins, 1999, p. 652.
23  L. Beinhart, *American Hero*, London: Arrow Books, 1995, p. 40.

## Chapter 7   Faultlines

1  A. Schlesinger, Jr, *The Disuniting of America*, New York: W.W. Norton and Co., 1991, p. 138.
2  G. Myrdal, *An American Dilemma*, New York: Harper & Brothers, 1944, pp. 1, 24 and 1022–33.
3  M. Dyson, 'Malcolm X', in M. Buhle, P. Buhle and H. Kaye, eds, *The American Radical*, London: Routledge, 1994, pp. 323–4.
4  D. Levi-Strauss, 'Floating Like a Butterfly', *Nation*, 25 January 1999, pp. 34–5.
5  S. Cone, 'Martin Luther King Jr', in Buhle et al., eds, *The American Radical*, p. 333.
6  T. Le Clair, 'The Language Must Not Sweat', *New Republic*, 12 March 1981, p. 27.
7  E. Warren, *The Memoirs of Chief Justice Earl Warren*, New York: Doubleday & Co. Inc., 1977, p. 292.
8  R. Gorman, *Yankee Red*, Westport, Conn.: Praeger, 1989, p. 11.
9  R. Lacey, *Ford*, London: William Heinemann Ltd, 1986, pp. 366 and 368.
10  H. Evans, *The American Century*, London: Jonathan Cape, 1998, p. 562.
11  M.J. Buhle, P. Buhle and H.J. Kaye, 'Introduction', in M.J. Buhle, P. Buhle and H.J. Kaye, eds, *The American Radical*, London: Routledge, 1994, pp. xv–xvi.
12  E. Morris, *Dutch: A Memoir of Ronald Reagan*, London: HarperCollins, 1999, p. 448.
13  Myrdal, *An American Dilemma*, p. 1075.
14  Ibid., p. 1078.
15  N. Mailer, 'St. George and the Godfather', in *The Time of Our Time*, Boston: Little, Brown and Co., 1998, p. 807.
16  Interview with B.W. Wells, 'Sommers on Deconstruction, Feminism', *Dartmouth Review*, 15 April 1998.

17   Cited in A. Ross and L. Cokorinos, 'Promise Keepers: A Real Challenge from the Right', *National NOW Times*, May 1997.
18   C. Harding, ed., *Wingspan: Inside the Men's Movement*, New York: St Martin's Press, 1992, cited in S. Biddulph, *Manhood*, Stroud: Hawthorn Press, 2000, pp. 53 and 27.
19   F. FitzGerald, *Cities on a Hill*, London: Picador, 1986, pp. 12, 41 and 67.
20   Myrdal, *An American Dilemma*, pp. 457–8.
21   Lacey, *Ford*, p. 363.
22   M. Gray, *Drug Crazy*, New York: Random House, 1998, p. 67.
23   D. Musto, *The American Disease*, New York: Oxford University Press, 1999, pp. 5–6 and 65.
24   S. Duke and A. Gross, *America's Longest War*, New York: G.P. Putnam's Sons, 1993, p. 85.
25   Gray, *Drug Crazy*, pp. 73–8 *passim*.

## Chapter 8   In Country

1    C. Crabb, *The Doctrines of American Foreign Policy*, Baton Rouge: Louisiana State University Press, 1982, p. 21.
2    A. Weinberg, 'The Historical Meaning of the American Doctrine of Isolation', *American Political Science Review*, 34:3 (1940), p. 547.
3    W.A. Williams, 'Vietnam and America: The Revival of an Anti-Imperial Mood?' in P. Melling and J. Roper, eds, *America, France and Vietnam: Cultural History and Ideas of Conflict*, Aldershot: Avebury, 1991, pp. 226–7.
4    G. Vidal, *Hollywood*, New York: Ballantine Books, 1990, p. 41.
5    W.A. Williams, 'The Legend of Isolationism in the 1920s', in H. Berger, ed., *A William Appleman Williams Reader*, Chicago: Ivan R. Dee, 1992, pp. 74 and 76.
6    H. Bowden, *American Indians and Christian Missions*, Chicago: University of Chicago Press, 1981, p. 116.
7    R.P. Beaver, *Church, State and the American Indian*, St Louis, Mo.: Concordia Publishing House, 1966, p. 34.
8    O.W. Esbree, 'Samuel Hopkins and His Doctrine of Benevolence', *New England Quarterly*, 8 (1935), p. 539.
9    R. Anderson, *The Hawaiian Islands: Their Progress and Condition under Missionary Labors*, Boston: Gould & Lincoln, 1864, pp. 115 and 390–1.
10   W. Hutchinson, *Errand to the World*, Chicago: University of Chicago Press, 1987, pp. 80, 7 and 77.
11   D. Healy, *US Expansionism: The Imperialist Urge in the 1890s*, Wisconsin: University of Wisconsin Press, 1970, p. 17.
12   L. Hartz, *The Liberal Tradition in America*, New York: Harcourt Brace Jovanovich, 1955, pp. 14 and 156.
13   In one notable encounter, on meeting representatives from Latin America, Quayle allegedly expressed regret that he could not talk to them in their own language – Latin. The Johnson and Kissinger comments are quoted

in K. Booth, *Strategy and Ethnocentrism*, London: Croom Helm, 1979, p. 135.

14 J. Hellman, *American Myth and the Legacy of Vietnam*, New York: Columbia University Press, 1986, p. x.

15 W. McNeill, 'The Care and Repair of Public Myth', *Foreign Affairs*, 61 (1982), pp. 1–13.

16 Hellman, *American Myth*, pp. 211–20 *passim*.

17 J. Baxter, *George Lucas: A Biography*, London: HarperCollins, 2000, pp. 245 and 334.

18 B. Hocking, 'Globalization and the Foreign–Domestic Policy Nexus', in A. McGrew, ed., *The United States in the Twentieth Century: Empire*, Hodder and Stoughton, 1994, p. 137.

19 W. Pfaff, 'The Question of Hegemony', *Foreign Affairs*, 80 (2001), pp. 221–32 *passim*.

# References

Anderson, R., *The Hawaiian Islands: Their Progress and Condition under Missionary Labors*, Boston: Gould & Lincoln, 1864.

Armstrong, K., *The Battle for God*, London: HarperCollins, 2000.

Barone, M., 'Our Country: The Shaping of America from Roosevelt to Clinton', in B. Shafer, ed., *Present Discontents*, Chatham, NJ: Chatham House Publishers, Inc., 1997.

Baxter, J., *George Lucas: A Biography*, London: HarperCollins, 2000.

Beaver, R.P., *Church, State and the American Indian*, St Louis, Mo.: Concordia Publishing House, 1966.

Beinhart, L., *American Hero*, London: Arrow Books, 1995.

Bly, R., *Iron John*, New York: Vintage, 1992.

Boorstin, D., *The Genius of American Politics*, Chicago: University of Chicago Press, 1953.

Booth, K., *Strategy and Ethnocentrism*, London: Croom Helm, 1979.

Bowden, H., *American Indians and Christian Missions*, Chicago: University of Chicago Press, 1981.

Bryson, B., *The Lost Continent: Travels in Small Town America*, London: Abacus, 1989.

Buhle, M.J., Buhle, P., and Kaye, H.J., 'Introduction', in M.J. Buhle, P. Buhle and H.J. Kaye, eds, *The American Radical*, London: Routledge, 1994.

Campbell, N., and Kean, A., *American Cultural Studies*, London: Routledge, 1997.

Caute, D., *The Great Fear*, New York: Simon and Schuster, 1978.

Chernow, R., *The House of Morgan*, New York: Simon and Schuster, 1990.

Cone, J., 'Martin Luther King Jr', in M.J. Buhle, P. Buhle and H.J. Kaye, eds, *The American Radical*, London: Routledge, 1994.

Cook, S., Du Bois, 'Democracy and Tyranny in America', in W. Havard and J. Bernd, eds, *200 Years of the Republic in Retrospect*, Charlottesville: University of Virginia Press, 1976.

Crabb, C., *The Doctrines of American Foreign Policy*, Baton Rouge: Louisiana State University Press, 1982.

Craven, A., *Civil War in the Making*, Baton Rouge: Louisiana State University Press, 1959.

Dos Passos, J., *USA*, Harmondsworth: Penguin, 1966.

Du Bois, W.E., *The Souls of Black Folk*, New York: W.W. Norton and Co., 1999.

Duke, S. and Gross, A., *America's Longest War*, New York: G.P. Putnam's Sons, 1993.

Dyson, M., 'Malcolm X', in M. Buhle, P. Buhle and H. Kaye, eds, *The American Radical*, London: Routledge, 1994.

Ellison, R., *Invisible Man*, New York: Random House, 1952.

Ellroy, J., *American Tabloid*, London: Arrow, 1995.

Esbree, O.W., 'Samuel Hopkins and His Doctrine of Benevolence', *New England Quarterly*, 8 (1935), pp. 534–50.

Evans, H., *The American Century*, London: Jonathan Cape, 1998.

Faludi, S., *Backlash: The Undeclared War Against American Women*, New York: Crown, 1991.

Fanon, F., *The Wretched of the Earth*, New York: Grove Press, 1963.

FitzGerald, F., *Cities on a Hill*, London: Picador, 1986.

Friedan, B., *The Feminine Mystique*, New York: Norton, 1963.

Frost, D., *'I Gave Them a Sword'*, London: Macmillan, 1978.

Gorman, R., *Yankee Red*, Westport, Conn.: Praeger, 1989.

Graham, K., *Personal History*, London: Weidenfeld and Nicolson, 1997.

Gray, M., *Drug Crazy*, New York: Random House, 1998.

Grazia, A. de, 'The Myth of the President', in A. Wildavsky, ed., *The Presidency*, Boston: Little, Brown and Co., 1969.

Halberstam, D., *The Best and the Brightest*, London: Pan Books, 1973.

Halberstam, D., *The Powers That Be*, New York: Alfred A. Knopf, 1979.

Haldeman, H.R., *The Ends of Power*, New York: Times Books, 1978.

Hammond, B., *Banks and Politics in America*, Princeton: Princeton University Press, 1957.

Hartz, L., *The Liberal Tradition in America*, New York: Harcourt Brace Jovanovich, 1955.

Hartz, L., 'The Nature of the Revolution', *Senate Committee on Foreign Relations, 90th Congress 2nd Session*, Washington, DC: US Government Printing Office, 1968.

Hawthorne, N., *The Scarlet Letter*, Harmondsworth, Penguin, 1983.

Healy, D., *US Expansionism: The Imperialist Urge in the 1890s*, Wisconsin: University of Wisconsin Press, 1970.

Hellmann, J., *American Myth and the Legacy of Vietnam*, New York: Columbia University Press, 1986.

Hitchens, C., *The Trial of Henry Kissinger*, New York: Verso, 2001.

Hocking, B., 'Globalization and the Foreign–Domestic Policy Nexus', in A. McGrew, ed., *The United States in the Twentieth Century: Empire*, London: Hodder and Stoughton, 1994.

Hofstadter, R., 'The Paranoid Style in American Politics', in *The Paranoid Style in American Politics and Other Essays*, Cambridge, Mass.: Harvard University Press, 1996.

Hutchinson, W., *Errand to the World*, Chicago: University of Chicago Press, 1987.

Johnson, P., *A History of the American People*, New York: HarperCollins, 1997.

Kehler, R., and Jezer, M., 'Campaign Cash: Dollars versus Democracy', in B. Miroff, R. Seidelman and T. Swanstrom, eds, *Debating Democracy*, Boston: Houghton Mifflin Co., 1999.

Kingdon, J., *America the Unusual*, New York: Worth Publishers, 1999.

Lacey, R., *Ford*, London: William Heinemann Ltd, 1986.

Le Clair, T., 'The Language Must Not Sweat', *New Republic*, 12 March 1981.

Lerner, M., 'John Marshall's Long Shadow', in F. Friedel and N. Pollack, eds, *Builders of American Institutions*, Chicago: Rand McNally & Co., 1963.

Levi-Strauss, D., 'Floating Like a Butterfly', *Nation*, 25 January 1999.

Lofgren, H., and Shima, A., *After Consensus*, Gothenburg: Acta Universitatis Gothoburgensis, 1998.

Lynd, S., *The Intellectual Origins of American Radicalism*, London: Wildwood House Ltd, 1973.

Lyon, P., *Eisenhower: Portrait of the Hero*, Boston: Little, Brown and Co., 1974.

Macaulay, T.B., *The History of England*, vol. 1, London: Dent, 1972.

McNeill, W., 'The Care and Repair of Public Myth', *Foreign Affairs*, 61 (1982), pp. 1–13.

Mailer, N., 'Huckleberry Finn – Alive at 100', in *The Time of Our Time*, Boston: Little, Brown and Co., 1998.

Mailer, N., 'St George and the Godfather', in *The Time of Our Time*, Boston: Little, Brown and Co., 1998.

Manchester, W., *One Brief Shining Moment: Remembering Kennedy*, Boston: Little, Brown and Co., 1988.

Mills, C., *The Power Elite*, New York: Oxford University Press, 1956.

Milner, C., 'National Initiatives', in C. Milner, C. O'Connor and M. Sandweiss, eds, *The Oxford History of the American West*, New York: Oxford University Press, 1994.

Morris, E., *Dutch: A Memoir of Ronald Reagan*, London: HarperCollins, 1999.

Morris, R., 'The Revolution and the Third World', in G. Billias, ed., *The American Revolution*, New York: Holt, Rinehart and Winston, 1980.

Musto, D., *The American Disease*, New York: Oxford University Press, 1999.

Myrdal, G., *An American Dilemma*, New York: Harper & Brothers, 1944.

Neustadt, R., *Presidential Power*, New York: John Wiley and Sons Inc., 1976.

Neve, B., *Film and Politics in America*, London: Routledge, 1992.

Nixon, R., *Six Crises*, New York: Pyramid Books, 1968.

Nixon, R., *RN: The Memoirs of Richard Nixon*, New York: Grossat & Dunlap, 1978.

Pfaff, W., 'The Question of Hegemony', *Foreign Affairs*, 80 (2001), pp. 221–32.

Robertson, P., *The New World Order*, Dallas: World Publishing, 1991.

Rockoff, H., 'The "Wizard of Oz" as a Monetary Allegory', *Journal of Political Economy*, 98 (1990), pp. 739–60.

Schlesinger, A., Jr, *The Imperial Presidency*, Boston: Houghton Mifflin Co., 1989.

Schlesinger, A., Jr, *The Disuniting of America*, New York: W.W. Norton & Co., 1991.

Schroeder, P., 'Congressional Bull****', in B. Murphy, ed., *Portraits of American Politics*, Boston: Houghton Mifflin Co., 2000.

Scott, I., *American Politics in Hollywood Film*, Edinburgh: Edinburgh University Press, 2000.

Smith, A., *The Wealth of Nations*, London: George Routledge and Sons, 1893.

Smith, A.L., 'Is There an American Culture?' in R. Maidment and J. Mitchell, eds, *The United States in the Twentieth Century: Culture*, London: Hodder and Stoughton, 1994.

Sommers, C.H., *Who Stole Feminism?* New York: Simon and Schuster, 1995.

Sperber, A., *Murrow: His Life and Times*, London: Michael Joseph Ltd, 1987.

Stein, R., and Bickers, K., *Perpetuating the Pork Barrel*, Cambridge: Cambridge University Press, 1997.

Stephanopoulos, G., *All Too Human: A Political Education*, London: Hutchinson, 1999.

Stowe, H.B., *Uncle Tom's Cabin*, New York: W.W. Norton & Co., 1994.

Tocqueville, A. de, *Democracy in America*, vol. 1, New York: Vintage Books edition, 1945.

Trescott, P., *Financing American Enterprise*, New York: Harper & Row, 1963.

Turner, F.J., *The Frontier in American History*, New York: Henry Holt, 1920.

Twain, M., *The Adventures of Huckleberry Finn*, Harmondsworth: Penguin, 1985.

Vidal, G., *Hollywood*, New York: Ballantine Books, 1990.

Walsh, J., 'American Soul-Searching: Talk Shows and the Culture of Confession', *Borderlines: Studies in American Culture*, 5:3 (1998), pp. 223–39.

Warren, E., *The Memoirs of Chief Justice Earl Warren*, New York: Doubleday & Co. Inc., 1977.

Warren, R.P., *All the King's Men*, New York: Harcourt Brace, 1946.

Weinberg, A., 'The Historical Meaning of the American Doctrine of Isolation', *American Political Science Review*, 34:3 (1940), pp. 539–47.

White, T., *Breach of Faith*, New York: Atheneum Publishers, 1975.

White, T., *America in Search of Itself*, New York: Warner Books, 1983.

Whitman, W., 'The Eighteenth Presidency', in *The Collected Writings of Walt Whitman*, vol. vi, edited by E. Grier, New York: New York University Press, 1984.

Williams, W.A., 'Vietnam and America: The Revival of an Anti-Imperial Mood?' in P. Melling and J. Roper, eds, *America, France and Vietnam: Cultural History and Ideas of Conflict*, Aldershot: Avebury, 1991.

Williams, W.A., 'The Legend of Isolationism in the 1920s', in H. Berger, ed., *A William Appleman Williams Reader*, Chicago: Ivan R. Dee, 1992.

Wills, G., *Under God: Religion and American Politics*, New York: Simon and Schuster, 1990.

Woodward, B., and Bernstein, C., *All The President's Men*, New York: Simon and Schuster, 1974.

Young, G., *From Sea to Shining Sea: A Present-Day Journey into America's Past*, Harmondsworth, Penguin, 1996.

# Index